Bison: Mating and Conservation in Small Populations

Methods and Cases in Conservation Science Series

Mary C. Pearl, Editor

METHODS AND CASES IN CONSERVATION SCIENCE

Tropical Deforestation: Small Farmers and Land Clearing in the Ecuadorian Amazon
by Thomas K. Rudel with Bruce Horowitz

Also related

PERSPECTIVES IN BIOLOGICAL DIVERSITY
Conserving Natural Value,
by Holmes Rolston III

Mary C. Pearl, Editor
Christine Padoch and Douglas Daly   Advisers

Bison: Mating and Conservation in Small Populations

Joel Berger and
Carol Cunningham

New York
Columbia University Press

Columbia University Press
New York   Chichester, West Sussex
Copyright © 1994 Columbia University Press
All rights reserved

Library of Congress
Cataloging-in-Publication Data

Berger, Joel.
Bison: Mating and conservation in Small Populations / Joel Berger and Carol
Cunningham.
p.   cm.—(Methods and cases in conservation science)
Includes bibliographical references and index.
ISBN 0-231-08456-0 (alk. paper)
1. Bison, American—South Dakota—Badlands National Park—
Reproduction.   2. Bison, American—South Dakota—Badlands National
Park—Germplasm resources.   3. Bison, American—Ecology—South
Dakota—Badlands National Park.   4. Wildlife conservation.
I. Cunningham, Carol.   II. Title.   III. Series.
QL737.U53B475   1994   93-45671
599.73'58—dc20   CIP

Casebound editions of Columbia University Press books
are printed on permanent and durable acid-free paper.

Printed in the United States of America
C 10 9 8 7 6 5 4 3 2 1

To our parents and for Sonja Sage

Contents

3. The Study and the Badlands Ecosystem

Contents ix

Part Two. Behavioral Ecology of Females and Males

4. Social Spacing and Land Use Systems

5. Population Features

Part Three. Insularization: Individuals, Populations, Ecosystems

9. Mating Asymmetries and Their Consequences

10. Bottlenecks and Lineage Mixing

Appendixes

Preface

What is man without the beasts? If all the beasts were gone, man would die from great loneliness of spirit, for whatever happens to the beast also happens to the man. All things are connected. Whatever befalls the earth befalls the sons of the earth.

Chief Seathl of the Duwamish Tribe, from a letter to the
President of the United States (1855)

Days of free-ranging large mammals are rapidly ending. Pere David's deer and Przewalski horses occur solely in manicured zoological parks; rhinos and elephants no longer roam without threat from poachers' bullets; and Yellowstone National Park is too small for its wintering elk and bison. Few places exist where unfenced prairies may be enjoyed. If the human population explosion continues, the earth will house more than 10 billion people in the next century, and the future for intact faunas is bleak. Virtually all large mammals will be found only in reserves.

In times past bison were a critically important ecosystem component, biologically and anthropologically. They provided food, clothing, and a focus for the art of native peoples and later for Euroamericans. They served as prey for wolves and lions. And they affected community structure, depositing urine and feces, removing and trampling vegetation, and occupying habitats from prairies to glaciers, deserts to forests. But the day of free-roaming bison is gone. Their classic and wanton extermination, promoted by white settlers and the U.S. government, on the once vast North American prairies during the nineteenth century is infamous. Bison are one of many textbook examples of species driven to the verge of extinction through callous human acts. Although North American bison were rescued from extinction last century, the likely fate of their descendants presents an unfortunate model for the future. Today's imperiled fauna suffer primarily from the loss of their habitats.

The plight of bison is symptomatic of many species today. Because background information spanning multiple generations is available, bison may serve as a general model for what might be expected of species that will suffer similar ecological problems and probably require intensive management in small reserves. In 1984 when we conceived of such a study, we asked three questions: (1) how might we best address some issue of fundamental importance in the area of conservation biology; (2) how might behavior be incorporated into the study; and (3) what type of species might profitably serve as a model? Numerous areas of conservation biology are of central importance, theoretically, empirically, historically, and ethically. One of the more timely issues concerns the extent to which a skew in breeding by some individuals affects the potential genetic structure of subsequent generations. Because information on this issue requires knowledge of a species' mating system, factors that affect it, and some knowledge of behavior per se, we decided our interests could best be met by addressing issues at the interface of conservation biology and behavioral ecology. Although in some instances deciding on a species to study is easier than selecting a question for study, we found the opposite to be true. Should we study bats, rodents, or elephants? Fascinating questions are regularly asked about these diverse taxonomic groups, but none of the groups seemed appropriate for us to study. Most species of bats and rodents are nocturnal and difficult to observe in the field. And given our professional backgrounds chances for funding seemed slim. The same was true of elephants. In addition to having low rates of reproduction and lengthy periods to first reproduction, they live in areas where we had no practical experience. To study mating we needed a species that was large enough to observe, had individuals that were morphologically distinguishable so that individual recognition was possible, occupied open habitat where observations would not be impeded by thick vegetation, and where measures of mating and births could be obtained.

Of North American mammals, the largest terrestrial species tend to be ungulates, but species like deer, elk, and moose vary in terms of ease relative to the criteria outlined above. Similarly, species found in deserts or on open prairies, such as bighorn sheep or pronghorn, were problematic because either other researchers were already involved in studies of mating biology or sites were too disturbed. Instead of finding "pristine" sites, we considered bison. Although the ecosystems they inhabit have been altered in one form or another at every site in the world, bison are found in reserves where information on the historical distribution of specific populations and transfers of animals is available. And by being situated exclusively in isolated reserves, bison typify what has already occurred to many of the world's larger mammals and portend the future— isolated reserves of varying sizes harboring a mere fragment of formerly widespread species. We spent nearly six months in Canada and the western United States looking for study sites, and our decision to choose bison at Badlands was largely fortuitous.

At most reserves bison reproduce well; as a consequence, a proportion of most populations are rounded up and auctioned to private citizens. To develop a study only to have known individuals removed did not make good sense; therefore we sought an area that was large enough to allow the population to grow, undisturbed by humans. The small parks could not make such concessions over multiple year periods, and the sensitive political environments in places like Yellowstone and Wood Buffalo National Park in Canada made the possibility of working there less attractive. While visiting Matt Rowe at Appalachian State University, we discovered an old copy of an *Audubon* magazine that described Badlands National Park and the more than three hundred bison that roamed freely over more than 250 km^2 federally designated wilderness area. Vehicles, indeed motors of any sort, are prohibited by law, and we thought it might be possible to study bison there without human interference. We had not visited Badlands when looking for sites in South Dakota, but we called Lloyd Kortge, the park's chief ranger, who encouraged the study and later ironed out details for an agreement in which bison would not be managed for four consecutive years.

During the initial planning and proposal-writing phases, bison loomed as attractive study animals for two additional reasons: we felt we could affect their management and still conduct basic work on their biology, and although studies of bison behavior, breeding, feeding, and history have been conducted, only that of Wendy Green and Aron Rothstein dealt with identified individuals for multiple year periods. (One of the premises of our research, that studies of the same individuals over extended periods will lead to novel finds, engendered cynicism common among funding institutions. Our first seven proposals were denied funding.)

Bison, we discovered, are interesting in their own right. They are the largest extant terrestrial mammals of the New World. They are a reminder of the huge concentrations of game once found throughout many savannas of Africa and Asia, and they were sources of myth, warmth, and food for various tribes of North American Indians. Although this book is about their behavioral ecology and conservation and must remain impersonal, we found bison to be both fascinating and beautiful. Bison in zoos are not the same as the bison we observed—frisky, aggressive, shy, social, powerful. Observing bison and other grassland denizens—on verdant prairies and among buttes, in wind, snow, cold, and heat—was an experience we will not soon forget. We hope this book inspires others to visit and appreciate bison, prairies, and other natural habitats—and to seek better ways to conserve our diminishing ecosystems and their species.

This book is divided into three major parts. "Big Animals in a Small World" introduces the major themes: mating, insularization, and bison. It also offers information about our study site, Badlands National Park in South Dakota, and the methods we employed. "Behavioral Ecology of Females and Males" is more directed, providing general material about bison natural history and specific details about mating biology, population size, and behavioral ecology. "Insularization: Individuals, Populations, Ecosystems" builds on material from the prior sections. It focuses on consequences of mating and insularization, but draws immediate links to conservation and places the results into the broader picture—contrasting what is known and what is not known about bison with that of other large mammals and their ecosystems.

Acknowledgments

Many people helped with our work and this book. In 1984 when we first conceived of the study Dirk Van Vuren and Valerius Geist suggested study sites. Lloyd Kortge helped us establish a research program at Badlands, and Mike and Marj Glass provided countless meals and showers, as well as warmth, data, and friendship. Mike rescued us from mud traps, dying Volkswagens, and other hurdles.

Our coworkers and field assistants included J'Amy Allen, Jim Berkelman, Michele Beucler, Kathy Betts, Sonja Browe, Rick Coleman, Lisa Ellis, Lybby Everest, Suzanne Fellows, Kim Furry, Marj Glass, Linda Kerley, Pete Kleinman, Monica Marquez, Mike Mooring, Rick Sweitzer, and David Wooster. Marj, Linda, Rick S., and David all worked two or more years. Without their long hours, near misses, blisters, and sunburns, the data base would have been meager indeed. Neal Berger, with his typical enthusiasm, visited us yearly. As usual, his companionship was well appreciated and brought many smiles.

Lee McClenaghan and Ernie Vyse were inspirational. They both contributed to the fieldwork, and Lee performed genetic analyses. Mike and Nancy Kock restrained and immobilized bison and processed samples into the wee hours. Judith Airy, Wendy Green, Don Klebenow, Stuart Nichol, Mary Peacock, Aron Rothstein, Matthew Rowe, and Pete Stacey all spent time watching bison with us, and they made stimulating, if unusual, suggestions about ways to enhance data collection.

The staff at Badlands National Park made us feel a part of their team, in particular, Bruce Besken, Dan Dearborn, Don Falvey, Nick and Sharon Geigle, Irv Mortensen, and Jay and Martha Shueler. Elsa and Lloyd Kortge were never too busy for us or our problems. Lloyd and Mike Glass also arranged meetings with Dan Dugan, who was most generous in allowing us the use of his cowshed for shelter and his land for better access to bison. Walt Heather granted passage across his property and offered us cookies, milk, and coffee.

Robert Ellis and John Malcolm, refuge chiefs for reserves managed by the U.S. Fish and Wildlife Service, were most cooperative in making unpublished material available. Dale Lott, Bob Rose, Gary Miller, Lew Carbyn, and Michael Stuwe all provided difficult-to-find references, manuscripts, or both. Access to the Archives of the New York Zoological Society's American Bison Collection was made available by the kindness of Fred Koontz and Steve Johnson.

Our analyses and interpretations of the data would have been far more simplistic had it not been for the suggestions of Robert Gibson, Steve Jenkins, Gary Vinyard, and John Wehausen. Peter Brussard, Dave Cameron, Mary Peacock, Pete Stacey, and Ernie Vyse helped hone two not-so-tidy chapters. Wendy Green and Aron Rothstein not only commented on numerous chapters but also shared the experiences and insights they gained from almost a decade of work on bison at Wind Cave National Park. Dan Rubenstein kindly read the entire manuscript. Others to whom we owe thanks include Fred Allendorf, Jeanne Altmann, Dave Armstrong, F. H. Bronson, Marco Festa-Bianchet, Jack Hogg, Rolf Ims, Petr Komers, Bob Lacey, Burney Le Boeuf, Bill Longland, Dale Lott, Martha McClintock, Brian Miller, Jan Murie, Lynn Rogers, Rich Rust, Allen Rutberg, John Seidensticker, Bill Shields, Andrew Smith, Lee Talbot, Dan Uresk, and Chris Wemmer.

The administration at University of Nevada, Reno, was not only understanding of our short stays at UNR while we disappeared to South Dakota for months on end, but also sympathetic during all phases of the writing. Jenny Frayer, Fred Gifford, Bernard Jones, and Ron Pardini all know how appreciative we are.

The research was supported by the Badlands Natural History Association; Great Pacific Iron Works; the National Geographic Society; the National Park Service; the University of Nevada, Reno; and the Wildlife Preservation Trust. Smithsonian Institution's Conservation and Research Center, through the help of Chris Wemmer, furnished the perfect atmosphere in which to write during the early stages of preparation.

Finally, our parents, the Bergers (Nathalie and Alvin) and the Cunninghams (Robert and Lorraine), have always been there when we've needed them. They instilled within us an appreciation for the importance of knowledge. How can we express what this has meant? Someday Sonja Sage will be big enough to read. This book is for her. It is also for Lari who will always be with us.

Bison: Mating and Conservation in Small Populations

PART ONE

Big Animals in a Small World

1. Natural History and the Twenty-First Century

> *We no longer destroy great works of art. They are treasured, and regarded as priceless value; but we have yet to attain the state of civilization where the destruction of a glorious work of Nature, whether it be a cliff, a forest, or a species of mammal or bird, is regarded with equal abhorrence.*
>
> H. F. Osborne 1912

The diversity of life and the survival strategies employed by different species on this planet are truly staggering. Parthenogenesis in small lizards and sessile plants, annual migrations of more than 5,000 km by monarch butterflies and caribou, moisture acquisition from desert fog by tenebrionid beetles, and large body size are but four of a marvelous array of tactics produced by millions of years of evolution. Julian Huxley remarked that size had a fascination all its own, but as we enter the next century many of the world's large mammals are threatened. Some are persecuted mercilessly; others are squeezed into progressively smaller areas where they encounter numerous problems. The present slaughter of elephants and rhinos for ivory and horns is reminiscent of last century's repugnant practice of killing bison for tongues and hides. Species the size of pandas, grizzly bears, and gorillas occur in isolated reserves where the nearest adjacent groups may be hundreds of miles away, effectively severing the spread of genes from one area to the next. Through meddling, reintroductions have occurred where Kenyan lions were mixed with those from Botswana, and the endangered Sonoran pronghorn was contaminated genetically in at least one Mexican reserve by hybridizing it with pronghorns from northern California. Although successes like the carefully planned reintroduction of Arabian oryx in Oman do occur (Stanley-Price 1989), the more common pattern has been demographic, genetic, and disease-related maladies that jeopardize continued survival. In the decades ahead the unending catalog of horrors will be exacerbated. Compared to the 1980s, they already are.

What lessons have been learned? To what extent can knowledge from past failures and successes be applied to future conservation programs? Because more than 95% of the world's mammals are polygynous, a system of mating in which only a small proportion of males obtain a majority of copulations, an inevitable consequence of limited space in isolated populations will be a high proportion of matings with relatives. Is this a problem? If so, how severe is it? Does it vary among species that differ in their histories, and what strategies might be employed to ameliorate this and other potential dilemmas we face?

These issues are the focus of this book. We use North American bison as a model and then enlarge our scope to include what is known or may be surmised for other large, similarly fated species. In essence this book is a hybrid, fusing and building on knowledge from two largely disparate fields, conservation biology and behavioral ecology. This chapter introduces some of the fundamental concepts of conservation biology, first by describing natural history and evolution, and then the nature of today's problems and those to be confronted in the future.

1.1 Why Study Natural History?

Natural history is the study of faunas or floras and their consequent relationships with biotic and abiotic factors. Today, it is mostly associated with the study of biodiversity. But why does natural history matter? Some scientists regard it as valueless description without rigor which even a novice could undertake, unlike genetics and modeling exercises. Others believe aesthetic and ethical justifications alone are sufficient (Ehrenfeld 1981; Ehrlich and Ehrlich 1981). Nevertheless, given that natural history has been sudied from other perspectives centuries (Zirkel 1938) and considerable monies, interest, and exploitation of it have occurred, some explanation of its significance seems appropriate.

Wild ecosystems have been converted for human use at rates estimated from 1 to 10 acres per second planetwide. The alterations we now experience exceed those that occurred 65 million years ago by orders of magnitude. Dinosaurs disappeared at the rate of one species every ten thousand years (Stanley 1985); estimates of today's extinctions range from one species per day to five hundred per year (Myers 1985). For mammals, the rates exceed those in the fossil record by a magnitude of from 700% to 7000% (Flesness 1989). Accurate estimates are impossible because most of this planet's species have yet to be named or even identified (Diamond 1985; Wilson 1988). But it is no longer debatable that the earth's biological systems are in rapid decay. Baseline natural history data, often gathered in ecological reserves, have been viewed as one of the critical ways in which to gauge and mitigate harmful alterations, although recent information casts doubt about the efficacy of many reserves for assuring the long-term persistence of species or even populations (Janzen 1983; Schaller et al. 1985; Western and Pearl 1989).

Such points aside, natural history is often thought of as the study of whole organism biology in the natural world (Willson 1984; Greene and Losos 1988). By definition, it could also refer to changes in the natural world over time. Many believe that natural history experienced its apogee last century, when the bulk of new species were described, but it may be more appropriate to include biological inventories as only one component of natural history. The continued importance of biological exploration is highlighted by efforts of numerous funding agencies, including the International Union for Conservation of Nature and Natural Resources, the Man and the Biosphere Program of UNESCO, the World Wide Fund for Nature, the National Science Foundation, the Smithsonian Institution, and a myriad of biodiversity initiatives. To conclude, therefore, that the study of natural history is the stuff of ancient naturalists or that it cannot be personally and professionally rewarding would be difficult.

1.2 Mating and Large Mammals

Many of the world's well-known megaherbivores share common life-history features, including large body size, low reproductive rates, and horns, antlers, or tusks (Owen-Smith 1988); they are also polygynous, a breeding system in which some males mate with more than one female, whereas others go mateless. Darwin (1871:232), with typical insight, claimed that "the practice of polygamy leads to the same results as would follow from an actual inequality in the number of the sexes; for if each male secures two or more females, many males cannot pair; and the latter assuredly will be the weaker or less attractive individuals." Most biologists agree that understanding the causes and the consequences of mating relationships is important: the former because they offer insights about selection pressures that have shaped past behavior, the latter because they affect copulatory dynamics that will shape the genetic material upon which future selection will operate. For instance, when access to mates is restricted by factors such as social behavior, the potential for genetic representation by some individuals over that of others is exaggerated beyond what might be expected under unaltered conditions. In small populations where males do not experience high turnover rates, all off-spring may be descended from a single dominant male. This scenario is of immediate conservation concern because levels of genetic relatedness within the population will be much higher than if genetically unrelated males were rotated for breeding with females. This concept will come as no surprise to those who breed livestock or manage captive populations. What is important to recognize is that the effects of a skew in mating success can be exacerbated when populations are isolated from one another.

The extent to which manipulations of breeding affect the genetic structure of populations has received much attention, primarily in zoological parks and small reserves (Ralls and Ballou 1986a), but large-bodied, free-roaming mammals have rarely fallen within the realm of such malleable systems. Large species present considerable challenges. They generally require vast amounts of space, and effects of different management regimes are usually difficult to assess because replicate populations are often unavailable. Principles developed for easier-to-study species are rarely applied to nomadic or mobile species such as white-eared kob, saiga antelope, pronghorn, springbok, and wildebeest (Child and Le Riche 1969; Pennycuick 1975; Fryxell 1987; Fryxell, Greever, and Sinclair 1988; Durant et al. 1988), which encounter problems because of poaching, political instability, and migration routes that are routinely severed by fences and agriculture. The problems faced by larger ungulates are even more intensive. Pere David's deer and Przewalski horses occur only in zoological parks, where gene flow is promoted by humans; rhinos and elephants face extinction because of human desire for their horns and tusks. Regardless of the ecological situations confronted by species with different life histories, individuals in small populations all face similar problems that arise because of their breeding systems.

Breeding Systems

Polygyny has been defined as a system in which "more females than males breed, with the result that variance in reproductive success is greater in males than in females. The greater the differences in variance, the greater the degree of polygyny" (Shields 1987:6). Monogamy, on the other hand, occurs when an equal number of males and females breed with just one partner and the degree of reproductive variance is much less than polygyny (Kleiman 1977; Shields 1987). These definitions are appealing because they do not rely on proximate mechanisms of spacing, consortships, pair bonds between individuals, or other behaviors. Only the consequences of mating are of immediate interest.

More than 95% of the world's mammals are polygynous (Kleiman 1977). Although data on the degree of variation in reproduction exist for only a handful of mammals (Chepko-Sade, Shields et al. 1987; Clutton-Brock 1988b), and to think that most studies of mating systems will result in such information is unreasonable, inferences about mating systems can be based on the distribution of the sexes, social groupings, and intrasexual aggression (Ralls 1976; Eisenberg 1981; Clutton-Brock et. al 1980). For instance, numerous species of tamarins are found in family groups with just a single adult pair and associated offspring (Goldizen 1987), whereas red howler and black-and-white colobus monkeys occur in groups with multiple females and usually a single adult male (Struhsaker 1975; Crockett and Eisenberg 1987). For species like bighorn sheep (Geist 1971a; Shank 1982; Festa-Bianchet 1988a) or moose (Miquelle 1989), where males and females are sexually segregated except for the breeding season, it is reasonable to conclude that polygyny characterizes the species, although little may be known about the degree of polygyny. Ancillary information that has bolstered such conclusions include observations on aggressive interactions, dominance, and the degree of sexual dimorphism, the latter in which a correlation between species with large ratios of variance in reproduction and degree of dimorphism exists (Emlen and Oring 1977; Alexander et al. 1979; Clutton-Brock, Guinness, and Albon 1982).

Mammalian breeding systems vary both spatially and temporally, from male congregations that attract females, to leks (Gosling 1986), to clumped females that are receptive sequentially to males (Berger 1989; Ims 1990), to widely spaced females that enter estrus at similar times, as in several monogamous primates (Hrdy and Whitten 1987). In the latter case direct competition among males may not occur because males remain exclusively with specific females. By and large the most common means by which mate access occurs is through the development of dominance relationships, but it is not the only means. In populations where individuals become familiar with one another, males with poor probabilities of breeding (e.g., subordinate, temporarily injured, young) may increase their rates of advertisement (see chapter 8); in others, they may trade potential breeding opportunities to feed in the most nutritious areas (Berger 1987) or move to peripheral regions and wait for another chance to mate (Gosling 1986). Other proximate effects of socially mediated competition include dispersal to areas where the potential for breeding is higher (Dobson 1982; Moore and Ali 1984), adoption of sneaky and satellite male strategies (Wirtz 1981, 1982), and formation of coalitions to oust or protect against rival males (Darwin 1871; Packer and Pusey 1982, 1983a). Whatever immediate tactic is taken, the ultimate force behind mating has been natural selection (Williams 1966; Wilson 1975). However, the effects of most interest to conservation biologists are those that result from socially restricted mating when dispersal opportunities are limited, habitats are fragmented, and populations are small.

Consequences of Polygyny

Breeding systems are, in essence, by-products of evolution; the behavior of individuals has been molded by natural selection, not by monogamy or polygyny per se. Nevertheless, because mating systems may constrain the breeding and migration of individuals, they can have striking demographic, ecological, and evolutionary effects. Adult sex ratios are often modified because males of polygynous mammals usually experience greater mortality than females (Ralls, Brownell, and Ballou 1980). The asymmetry has been attributed to at least four factors: (1) higher costs (including injuries) associated with male reproductive competition, (2) greater susceptibility of males to nutritional stress, (3) higher rates of male emigration, and (4) sex differences in maternal investment. Mixed support exists for all of these (Ralls, Brownell, and Ballou 1980; Michener 1980; Clutton-Brock and Albon 1982). An additional possibility is that females are more numerous at birth than males, but the evidence argues against this; for most species, the sex ratio at birth approaches parity (Clutton-Brock and Iason 1986).

With respect to sexually dimorphic ungulates such as moose, bighorn sheep, and red deer, one of the more striking spatial effects concerns the extent to which males and females occupy different habitats. Although precisely how these differences relate to polygyny is still unclear, three classes of explanations have been suggested: (1) the sexes differ in predator avoidance strategies (Geist and Bromley 1978; Geist and Bayer 1988); (2) the sexes differ in parental investment, with females selecting areas to enhance nutritional gains for their young (Clutton-Brock, Guinness, and Albon 1982; Festa-Bianchet 1988a); and (3) the nutritional demands of males and females differ because of allometric scaling (Bowyer 1984; McCullough, Hirth, and Newhouse 1987). Distinguishing among these has been difficult (Miquelle 1989; Berger 1991a), but what is important is that mechanisms of social competition upon which selection has acted have obvious effects at the ecosystem level—in this case, the use of different areas by males and females.

Mating systems can also have strong effects on the direction of selection and vice versa. The degree of polygyny will be dependent on variables such as breeding sex ratio and environmental conditions. Although this may be of *basic* interest from the perspective of evolutionary mechanisms, one goal of conservation biologists is to minimize the potential role of genetic drift in populations that have been reduced in size because of humans. Relationships between quantitative genetics and processes such as sexual selection have long been studied, but influences of variation in reproductive success have rarely been used in the development of models with application to conservation (Barrowclough and Rockwell 1993). For instance, if differences in reproductive success or survival were due exclusively to phenotypic variation, selection would not occur and the opportunity for selection would be equivalent to the "opportunity for genetic drift" (McVey 1988). Thus knowledge of some of the evolutionary processes affecting mating systems can be applied directly to the study of small polygynous populations.

Genetic variation is a function of population size, structure, and stochastic events. In many populations, especially those such as large terrestrial animals, which require large amounts of space, the genetic variation present will inevitably result from the degree of disturbance suffered at the hands of humans. For instance, in species where predation and juvenile mortality exert negligible influences on survival, any individual differences in male reproduction will arise because of differential access to mates (Berger 1986). Two classes of species have become the focus of attention for genetic management, and for both classes long-term goals are to preserve as much genetic variation as possible. The first category, small captive populations that include species such as black-footed ferrets and Przewalski horses, is usually managed in ways to minimize the loss of genetic diversity and to facilitate reintroduction into large reserves (Ralls and Ballou 1986a, 1986b). The second class is represented by widely distributed but uncommon species whose demographic survival is not in immediate jeopardy, but whose long-term evolutionary potential may be limited by low levels of genetic variability. Cheetahs, pronghorn, bighorn sheep, and bison are examples.

1.3 Insularization and Conservation

Because many of the world's species no longer occur in continuous undisturbed environments, their distributions are referred to as fragmented; those occupying disjunct habitats, whether disturbed by humans or not, may be referred to as insular, or allopatric, populations. When populations become fragmented and successful dispersal from one area to another becomes problematic, population viability may become questionable, especially when population sizes are reduced or the available habitat is small. Populations or species that fit the above picture are of greatest concern because demographic jeopardy is exacerbated (Soule 1980). Principles of island biogeography have been applied with these species in mind.

Insights to the Past and Future

Darwin (1859) and Wallace (1876) were among the first to consider effects of time, isolation, and local environment not only on speciation and local adaptation but also on extinction. The concept in its most elementary form is that larger areas will contain more species and larger populations than smaller areas. If an area under consideration is islandlike (i.e., unsuitable habitat surrounds it) and distant from colonizing sources, a relationship will exist between extinction and immigration (MacArthur and Wilson 1967; Brown 1971). An example from the Sunda Shelf is illustrative. Three present islands, Sumatra, Borneo, and Java, were connected to the adjacent Malay Peninsula during the Pleistocene. The islands now differ in the composition of their large mammal communities (Terborgh 1974; Diamond 1980). Tigers are absent from Borneo, but not from the other two islands. Orangutans do not occur on Java, but are present on Borneo and Sumatra. The Malay tapir is found only on Sumatra, as is the Siamang gibbon (Terborgh 1974). The present patterns presumably arose as a consequence of stochasticity in immigrations and extinctions.

Large oceanic islands and large insular parks harbor relatively greater numbers of species than smaller areas. New Zealand and Serengeti National Park have species diversity exceeding that of smaller islands in the Hawaiian archipelago or Yellowstone Park (Berger 1991b). Of more immediate concern is that virtually all of the world's national parks are too small to allow for mammalian speciation given the magnitude of area required for speciation (Soule 1980). Endemic mammals of the world's

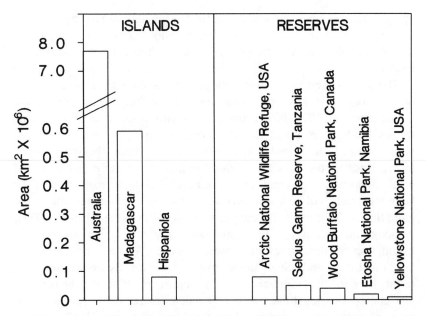

FIGURE 1.1. Comparison between the sizes of true islands upon which mammalian speciation events have occurred and the world's largest nature reserves. Taxonomic groups for speciation are marsupials, lemurs, and insectivores. Modified from Soule 1980.

largest islands, Australia and Madagascar, have experienced speciation, but wildlife refuges and national parks are quite tiny by comparison (see fig. 1.1). They are unlikely to provide the space needed for the evolution of unique forms, even assuming complete protection for millions of years. The smallest island on which autochthonous speciation is known to have occurred is Hispaniola where solenodon are found, but even reserves the size of the Arctic National Wildlife Refuge and the Selous Game Reserve are representative of less than 0.5% of the world's parks. And they may simply be too small for the evolution of new life forms.

Perhaps worrying about the size of areas needed to facilitate long-term evolutionary events is foolish, particularly in light of human population growth and the difficulty of forecasting events for longer than several decades. In the 1930s about 2 billion people inhabited the earth (Ehrlich 1968); in the early 1990s the population exceeded 5 billion. By the beginning of the twenty-first century nearly sixty cities will have more than 5 million people; only seven cities had that many in 1950 (Western 1989). Nearly 95% of the world's population increase will be in developing countries, and the world's projected population size by the year 2100 is from 10 to 14 billion. Looking at trends over the short term may be a more prudent way to guide the future direction of conservation events.

The first explicit use of island biogeographic theory for the conservation of mammals involved extinction rates of large mammals on the Sunda Shelf in 1974 (see above), ideas later applied to shorter time frames for large mammal faunas of nineteen African savanna national parks. Soule, Wilcox, and Holtby (1979) used the term "benign neglect" in reference to the idea that without human intervention extinction of local faunas would be rapid. For the average 4,000 km^2 park, 11% of the large mammals will be lost in fifty years, 44% in five hundred years, and more than 75% in five thousand years (Soule, Wilcox, and Holtby 1979). Although the accuracy of these predictions has been questioned because assumptions of insular equilibria were violated (Western and Ssemakula 1981) and the Sunda Shelf model may not be directly comparable, the results have led to simulations and new empirical tests at both the community and species level (see table 1.1). For instance, using park size and years of protection as independent variables, Newmark (1987) showed that both variables accounted for 71% of the variation in the remaining species. Similar findings are now available for Canadian parks (Glenn and Nudds 1989).

Historical data have also been valuable in projecting rapid changes, especially since they offer ways to examine species persistence without simulation. Bighorn sheep in deserts of the southwestern United States highlight the magnitude of demographic jeopardy that results from small population size. All populations with fewer than fifty individuals experienced extinction within fifty years, whereas populations with one hundred animals or more persisted for up to seventy years (see fig. 1.2). Such results indicate that population size can be used as a marker of persistence trajectories; they also suggest that local extinction in this species could not be overcome because fifty individuals failed to constitute a long-term viable population. Although paradigms based on size-area relationships and historical data have been applied to conservation at the community-level perspective, they represent only two of several ways to project species persistence. Spatial requirements, simulations of genetic diversity in isolated populations, and empirical assessments, all for single species, have been employed to examine short- and long-term persistence probabilities for species such as black-footed ferrets, bighorn sheep, and grizzly bears, all of which may occur in disjunct populations (see table 1.1).

TABLE 1.1.

Summary of studies applying predictions of island biogeography (PIB) to conservation biology of mammalian populations

Theme	Location	Result	Data	Reference
Community-level				
National parks as islands	East Africa	Faunal collapse likely without human intervention	E–S	Soule, Wilcox, and Holtby 1979
Savanna reserves as faunal enclaves	East Africa	Landscape and habitat diversity, not PIB, explain patterns for most species	E–S	Western and Ssemakula 1981
Parks as disturbed islands	East Africa	Intense management needed to maintain viable populations	E–S	East 1981, 1983
National parks as land-bridge islands	Western North America	Park area and time since established account for 71% of extinctions	E	Newmark 1986, 1987
Parks as islands	Canada	Smaller parks less likely to fit PIB than larger parks	E	Glenn and Nudds 1989
Land-bridge montane communities	Great Basin Desert, U.S.	Populations on small mountains experience more frequent losses	E	Brown 1971; Diamond 1984
Land-bridge montane communities	Great Basin Desert, U.S.	Predicted and observed population persistence probabilities fit expectations	E–S	Brown 1971; Belovsky 1987
Land-bridge Pleistocene islands	Bass Strait Islands, Australia	Higher extinction rates of herbivorous marsupials on smaller islands	E	Diamond 1984
Species retention on semi-isolated mountains	Rocky Mountains, U.S.	Losses inversely related to area size (human disturbance included)	E	Picton 1979
Insular communities in old-growth forests	Northwest USA	Species persistence related to size of available patches	R	Harris 1984
Biotic diversity and park size	U.S.	Largest parks do not contain greatest diversity	R	Schonewald-Cox 1983

TABLE 1.1. (Continued)

Theme	Location	Result	Data	Reference
Species-level				
Tigers	Java/Bali, Indonesia	Small populations have high extinction probabilities	E	Seidensticker 1987a
Grizzly bears	Rocky Mountains, U.S.	Persistence of isolated populations improbable	S	Harris, Maguire, and Shaffer 1987
Black-footed ferrets	Wyoming, U.S.	Disease-promoted extinction in wild; populations below 120 not likely to survive long term in wild	S	Clark 1989; Harris, Clark, and Shaffer 1989
Bighorn sheep	Deserts of U.S.	All populations smaller than 50 extinct within 50 years	E	Berger 1990

E = empirical data; S = simulation; R = review

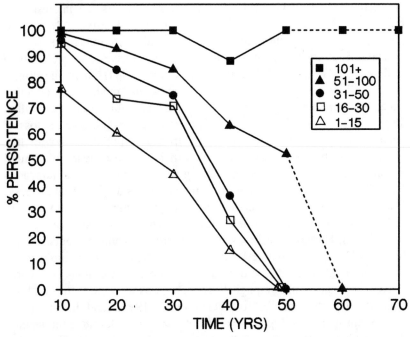

FIGURE 1.2. Relationship between time and the percent persistence of bighorn sheep populations. The number of individuals in five size categories is shown. From Berger 1990.

Small Populations and Genetic Structure

The rates at which small populations lose heterozygosity is roughly proportional to their size. Measures of population size based on the members that effectively contribute genes to subsequent generations are important as constructs because they provide standard ways to compare population structure across species or populations (Wright 1978). Effective population size (N_e) has been defined as the size of an ideal population that loses the same amount of genetic variability as an actual population under consideration (Crow and Kimura 1970). Under real-world conditions, mating is not panmictic and polygyny reduces N_e far below actual population size. When populations contain a small number of breeding individuals, the random loss of genetic diversity may occur due to chance mating, a process known as genetic drift. This occurs because small samples of zygotes in successive generations are few enough to produce random fluctuations in alleles with the result that alleles are either lost by chance or fixed (Grant and Grant 1990). Because managers are interested in preserving populations and genetic variability, identifying N_e is important, as is gaining knowledge about past and future influences. The serious consequences of a loss of genetic variation are well known (Falconer 1981; Lasley 1978; Mitton and Grant 1984), including diminished abilities to cope with changing conditions, reduced reproductive capacities, diminished growth, and increased mortality (Ralls and Ballou 1983; Allendorf and Leary 1986). Numerous factors promote the loss of heterozygosity. When gene flow is restricted in populations with low N_e's, mating between close relatives will be a consequence of limited dispersal and result in offspring with a greater proportion of homozygous loci. The population will, therefore, increase in its degree of relatedness. But homozygosity and inbreeding are not synonymous as homozygosity can increase in disjunct populations even when close relatives do not mate (Ralls, Harvey, and Lyles 1986). A small population founded by a historically large one may retain only a small proportion of heterozygosity and, with continued genetic drift, become more homozygous (Allendorf 1986; Lande and Barrowclough 1987). This was found to be true in lions from the Ngorongoro Crater (Packer et al. 1991), and Indian rhinos may retain unusually high levels of heterozygosity despite experiencing demographic contractions (Dinerstein and McCracken 1990). On the other hand, inbreeding per se may not have deleterious consequences in species that are already inbred (e.g., Speke's gazelle; Templeton and Read 1983), although evidence from captive populations and domestic species supports the opposite view—that matings between close relatives result in increased mortality (see Lacy, Petric, and Warneke 1993). Most scientists agree that the reduction of genetic variation in species today is the specter of death tomorrow; thus the prudent tactic is to conserve as much variation as possible (Lasley 1978; Falconer 1981; Ralls and Ballou 1983; Brussard 1991).

1.4 Model Species and Bison

A major goal of most conservation organizations is to conserve uniqueness. Although large mobile mammals would not rank as the first choice of many ecologists as organisms with which to model and test ecological and evolutionary principles, the earth is full of unique organisms. To ignore large mammals because sample sizes might be small or logistical problems large is to sacrifice opportunities to learn more about natural variation and to engender involvement by a public largely sympathetic to many conservation issues, if for no reason other than they recognize the species at stake. For a species or system to be useful as a model, biological features must be applicable to a wide array of topics. To use a monogamous species as a mammalian model would make little sense when more than 95% of the world's mammals are polygynous (Kleiman 1977). But to claim that a single polygynous species is representative of nonmonogamous breeders would be equally unreasonable, as species vary widely in the degree to which they are polygynous. We adopted bison, which appear to be a good model for seven principal reasons:

1. *Space, visibility, and public awareness.* Time is running out for long-term studies of large mammals. As human populations proliferate, the space needed by large mammals becomes less plentiful, and at some point it will be impossible to address certain issues simply because populations will be too managed. If we are to make recommendations to developing countries about their resources and conservation strategies, it seems prudent to select a well-known species that Americans nearly depleted and have now restored. What is desperately needed is a long-term success story. Bison were among the first animals to be relocated and saved. Their plight last century has been chronicled and remains well known. Although bison now exist in multiple isolated reserves, they are symptomatic of many present species and serve as a grim reminder for the future.

2. *Fragmented populations and insular ecosystems.* Unlike many species, bison are not in demographic jeopardy. They are distributed widely. However, their past ecosystems are mostly destroyed, and gene flow among populations does not occur except in cases of human intervention. Because many other species already exist in situations not unlike bison and others will experience similar fates in the near future, information on bison should enhance knowledge about insularization effects.

3. *Availability of domestic counterparts.* The availability of closely related species makes it possible to rely on a wealth of detailed, and often experimental, information. Although little work has been conducted on bison physiology, digestion, genetics, or reproduction, an enormous literature is available for cattle.

4. *Prior data bases.* For many species the absence of solid preliminary data means that techniques, sampling methods, field logistics, and other problems must be resolved. This is not the case

for bison. Rutting behavior, female relationships, and feeding
ecology have all been investigated (see chapter 2). More important, perhaps, historical records are available not only on
past distribution but also on founding herd sizes, transplants,
and reintroductions.

5. *Data collection and handling*. As with many wild species, bison
can be observed reasonably easily once they become habituated.
Distinct individual differences also exist, which facilitate identification in the absence of artificial marking. In addition, bison,
unlike many other large mammals, can be regularly restrained at
some sites because capture traps with scales have been established and remain in place from year to year. Hence, size and
weight relationships and ages can be determined, nondescript animals can be marked with tags, and genetic sampling can be carried out.

6. *Reproductive data*. Gathering reproductive data for most wild
mammals is difficult. Females with offspring are often secretive,
young may be secluded, and monitoring juvenile survival is expensive or impossible. Male copulatory success is usually anything but obvious. Bison copulate and bear young in open environments where visibility is often great, allowing data to be gathered on the breeding biology of known individuals.

7. *Suitability of study sites and interagency cooperation*. Whereas
many species can be studied at multiple locations, bison are
highly restricted to managed sites (see chapter 2). To develop
studies where known individuals may be hunted and valuable
data lost would make little sense. Likewise, to select areas
where intensive management or human populations regularly dis-
turb animals would be imprudent. Although the majority of sites
occupied by bison in the United States fit into these categories,
Badlands National Park does not. The bison occur in a federally
designated wilderness where roads are prohibited, and the area
is seldom visited by people on foot. Our choice of site was
strongly influenced by the cooperation we received from the National Park Service. The agency provided almost unlimited logistical coordination, including marking, handling, weighing, and
immobilizing animals, as well as providing employee assistance, horses, and vehicles. Such good working relationships obviously enhance data collection but are sometimes difficult to
maintain, particularly when the target species are popular with
the public (Craighead 1979; Chase 1986; Clark 1989).

1.5 Goals and Format of the Book

In using bison as a study animal, we have three goals. First, we present new data about behavioral ecology with the caveat that bison of the twentieth century may already differ from those of past eras. That we do not know more about bison behavior of the past is unfortunate. But understanding their present mating system and determining how to project its effect on subsequent population structure is what is important for the future. Second, we analyze our data in ways to aid bison conservation. Third, we attempt to show that behavioral ecology can be studied in a conservation framework so that large mammals that survive until the twenty-first century will have a better chance of surviving into the twenty-second century and beyond.

In numerous areas our behavioral observations are interpreted within an evolutionary context, some of which will have little immediate relevance to conservation. We justify this on two principal grounds. First, if every study was designed to uncover only facts of direct relevance to conservation, many topics studied today might have been avoided. Questions about dispersal, mechanisms of inbreeding avoidance, sexual selection, and mating systems might have been sacrificed as being "too behavioral." But investigations into each of these four areas have produced new insights into population structure and selection pressures, issues that are now of direct relevance to the conservation of genetic diversity at species, population, and individual levels. Second, issues like sexual segregation, habitat use, movements, and feeding behavior may have questionable application to conservation simply because the link to a species population structure seems tenuous. But issues that deal with land or space use provide insights about how individuals economize time and food, and thwart rivals. They also tell us something about other organisms in the ecosystem. When one's goal is not just to save individual species, but to investigate complex ecological processes such as migration or predator-prey relationships (e.g., black-footed ferret–prairie dog), knowing something about how bison use their space may eventually apply to other components of the ecosystem. We do not claim that study of a single species for a short time frame in one area will solve all or even many conservation problems; we do believe empirical results can be applied in numerous ways to the conservation of large mammals. We develop a perspective based on a five-year study and seventy-five years of historical information about a long-lived mammal surviving in isolated populations.

The next two chapters are introductory in nature, describing bison historically and in their current distribution (chapter 2), then providing features of our study—its methods, background, and the Badlands population (chapter 3). We next deal with land use systems of bison and other large mammals (chapter 4), population regulation and impacts of modern man (chapter 5), and essential aspects of breeding biology, such as reproductive synchrony and gestation adjustment, as well as relationships between body size, weight, and age (chapter 6). In the next two chapters (7 and 8) information about female and male behavior, reproductive success, and tactics to enhance mating opportunities is given. Chapters 9 and 10 discuss consequences of socially restricted mating, genetic variation, and possible effects of lineage mixing in the small Badlands population. The final chapter (11) deals with the demise of many large animals, options for bison, and some immediate conservation issues , including the degree of human manipulation necessary to balance ecological processes and socioeconomic issues. In a real-world sense, conservation will be infinitely more complex than merely melding concepts in behavioral biology, demography, and genetics. Ultimately it will be shaped by economics, politics, and education, although we hope that conservation efforts will lead, rather than follow, economic, political, and education issues of the future.

1.6 Summary

1. This chapter introduces the basic ideas and format of the book.
2. Natural history has proved to be a fertile area for study because it offers a fuller understanding and appreciation for the earth's living organisms. This enhanced knowledge about species and processes critical to their sustenance can be useful in inhibiting ecosystem degradation.
3. Knowledge about ecological changes in the past has been used in the development of theory pertaining to conservation biology. Among the major conceptual advances applied to conservation have been island biogeography and population viability analysis, both of which are predicated on an understanding of demography, ecology, and historical geography. For populations restricted to isolated reserves, knowledge about animal behavior and population genetics will also be useful in the implementation of sound management.
4. Large-bodied mammals are especially vulnerable to effects of

habitat fragmentation, if only because they require a lot of space. When populations of such species become isolated and when populations are small, an increase in the level of inbreeding will occur as relatives are forced to mate with one another. When the species is characterized by polygyny, a few dominant individuals may sire most offspring, leading to a further increase in the mean relatedness of the population.

5. Big mammals with migratory habits have been especially difficult to fit within the more conventional conservation models because experimental populations have not been readily available for study, replicates are hard to find, and difficulties arise in their management because of interagency conflicts. Nevertheless, because of the public's interest in large mammals, unusual opportunities to develop public support for species and ecosystem conservation exist.

2. Bison of the Past, Present, and Future

Once we were happy in our own country and we were seldom hungry, for the two-leggeds and the four-leggeds lived together like relatives, and there was plenty for them and for us. But the Wasichus [whites] came, and they made little islands for us and other little islands for the four-leggeds and always these islands are becoming smaller.

Black Elk, ca. 1875

Two species of bison exist: the European bison, or wisent, and the North American bison with two recognized subspecies, plains and wood bison. The bison of today are not quite like those of yesterday. They no longer roam vast unfenced prairies; the impacts of nonhuman predators have been negligible for more than a century; and the catastrophic reduction of populations to minute remnants of their former abundance may have produced genetic changes. The present wisent are all descended from twelve animals (Slatis 1960; Olech 1987), whereas more than sixty-five hundred plains bison were shipped to northern Canada, where they hybridized with wood bison (van Zyll de Jong 1986; Carbyn et al. 1993). The subsequent discovery of a few remaining presumably pure wood bison precipitated the shipment of eighteen animals 300 km north to a reserve in the Northwest Territories (Calef 1984), but the extent to which these animals may have already been inbred remains unknown (Geist 1990). Plains bison were fractured into multiple tiny isolated populations. In *The Last of the Buffalo* George Bird Grinnell rekindles the shame of one hundred years ago: "As I gaze at these relics [skulls] of the past, they take life forms before my eyes. The matted brown hair again clothes the dry bone, and in the empty orbits the wild eyes gleam. Above me curves the blue arch, away on every hand stretches the yellow prairie, and scattered near and far are the dark forms. . . . Heads down and tails in air, they rush away from their pursuers . . . till the black mass sweeping over the prairie numbers thousands" (Grinnell 1892:267).

Although the herds of today are not ecologically quite the same, bison are among the first success stories of American conservation (McHugh

1972). They were reintroduced into former ranges and later reestablished in disjunct populations for protection against catastrophe. Initial preservation efforts, once championed by nongovernment organizations such as the New York Zoological Society through the American Bison Society, were later assumed by the U.S. government. In this chapter we offer a brief overview of the largest terrestrial mammal of the New World, presenting information on bison paleohistory, relationships with native Americans, and the carnage of the 1800s. We also discuss conservation achievements of the early twentieth century and summarize the present distribution of bison.

2.1 Bison Origins

Bison are bovids, members of the subfamily Bovinae. The oxlike tribe includes the true buffalo, both African and Asian, wild cattle, and bison (Sinclair 1977; McDonald 1981). Ecologically, the Bovini comprise some of the least-known species of surviving large mammals, kouprey, banteng, gaur, tamarou, and anoa (Popenoe 1983). Based on morphological criteria, the taxonomic status of some species remains questionable, but systematic relationships for Asian water buffalo, bison, and yak have recently been examined using mitochondrial (mt) DNA (Miyamoto, Tanhauser, and Laipis 1989). The family has been known since the early Miocene (Pilgrim 1947), with the genus *Bison* first appearing on the Asian subcontinent around the Pliocene-Pleistocene border (Geist 1971b; McDonald 1981). Whereas most species in the subfamily evolved and remain in warm, moist, and tropical/subtropical environments, both bison and yak radiated into cold northern climes (Schaller 1976, 1977; Geist and Karsten 1977).

Various scenarios have been proposed for examining relationships between the paleohabitats of different bison species and their social groupings as well as morphological changes over time. Using modern analogues, McDonald (1981) suggested that bison occupied three different habitat types during the late Quaternary: forests and woodlands, savannas and wooded steppes, and open grasslands, with different ecotypes varying in their behavior and morphological adaptations. Geist (1971b, 1983) and Geist and Karsten (1977) indicated that changes in body size, secondary sexual traits, and pelage and hair patterns are tied to dispersal into previously uncolonized habitats. Guthrie (1990) summarized bison history in relation to body size and geography, focusing particularly on the ecology of the extinct steppe bison.

2.2 Brief History: Humans, Extermination, and Early Conservation

Evidence of human predation on bison during the Holocene is widespread, from Texas to Alberta and Minnesota to Siberia. Bison bone beds were once thought of as mass natural kills (Wilson 1978), but detailed accounts of hunting procurement, processing, and subsistence patterns substantiate human involvement (Davis and Wilson 1978; Frison 1978; Speth 1983; Guthrie 1990). Bison were harvested at least fifty-five hundred years ago at the Heads-Smashed-In site in southern Alberta. They were driven for as much as 6.5 km toward and over cliffs that were 10 to 15 m high and extended across a 300-m lateral distance; excavation depths reach nearly 10 m (Reeves 1978). Folsom projectile points more than ten thousand years old have been recovered from Wyoming's Hell Gap site (Irwin-Williams et al. 1973), and bison procurement on the northern prairies included driving animals through arroyos and ravines and over cliffs (Frison 1978).

Not surprisingly, kill sites varied in the proportion of adult males and females. Like many large temperate ungulates (Geist and Petocz 1977; Bowyer 1984), adult male and female bison segregate from one another throughout much of the year (see chapter 4). Because ungulate females of North American prairies are more gregarious than males (Berger and Cunningham 1988), human hunters of the Holocene may have found it economically desirable to design harvest tactics toward one sex or the other. For instance, bulls were preferred on the southern plains of New Mexico, whereas cows and calves were the favored victims on the northern plains, preferences that may have arisen as a consequence of sex differences in physiological condition, available fat, and vulnerability (Speth 1983). Humans had profound effects on paleomegafauna mammals including bison (Reher 1978), nevertheless numerous large species persisted at specific sites, possibly as a result of a less nomadic, more sedentary pattern of later human occupation (Martin 1984). Regardless of why bison survived the blitzkrieg, once the harvest by the Euroamericans began the cultural identities of North American Indians were lost.

Relationships with North American Indians

The deliberate slaughter of bison and Indians has been the topic of much writing, and no summary could do justice to this insidious period. When the nineteenth century began, bison were still very much a part of Indian

life. The masks, shields, and headdresses worn by the Gros Ventre and
Cheyenne were made from hair, hides, and horn. Scrapers and paint-
brushes used by the Sioux came from bone, and they, like the Comanche
and Kiowa, adorned hides with drawings of bison and other prairie scenes
and memories. The Shoshone also depicted bison on elk hides. The
Blackfoot employed enormous half-pint spoons made from horns; the
Sioux made bison incisors into necklaces. To attract bison, the Assiniboin
erected skulls on rock piles, and the Mandan danced in elaborate ceremonies for days (Barsness 1977).

Bison were hunted on horseback, snowshoes, and foot, on prairies, in
canyons, on mountains; arrows, spears, and later guns were used in the
hunt. Deep gullies, water courses, and snow-drifted ravines were preferred sites for stalking (Arthur 1975). Catlin wrote of the relationship
between the Blackfoot on the upper Missouri near the mouth of the
Yellowstone River and bison: "The buffalo herds, which graze in almost
countless numbers on these beautiful prairies, afford them an abundance
of meat; and so much is it preferred to all other, that the deer, the elk,
and the antelope sport upon the prairies in herds in the greatest security;
as the Indians seldom kill them, unless they want their skins for a dress."
(Catlin 1841:18). In Canada native Americans also found bison abundant.
In 1865 explorer John McDougall described them on the northern plains:
"more buffalo than I ever dreamed of before. The woods and plains are
full of them. During the afternoon we came to a large round plain,
perhaps 10 miles across, and as I sat on the summit of a knoll looking
over this plain, it did not seem possible to pack another buffalo into the
space. The whole prairie was one dense mass" (McDougall 1898:95).

Neither bison nor North American Indians were to survive ecologically
for much longer. By 1875 bison populations plummeted; Indian tribes
of the northern U.S. prairies were forced onto reservations; and the
socioeconomics of wildlife destruction and loss of cultural identity were
noted:

> The mere loss of food, however, is not the only evil which has resulted
> from this wastefulness and wantonness. Many of the wild Indians of the
> plains, deprived of their ordinary sustenance, Government rations not
> being forthcoming, and driven to desperation, have taken to the warpath.
> . . . In 1873, when the settlers in Kansas were suffering from the destruc-
> tion of their crops by the ravages of the grasshoppers, troops were consid-
> erately sent by the government . . . to kill meat for the starving families.
> When the soldiers arrived . . . there was little meat for them to kill, as the

TABLE 2.1.

Summary of major papers or books on bison history, anthropology, biology, and economics

Distribution	1, 2, 9, 19, 21, 27, 31, 32, 37, 39
Paleoecology	10, 11, 13, 14, 17, 26, 30, 35
History/ethnohistory	1, 2, 9–12, 16, 19, 21, 23, 27, 30, 31, 32
Behavior	4, 6, 7, 13, 15, 24, 25, 27, 28, 30, 31
Ecology	5–8, 12, 27–32, 37, 38, 40
Habitat	1, 2, 19, 27, 30–32
Reproduction	4, 12, 30, 33, 34
Art	3, 9, 27
Economics	18, 20

1—Allen 1875; 2—Arthur 1975; 3—Barsness 1977; 4—Berger 1989; 5—Berger and Cunningham 1988; 6—Carbyn and Trottier 1987; 7—Carbyn and Trottier 1988; 8—Coppock et al. 1983; 9—Dary 1974; 10—Davis and Wilson 1978; 11—Frison 1978; 12—Fuller 1966; 13—Geist 1971a; 14—Geist and Karsten 1977; 15—Green, Griswold, and Rothstein 1989; 16—Grinnell 1892; 17—Guthrie 1990; 18—Hawley 1989; 19—Hornaday 1889; 20—Jennings and Hebbring 1983; 21—Krasinski 1967; 22—Krasinski 1978; 23—Kyrsiak 1967; 24—Lott 1979; 25—Lott 1981; 26—McDonald 1981; 27—McHugh 1972; 28—Meagher 1973; 29—Oosenbrug and Carbyn 1985; 30—Reynolds, Glaholt, and Hawley 1982; 31—Reynolds and Hawley 1987; 32—Roe 1970; 33—Rutberg 1984; 34—Rutberg 1986a; 35—Skinner and Kaisen 1947; 36—Speth 1983; 37—Van Vuren and Bray 1983; 38—Van Vuren and Bray 1985; 39—Van Vuren and Bray 1986; 40—Whicker and Detling 1988

"buffalo-skinners" had anticipated them, and had slaughtered nearly every buffalo in the district. . . . The evils to the citizens of the United States arising from this wholesale and wanton destruction of the buffalo . . . may be summarized as follows: Principal Indian tribes on the plains being deprived of their annual supply of food for the winter, and only receiving short rations on the reservations, driven on the war path.

(Dodge 1875, quoted in Allen 1875b)

Extermination

The chronology of bison losses has been recorded numerous times and need not be repeated (see table 2.1). On the prairies of west Texas, Catlin wrote of his own despair 150 years ago:

We are snuggly encamped on a beautiful plain, and in the midst of countless numbers of buffaloes. . . . For several days the officers and men have been indulged in a general license to gratify their sporting propensities; a scene of bustle and cruel slaughter it has been to be sure! From morning till night, the camp had been daily deserted; the men having dispersed in little squads in all directions, and are dealing death to these poor little creatures to a most cruel and wanton extent, merely for the pleasure of destroying, generally without stopping to cut out the meat. During yesterday and this day, several hundreds have undoubtedly been killed, and not so much as the flesh of half a dozen used. Such immense swarms of them are spread over this tract of country; and so divided and terrified have they become, finding their enemies in all directions where they run, that the poor beasts seem completely bewildered—running here and there, and as often as otherwise, come singly advancing to the horsemen, as if to join them for their company, and are easily shot down. In the turmoil and confusion . . . they have galloped through our encampment, jumping over our fires, upsetting pots and kettles, driving horses from their fastenings, and throwing the whole encampment . . . into alarm.

(Catlin 1841:345)

Early Conservation Efforts and Popularity

Plains Bison.

The first report of captive bison came from Quebec around 1750, where they were kept with cattle, and from the Carolinas: "When grown up they were perfectly tame, but at the same time very unruly, so that there was no inclosure strong enough to resist them if they had a mind to break through it" (Kalm, no date, quoted in Allen 1875a). But the first serious attempts to preserve the species and to conserve genetic diversity and wildness were promoted in the 1800s by William Hornaday, although several ranchers also captured calves that would later serve as founders for numerous populations (Garretson 1934; Malcolm 1983). Hornaday led an expedition in 1886 to the Missouri–Yellowstone Divide in Montana to gather live bison for propagation in zoos (Hornaday 1889). Animals were displayed on the mall at the Smithsonian Institution in Washington, D.C., from 1889 to 1891. Hornaday, later working for the New York Zoological Society, helped establish the American Bison Society; as its first president, he conducted extensive mail censuses to determine remaining population sizes, both in captivity and in the wild.

His insightful 1906 letter could have been written today and applied to any number of species:

There are many questions which should at once be considered . . .(1) Is it safe to assume that bison can be preserved for the next 500 years? . . . (2) In view of the uncertainty of human life, of the changes in fortune and in policy toward existing herds . . . , is it possible to secure permanency in the maintenance of buffalo herds not owned by states, or the national government? (3) . . . to provide against local failures, and possible outbreaks of contagious disease, it seems desirable that several Bison herds should be established, in widely separated localities. How many herds do you think should be so established?

(American Bison Society)

In 1905 two government herds existed, the National Zoological Park's and those in Yellowstone National Park (Garretson 1934). In the next eight years, federal reserves were established at the Wichita Mountains (Oklahoma 1907), at the National Bison Range (Montana 1908), at the Niobrara Reservation (Nebraska 1913), and at Wind Cave Park (South Dakota 1913) (American Bison Society) (see appendix 2).

Wisent.

Wisent were extinct in Sweden by the eleventh century and in France by the fourteenth (Kyrsiak 1967). In Poland's Bialowieza Forest they were reduced from about seven hundred animals in 1908 to zero by the end of World War I (Ahren 1926). Although the world's wisent population was reduced to twelve founders (Slatis 1960), by 1924 it had rebounded to sixty-six with help from the International Society for the Preservation of the Wisent, which maintained pedigrees for animals housed at different zoos (Ahren 1926). In 1929 animals were placed on a reservation and then reintroduced to Bialowieza in 1952; wisent now roam in parks in the Soviet Caucuses and in Poland (Zabinski 1976; Krasinski 1967, 1978).

Wood Bison.

Wood bison followed nearly identical historical paths as plains bison and wisent. First noted by Samuel Hearns in the 1770s during explorations of northern Alberta and the Northwest Territories, they were described in the 1880s as "nearly a thing of the past. A few still remain scattered over a wide district. Could some means be devised to protect them for several years, they would probably soon multiply and become a source of food supply and revenue to the natives" (Ogilvie 1890). Historical accounts are summarized by Soper (1941), Fuller (1966), and Oosenbrug and Carbyn (1985).

In 1893 the Canadian parliament passed the first legal protection actions, and by 1911 "buffalo" ranger patrols began. Wood Buffalo National Park was established in 1922 when the bison population size was thought to be 1,500 (Fuller 1966). From 1925 to 1928, 6,673 plains bison (mostly yearlings and two-year olds) from Buffalo Park in Wainwright, Alberta, were shipped for introduction into Wood Buffalo National Park.

That regrettable decision promoted hybridization between two subspecies; at the time, it was a sensitive, highly polarized, controversial action, opposed by Canadian and American conservationists (Harper 1925; Howell 1925) It has been called "one of the most tragic examples of bureaucratic stupidity in all history" (Barbour, quoted in McHugh 1972). The issue remains volatile (Carbyn, Oosenbrug, and Anions, 1993).

Tuberculosis was later discovered in the population, which had peaked in the 1930s at around twelve thousand to fifteen thousand animals and later crashed (Fuller 1966; Tessaro 1989). In 1959 an isolated population suspected of being "pure" (i.e., nonhybridized) wood bison was found in the northwestern portion of the park, and in 1963 eighteen nondiseased animals were transplanted about 300 km north to the Mackenzie Bison Sanctuary along the northwestern border of the Great Slave Lake, where the population now numbers more than twenty-five hundred (Calef 1984; van Zyll de Jong 1990) (see fig. 2.1). The possible existence of nonhybridized populations in other areas has been raised (Van Camp 1989).

Like bison of North American prairies and wisent, wood bison have not escaped a tumultuous past. The largest population, about forty-five hundred animals in Wood Buffalo National Park (see photo 2.1), are now hybridized with plains bison and riddled with disease; controversy is likely to beset all management actions (Geist 1990; Carbyn, Oosenbrug, and Anions 1993). The extent to which the presumably isolated 1959 population was buffered from gene flow by hybrids is unclear. Nevertheless, individuals from some populations retain morphological characters reminiscent of "pure" wood bison (van Zyll de Jong 1986), and recent analyses employing DNA suggest that wood and plains bison are genetically distinct units (Bork et al. 1991).

Popularity.

Bison have many faithful followers. More than fifty books have been written about them; two private societies—the National Buffalo and American Buffalo associations—hold annual meetings; and a National Buffalo Hall of Fame exists in Tucson, Arizona. Bison once graced the American nickel. They are the symbol of the Chicago Zoological Society, the United States Department of Interior, and the American Association for Zoological Parks and Aquaria, and they adorn labels of Calgary Beer. They are featured in sports, from the University of Colorado's football team, the Buffaloes, to the Buffalo Bisons (minor league baseball) and the Buffalo Bills (professional football). They have been depicted on stamps, in advertisement, on railroad bridges, in paintings, and in sculp-

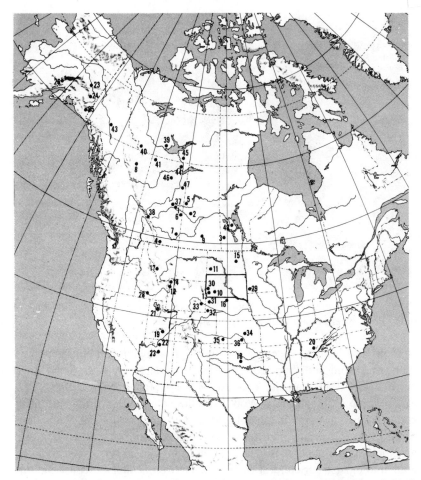

FIGURE 2.1. Distribution of extant bison populations managed by federal, state, or provincial governments. Numbers refer to specific populations listed in table 2.2. South Dakota is outlined; the Badlands population is number 10.

ture. They are marketed, registered, vaccinated, certified, and consumed as steak and burgers; they are bred with domestic stock (beefaloes and cattaloes), and hunted legally (though not in national parks) and illegally. They are sold live at auctions and are the subject of increasingly feverish legal disputes. Their bone beds are ransacked on the northern prairies.

Native Americans stock their lands with bison and use their products commercially and ceremonially; chic boutiques in Santa Fe, Los Angeles, and Rapid City sell decorated skulls to tourists; robes can be purchased

PHOTO 2.1. Female bison in thickly vegetated section of Wood Buffalo National Park, where group sizes tend to be small

from private dealers; woven bison "wool" is available, and buffalo chips (dung) are sold and flipped in contests. The largest private herds have more than 3,000 animals, and public herds range from 2,800 (Yellowstone) to 4,500 animals (Wood Buffalo National Park). Indeed, bison enthusiasts wear many hats. Not least among their followers is a devout cadre of academicians and managers—paleoecologists, ethnohistorians, anthropologists, ecologists, behaviorists, range managers, veterinarians, epidemiologists, agricultural scientists, environmentalists, conservationists, and politicians.

2.3 Extant Bison in Isolated Reserves

Bison are found in reserves of various sizes throughout North America (see fig. 2.1). In the United States bison have been prevented from recolonizing historic habitats, although this has happened in subboreal habitats of Canada (see below). A variety of logistical concerns restrict bison to isolated reserves. These include the size of individual animals (males attain weights in excess of 1,000 kg), the space required to sustain a herd, potential danger to humans, damage to agriculture, possible competition with other species, and spread of disease. Every extant herd owes its existence to human intervention, and now human intervention prevents gene flow from occurring naturally between any of the populations.

National Bison Range, Montana

The range was established in 1908 with land purchased by the U.S. government from the Salish, Kootenai, and Pend d'Oreille tribes. Bison were introduced into the area, as were white-tailed deer and pronghorn in 1910, elk in 1911, mule deer in 1918, and bighorn in 1922. Populations flourished, and by the mid-twenties more than 700 bison and 600 elk roamed the 18,542 fenced acres. Management was then established to keep populations at modest sizes, and to prevent overgrazing a rotation grazing system was begun in 1965 with bison shifted among 8 units (Cates 1986). Animals are culled annually for public auction in the fall to maintain a stable population between 300 and 350. One of the most famous inhabitants was Big Medicine, an albino bull that resided there for twenty-six years (see photo 2.2).

Yellowstone National Park, Wyoming

Yellowstone's bison population is often said to exist without human interference, governed only by processes of natural regulation (Cole 1972; Meagher 1974; Despain et al. 1986), but the group was precariously close to extinction at the turn of the century when food-supplemented, penned animals were added to enlarge the population (Meagher 1973). Most notable among contemporary problems is that many bison in the park's northern herd migrate regularly to areas outside the park despite control efforts by helicopters, rubber bullets, fences, and cattle guards (Meagher 1989a, 1989b). Once in Montana, the bison are shot. In 1988–89 this policy resulted in the killing of more than 550 animals and reduced the northern herd by more than 50%. Such actions resulted in media outcries and the development of alternate management scenarios (Vetter 1991; Peterson, Grant, and Davis 1991).

The issue is that bison have brucellosis, a bacterial disease that causes abortion in cattle (Thorne, Meagher, and Hillman 1991), and upon leaving the park bison may encounter cattle ranches. The potential for disease transmission exists, but actual cases have not been documented. Although the U.S. Department of Agriculture conducts a brucellosis eradication program in all fifty states, the State of Montana initiated a program in

PHOTO 2.2. "Big Medicine," a mostly white male bison from the National Bison Range, Montana (Courtesy of New York Zoological Society)

1985 allowing hunters to kill bison that stray into the state. Because elk also have brucellosis and outnumber bison by about 15:1, numerous groups argue that the control of bison is a Band-Aid solution to the larger problem of insularization of national parks. Problems of this sort have plagued the Greater Yellowstone Ecosystem since the park's inception in 1872 (Chase 1986), and in the absence of congressionally mediated legislation at the ecosystem level, neither swift nor easy solutions to problems created by the migrations of large herbivores are likely to be forthcoming (Berger 1991a). Currently, the National Park Service, the U.S. Forest Service, and the State of Montana are considering alternative ways to manage bison (Yellowstone bison 1990).

Jackson Hole, Wyoming

Bison occurred in the Jackson Hole area until about 1840. After a 108-year absence, they were returned in 1948 by the Wyoming Game and Fish Commission, which purchased 22 from Yellowstone Park and maintained them at a fenced preserve. Because of an outbreak of brucellosis, these animals were destroyed in 1963, but new animals were secured from North Dakota in 1964. In 1968 they escaped from enclosures, and 9 animals were permitted to roam freely, spending most of their time in Teton National Park. The herd, which consisted of only 15 animals by 1975, wintered at the National Elk Refuge adjacent to Teton National Park. Although the bison still used Teton Park during summers, the population expanded and continued to forage at the elk refuge during winter (Environmental assessment 1986). By 1992 the population had expanded to nearly 150 bison.

Four issues cloud bison management in the Teton area. First, bison roam in and out of the park, using land managed by four agencies—the National Park Service, Wyoming Game and Fish Department, U.S. Forest Service, and U.S. Fish and Wildlife Service. Second, bison carry brucellosis (as do elk in the area) and have the potential of impacting the local cattle industry. Third, elk are intensively managed while at the elk refuge; during the winter the U.S. Fish and Wildlife Service provides supplemental food (Boyce 1989). Allegations of competition between the bison and 7,000 elk for these rations prompted bison control (Environmental assessment 1986). Fourth, nongovernment organizations, the media, and the public have all become involved in the management controversy. Currently, a small number of bison are hunted on elk refuge and other public lands, primarily by Wyoming residents.

Henry Mountains, Utah

Although plains bison are often thought of as inhabitants of open prairie environments, bones have been recovered recently from alpine and subalpine areas in mountains of Utah, Wyoming, and Colorado, and a free-ranging population migrates from 1,000 to 1,500 m up to about 3,500 m in the Henry Mountains of southern Utah. The herd stems from a 1941 transplant of eighteen bison from Yellowstone National Park to lands administered by the Bureau of Land Management. Habitats vary from sagebrush and grasslands at lower elevations to discontinuous forests of spruce, fir, and aspen. Bison are hunted in the Henry Mountains and remain extremely wary of humans. "Detection of a person by either sight or smell usually caused a stampede. Once stampeded, bison ran an average of 1.8 km . . . range = 0.8-5.0" (Van Vuren 1980). In the late 1980s the population approached five hundred animals (van Zyll de Jong 1990). The major management issues concerning this population include potential competition with cattle for food and assessment of population status (Van Vuren and Bray 1983, 1986).

Custer State Park, South Dakota

Custer State Park, managed by the State of South Dakota, has about 1,400 bison in one of the most heavily manipulated populations. Animals are maintained for viewing by the public and about $200,000 per year is generated by bison. These revenues are used in park management activities that include: (1) culling "undesirable" animals, (2) midwinter weaning of calves to promote higher conception rates in cows, (3) removal of cows ten years of age or older, (4) guided hunts for males ten years or older, and (5) an annual bison auction (Walker 1987).

Alaskan Populations

Bison were extinct when the first explorers of European descent visited Alaska, but bison are believed to have been extant as recently as five hundred years ago (Peek, Miquelle, and Wright 1987). Twenty-three animals from the National Bison Range were introduced into Alaska in 1928, and four free-roaming populations currently occur: the Farewell (180 animals), Chitna (50), Copper River (100), and Delta (375) (Miquelle 1985; Dubois 1987; Peek, Miquelle, and Wright 1987). The Delta population has been particularly problematic because of its migratory tendency and subsequent consumption of barley and other grains spread out over thousands of acres, the result of the Delta Agricultural Project (see photos 2.3 and 2.4).

Wood Buffalo National Park, Canada

Because of hybridization and continued problems associated with anthrax and brucellosis, one of the boldest plans calls for removal of all bison in the park and later restocking with "pure" wood bison, an action that is both highly controversial and unlikely to be easily implemented (Redhead

PHOTO 2.3. Overview of agricultural conversion of forested areas to barley fields near Delta Junction, Alaska. Alaska Range in background.

1987; Tessaro 1989; Gainer and Saunders 1989; van Zyll de Jong 1990; Geist 1990).

Mackenzie Bison Reserve, Canada

The population of the Mackenzie Reserve has increased from 18 in 1963 to more than 2,500 in 1989 (van Zyll de Jong 1990). Groups as large as 73 (in 1983) and 217 (in 1984) have been observed, and radio-tracking data indicate that animals have colonized areas up to 70 km away (Environmental assessment 1987). In the interest of tourism, resource development, bison management, and continued conservation efforts, nonconsumptive and consumptive uses are planned.

Populations of Former Soviet States

European bison became extinct on the steppes of the Ukraine by 1920. Reintroduction began in 1965 when fifteen animals were placed at the Tsumansky State Hunting Farm in the Volynsky region. Between 1965 and 1976 bison were reestablished in six areas with populations varying from ten to forty-eight: Bakhchisarai, Crimea (fifteen animals), Buko-

PHOTO 2.4. A mixed group of bison grazing
in the barley fields shown in photo 2.3

vina, Chernovtsy (thirty), Zalesck, Kiev (ten), Maidan, Lvov (twenty-
two), Tsuman, Volyn (forty-eight), and Kolkov, Volyn (ten) (Boldenkov
1977). One park, the Kavkazsky in the Caucasus Mountains, designated
an International Biosphere Reserve in 1979, has an estimated population
of twelve hundred (Chadwick 1988).

La Margeride Reserve, France

Bison have been extinct in France for more than two thousand years, but
a small population of thirty animals of Polish descent were reintroduced
in 1990 to the La Margeride, a forested granite plateau in the northeast.
Several fenced areas are planned to promote tourism and research on
bison (Maury 1990).

2.4 Future Bison

Given the present distribution (see fig. 2.1), number of recent reintroductions, and historical and current efforts to prevent extinction (see table 2.2), bison enjoy opportunities for continued survival much greater than those of many large mammals. But because bison are isolated in many small reserves, gene flow between populations can occur only through artificial migration aided by human efforts. In addition, genetic variability appears low (Cronin 1986; McClenaghan, Berger, Truesdale 1990; Bork et al. 1991), which limits the potential for future evolutionary change. This situation arises when populations deplete their genetic variability because of bottlenecks or chance events in small isolated groups, a particularly precarious situation when rare alleles maintained by selection are lost (Frankel and Soule 1981). If individuals in a population or species are genetically homozygous, little opportunity for natural selection to operate exists, thus inhibiting evolutionary adaptations to changing conditions. Although bison are no longer in demographic jeopardy, they are among the best examples of a species where future management decisions can be designed to minimize the loss of any further genetic diversity.

Unlike captive breeding programs, which incorporate extensive demographic and genetic planning (Beck and Wemmer 1983; Foose and Foose 1983), management approaches for bison have only recently addressed these issues (Knutsen and Allendorf 1987; Shull and Tipton 1987). For instance, the JA Ranch herd, started from six animals in western Texas, has never been mixed with bison from other populations. The Bison Specialist Group of the IUCN recommends that small bison herds be managed to ''ensure the long-term survival of herd[s] and genetic integrity'' and that isolated herds with unique heritages, such as the one at the JA Ranch, be managed ''based on principles of genetic conservation'' (Frey, quoted in Pucek 1992).

Economics will also have a bearing on the continued survival of bison, which attract hunters, as well as visitors to national parks (Jennings and Hebbring 1983; Hawley 1989). One of the more radical possible scenarios involves human cultures, economic considerations, and the ecology of the northern prairies in the United States. Because human populations in rural areas of eastern Montana, Wyoming, and North and South Dakota have been declining and experiencing economic hardships for nearly half a century, one proposition has been to convert the area into a ''buffalo commons''—a vast national park restored with bison and other large mammals for viewing, harvesting, and promoting tourism (Popper and Popper 1987; Mathews 1992).

TABLE   2.2.
Distribution and status of U.S. and Canadian populations of bison*
on public lands

Location	Population size	Status
Bison bison bison in Canada		
1 Elk Island National Park	340	Fenced, artificial regulation of population
2 Prince Albert National Park	55	Free-roaming
3 Riding Mountain National Park	46	Display herd only
4 Waterton Lakes National Park	23	Display herd only
5 Primrose Lake Weapons Range	50	Free-roaming
6 Wainwright Military Reserve	14	Display herd only
7 Suffield Military Reserve	16	Display herd only
8 Pink Mountain (crown lands)	500	Free-roaming
9 Buffalo Pound Provincial Park	15	Display herd only
Bison bison bison in United States		
10 Badlands National Park	500	Free-ranging in wilderness area, controlled beyond
11 Theodore Roosevelt National Park	550	Managed by roundups
12 Grand Teton National Park	120	Limited harvest beyond park border
13 Wind Cave National Park	410	Managed by roundups
14 Yellowstone National Park	2,500	Harvested when beyond park boundaries
15 Sulley's Hill NWR	35	Artificially controlled
16 Fort Niobrara NWR	380	Managed by roundups
17 National Bison Range	450	Managed by roundups
18 Wichita Mountains NWR	700	Managed by roundups
19 Henry Mountains	400	Free-roaming, limited annual harvest
20 Land-Between-the Lakes Park	70	Fenced, managed herd
21 Antelope Island State Park	470	True island herd, managed by roundups
22 House Rock Ranch	130	Limited harvest
23 Raymond Ranch	110	Limited harvest
24 Delta Junction	450	Limited harvest, free-roaming
25 Copper River	120	Limited harvest, free-roaming
26 Chitina	70	Limited harvest, free-roaming
27 Farewell	275	Limited harvest, free-roaming
28 Three-Islands State Park	5	Display herd only
29 Blue Mounds State Park	65	Managed
30 Custer State Park	1,400	Managed by roundups and harvest
31 Fort Robinson State Park	325	Managed by round-ups
32 Wild Cat Hills State Park	10	Display herd only
33 Hot Spring/Glendo State Park	45	Managed
34 Maxwell State Game Refuge	240	Managed by roundups
35 Garden City State Game Refuge	135	Managed
36 Kingman State Game Refuge	15	Display herd only
Bison bison athabascae in Canada		
37 Elk Island National Park	222	Fenced, artificial regulation of population
38 Banff National Park	10	Display herd only
39 Mackenzie Bison Sanctuary	2,405	Free-roaming

TABLE   2.2.   (Continued)

Location	Population size	Status
40 Nahanni-Liard (crown lands)	50	Free-roaming
41 Hay-Zama (crown lands)	29	Managed in fenced area
42 Waterhen (crown lands)	200	Managed in fenced area
43 Nisling River	61	Free-roaming
Bison bison hybrids (and uncertain status)		
44 Wood Buffalo National Park	4,500	Free-roaming
45 Slave River Lowlands	200	Free-roaming
46 Wabasca River	150	Free-roaming
47 Firebag River	20	Free-roaming

Based on van Zyll de Jong 1990
NWR = National Wildlife Refuge
Numbers refer to locations on map in figure 2.1.
*As this book went to press, the genus *Bison* was changed to *Bos*.

2.5 Summary

1. The evolutionary origins of bison and subsequent relationships
   with paleohumans in North America are briefly described. Native Americans hunted bison on horseback, snowshoes, and
   foot; they used bison ceremonially as well as for food and other
   products. The annihilation of plains bison during the nineteenth
   century was coupled with the destruction of prairie Indian cultures. Wisent and wood bison experienced similar fates.

2. The private sector, and later, the federal government, contributed to the conservation of bison. Strategies included reintroduction into multiple reserves, establishment of large population
   sizes, and some shipment of animals to increase gene flow. Bison today are fragmented into more than fifty public reserves
   and marketed for tourism, as well as for food and other
   products.

3. Most bison are found in small, heavily managed populations.
   The most pressing management problems include isolation, restriction to small tracts of land (which results in rapid population
   growth and subsequent culling), and the potential for harmful effects on the livestock industry through the transmission of brucellosis or other diseases.

3.   The Study and the Badlands Ecosystem

At the horizon, at the end of an immense plain and tinted rose by the reflecting of the setting sun, a city in ruins appears to us, an immense city surrounded by walls and bulwarks, filled by a palace crowned with gigantic domes and monuments.

E. de Girardin, 1849

When the bulk of white travelers descended on North America's central prairies during the mid-nineteenth century, an ocean of grasses confronted them, pierced only by ribbons of trees along water courses stretching from Minnesota and Kansas to the Rocky Mountains and from Manitoba and Saskatchewan to Texas. In 1820 Steven Long of the U.S. Army referred to this area as the Great American Desert, and Teddy Roosevelt (1899:198) later wrote: "Far-reaching, seemingly never-ending . . . their very vastness and loneliness and their melancholy monotony have a strong fascination. . . . . The landscape seems always the same, and after the traveller has plodded on for miles and miles he gets to feel as if the distance was indeed boundless."The scenes that Roosevelt and others described were short lived. Towns sprang up, promoted in part by land made available by the federal government for homesteading, and their names reflected the animals of prairie environments: Eagle Butte, Elk Point, Buffalo, Bison, Buffalo Gap, and Porcupine. Plows, fences, farms, and cattle were soon to replace elk, wolves, grizzlies, bison, even black-footed ferrets, which in 1988 went extinct in the wild as the result of distemper. (Ferrets were reintroduced in Wyoming in 1992). Poisoned prairie dogs, plunging aquifers, pesticide infiltration, and accelerated soil erosion are all signs of recent abuse.

Although pristine prairies are but distant memories, one of the best places to experience relict grasslands is at Badlands National Park in South Dakota. Bison occur as diminutive blotches on horizons, vanish among jagged labyrinths of vertical pinnacles, and roam far from traffic jams and manicured lawns. Other prairie denizens are also present. Burrowing owls, prairie dogs, swift foxes, badgers, pronghorn, two species of deer, sharp-tailed grouse, and long-billed curlews make Badlands their home. Wolves no longer coexist with bison, but large expanses of prairie habitats enable bison to maintain discrete seasonal home ranges. Although re-creating historical patterns about how (or whether) bison migrated across continental prairies is not possible, bison in Badlands may tell us something about the future of polygynous species isolated in reserves. In this chapter we describe the study, the prairies and the Badlands ecosystem, methods of data collection and analyses, and other pertinent aspects of the project.

3.1 The Study

We began our work at Badlands in February 1985 and gathered the last field data in October 1989. We and our crew spent nearly 8,750 hours observing bison. The population expanded from 300 to about 775 animals; in late 1989 it was reduced to about 400 animals. Roundups still continue as "excess" animals are given to other reserves and Native Americans that maintain bison.

The U.S. National Park Service administers Badlands National Park and they agreed not to manipulate the population during the first four years of study, an arrangement that was crucial if we were to gather enough data on the breeding biology of known individuals over multiple year periods. At other sites the amount of space available is either too small to permit such an agreement, or hunting, usually for large males, makes it impossible to assess the reproductive performances of individual males that otherwise might live much longer lives. The willingness of the Park Service to support research prompted our decision to use Badlands as a study site.

Our study dealt with more than two hundred known animals, some from birth to death. However, the life span of bison is well over five years; therefore our work covered only a portion of the lives of most of Badlands' bison. Long-term studies are necessary if generalizations at the interface of demography and social interactions are to be valid because population processes affect behavior and behavior affects population processes. Clearly, field studies cannot be conducted like those in the laboratory. Twenty-year studies of elephant seals or red deer cannot easily be replicated, and if they could, environmental and demographic conditions would almost certainly be different. Fortunately, the comparative method allows for contrasts with only a few variables, and it is the only practical way in which ecological contrasts can be made.

PHOTO 3.1. Winter overview of broken topography in the northwestern corner of Badlands National Park. *Right-central part of photograph,* note small, herd of female bison and young.

3.2 The Prairie and Badlands Ecosystem

Overview

The term *badlands* refers to rough, gullied topography bisected with deep arroyos. Such landforms occur throughout the world from the Gobi and Namib deserts to the Middle East and central Australia. In North America they include areas of southern Alberta, California, Nevada, Wyoming, Montana, and the Dakotas. The badlands we refer to are part of the White River badlands, first described for their geological resources (O'Hara 1920), and contain Badlands National Park (see photo 3.1). The reserve was established in 1939 by presidential proclamation as a national monument "to preserve the scenic and scientific values of a portion of the White River Badlands and to make them accessible for public enjoyment and inspiration." In 1978 it was changed to a national park, containing

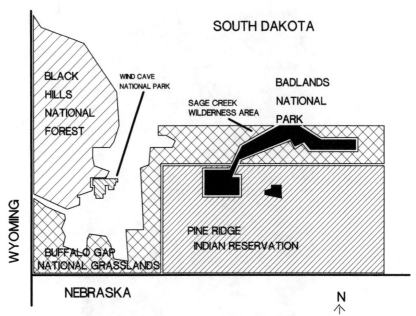

FIGURE 3.1. Location of the Badlands (in black) and prairie ecosystems in southwestern South Dakota.

approximately 1,000 km². The park is bounded by Buffalo Gap National Grasslands, which covers an additional 2,300 km² and extends to the Wyoming border and into Nebraska (see fig. 3.1). The park is adjacent to the Pine Ridge Indian Reservation to the south and to pockets of private land. The national grasslands are managed by the U.S. Forest Service (USFS), and like most USFS lands multiple use edicts, including heavy livestock grazing, are practiced. The reduction of grasses on lands adjacent to the park and the occasional intense planting of crops against its borders creates the impression that the park's rich grasslands really are an island divorced from altered landscapes surrounding it (see photo 3.2). This is literally true for Badlands' bison, which are restricted from the nearest neighboring populations at Wind Cave National and Custer State parks in the Black Hills by impenetrable borders. Dispersal is not precluded for other species, even for the ungulates (bighorn sheep, pronghorn, mule and white-tailed deer), which move onto the national grasslands or the Pine Ridge Reservation.

The Badlands ecosystem falls within the mixed-grass realm and varies in altitude from about 800 to 1,100 meters. Vegetation includes a wide spectrum of grasses—western wheat grass, green needle grass, blue

PHOTO 3.2. Rolled bales of prairie grasses on private land adjacent to the western border of Badlands National Park. Top half of photo is the park.

grama, needle and thread grass, big bluestem, buffalo grass, and muhly—and shrubs, forbs, and cacti—fringed sage, snowberry, common choke-cherry, silver buffaloberry, prairie turnip, bush morning glory, Dakota verbena, penstemon, small soapweed, yucca, common prickly pear, and Missouri pincushion. Trees are limited primarily to watercourses and include cottonwood, American and slippery elm, green ash, common hackberry, and Rocky Mountain juniper. Additional information on prairie vegetation (Larson and Whitman 1942; Clark 1974; Johnson and Nichols 1982; Weedon 1990) and the history of the park (Sheire 1969; Mattison and Grom 1970; Shueler 1989) is available.

The Sage Creek Wilderness Area

At Badlands the Sage Creek Wilderness Area (Sage Creek WA), established in 1976, covers 64,144 acres; motorized vehicles and machines are prohibited.The area contains two permanent springs, several ephemeral watercourses, including Sage Creek itself, and fencing around 80% to 90% of its borders. The unfenced areas are steeply eroded ridges and barren pinnacles that are usually effective barriers to bison. Approxi-

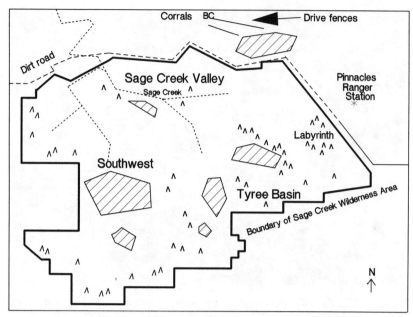

FIGURE 3.2. Schematic overview of the 64,144-acre Sage Creek Wilderness Area in the northwestern portion of Badlands National Park and features mentioned in the text, including *striped areas,* major prairie dog towns; *dotted lines,* stream drainages; *dashed lines,* roads; *BC,* base camp; and buttes and pinnacles as designated.

mately ten man-made dams may, depending on weather conditions, maintain water year-round or be dry.

The Sage Creek WA is composed of three major geographical regions: (1) Sage Creek Valley—containing rolling hills, juniper forests, woody draws, a few prairie dog colonies less than 10 ha in size, Sage Creek, labyrinths of mud-caked hills, and the majority of dams; (2) Tyree Basin—comprising mostly level areas with several large (>2 km²) prairie dog towns speckled generously with table tops, short dry riverbeds, and pinnacles as well as three dams; and (3) the Southwest—the most remote of the areas, with sizable (>3 km²) prairie dog towns, relatively flat grasslands, extensive pans, mesas, and buttes, and ephemeral convoluted watercourses (see fig. 3.2).

Few people visit Sage Creek WA, which is surprising given that more than 1 million people visit Badlands annually. Most visitors spend less than four hours in the park, usually driving its roads on their way to the Black Hills or other areas to the west (Mortenson 1988). Those who see the wilderness area usually drive on the dirt road bordering its northern flank. In our five years of fieldwork, we saw people in Sage Creek Valley less than a dozen times annually, only twice in Tyree Basin, and once in the Southwest. The Sage Creek WA is a paradise, a prairie environment par excellence, for those willing to hike trailless corridors.

Fauna

Badlands and the Buffalo Gap grasslands overlap to a great extent in their fauna. Some of the more obvious smaller mammals include 4 species of rabbits (desert and eastern cottontail, white- and black-tailed jackrabbits), porcupines, spotted ground squirrels, meadow and prairie voles, northern grasshopper mice, Ord's kangaroo rats, and black-tailed prairie dogs. The more notable carnivores are badgers, bobcats, coyotes, striped skunks, swift fox, and long-tailed weasels. Grizzlies, and wolves, not uncommon in the 1850s and early twentieth century, respectively (Meek 1853; Dalrymple 1919; Borman 1971; Knowles 1919), are now absent, as are black-footed ferrets. We saw a beaver just outside the southwest corner of the park in 1985, but none since, and a couple of elk passed by the northwest edge of the park in 1987. A puma with kittens was observed in the park in the early 1980s (Kortge, pers. comm. 1985), but we never found evidence of pumas. Pronghorn and mule deer are abundant; white-tailed deer are uncommon, but occur just outside the park in the more thickly vegetated regions adjacent to the northern and western boundaries. The Audubon's race of bighorn sheep became extinct during the 1920s and was replaced by the Rocky Mountain subspecies in the 1960s; it has expanded its range within the park and increased from 22 to more than 125 animals. Additional information on mammals of the region is found in Turner (1974) and Jones et al. (1981).

The grassland avifauna is spectacular, and a simple listing cannot do it justice. Species include long-billed curlews, kingbirds (eastern and western), chestnut collared longspur, sparrows (chipping, field, lark, vesper, and grasshopper), gray-crowned rosy finch, Lazuli bunting, black-headed grosbeak, northern and loggerhead shrikes, warbling vireo, yellow-breasted chat, owls (long-eared, short-eared, great horned, and burrowing), eagles (golden and bald), prairie falcons, kestrels, northern harriers, and Swainson's and Ferruginous hawks. Depending on the season, ravens, crows, black-billed magpies, turkey vultures, blackbirds, and cowbirds were frequent visitors.

Weather and a "Typical" Annual Cycle

Like ranchers everywhere, those in the Badlands ecosystem are fond of saying there is no such thing as a typical year. We are inclined to agree. Drought and wet years alternate in unpredictable fashion, and extreme fluctuations in precipitation and temperature are not uncommon. At the Badlands Visitor Center, 55 km to the east of Sage Creek WA, temperatures have reached +47°C. Because the wilderness area is mostly contained within a large basin with denuded areas full of clay and stones, little shade, and a great deal of reflection, it is probably hotter there than official records from elsewhere suggest. And although blizzards on the northern plains are legion, it is the cold and rapid changes in temperatures that have received more attention. At Badlands temperatures have plunged as low as −41⁰C, and in Spearfish, about 150 km to the northwest, ambient temperature changed 27°C (49°F) in *two* minutes, from −20°C (4°F) to 7°C (45°F) in January 1943. The temperature returned to −20°C in less than thirty minutes (Miller 1986). Although the northern plains are in the center of the temperate zone, temperatures are hardly temperate (Jones et al. 1981), with extreme heat in the summer and bitter cold during the winter. During our study the mean high for July was 36°C; for January, the mean low was −12°C.

Average precipitation at park headquarters is 40 cm. Most precipitation occurs in May and June, during heavy and occasionally violent thunderstorms that are often accompanied by spectacular lightning and sometimes hail. Snowfall is generally light, averaging only about 60 cm per year. Because the northern plains experience year-round winds, the sporadic snowfalls result in bare patches of ground, but snowdrifts pile up to 5-m deep in ravines. Cattle and bison have drowned en masse by wandering onto frozen ponds to avoid the drifts.

Winter at the Badlands is sterile, with few signs of life other than tracks and swirling marks in the snow. Most birds are gone; porcupines form lifeless groups nestled among tree branches; arctic air envelops the park at unpredictable intervals; and the yelps of coyotes are one of the few sounds that pierce the silence or blend with the wind. Pronghorn and mule deer form large groups that sometimes mix among the bison, a scene reminiscent of herds grazing on an African savanna.

Spring arrives with intense wind. Melting snow and rain turn frozen grasslands into fields of mud. Gumbo, as it is called, cakes onto one's feet and can turn legs into teetering stilts. The unwieldy, several-kilogram mass makes hiking difficult; moving even a couple of kilometers is frustrating and limits access to the Southwest and Tyree Basin. Warmer weather also brings a new wave of life. Meadowlarks arrive; sharp-tailed grouse dance; porcupines scurry across open prairies in search of emergent new grass; sandhill cranes and bald eagles migrate overhead. In early April bison drop calves and conspicuous herds form. The prairie attains its greatest splendor in May. Trees bud, flowers emerge, and grasses are verdant. By June woody draws are alive with mosquitoes and dreaded ticks. Milkweed beetles, butterflies, leopard frogs, painted tur-tles, rubber boas, rattlesnakes, and the bleating calls of bighorn lambs all signal life.

During summer the moisture is sucked from grasses. Chiggers are thick, and the remains of ephemeral alkali ponds crack under the glaring sun. Distant tabletops and buttes become blurred in the heat. Sweat bees attach themselves to moisture-rich areas on sitting humans, stinging them when they stand; grasshoppers cut holes in nylon tents with razorlike mandibles. Most vertebrate life retreats to the shade of dawn and dusk. Tinder-dry vegetation explodes, ignited by lightning. In 1988 fires scorched every mountain range between the Badlands and the Idaho border—the Black Hills, the Bighorn Mountains, the Absaroka, and the Yellowstone Plateau. Haze from billowing smoke obscured the sky. The air is perforated by the sweet scent of urine-soaked soil, and the grunts and bellows of bison announce the rut. Clouds bring welcome relief for weary, sunburned fieldworkers as critical periods of unrelenting data collection begin.

A freshness on the parched landscape arrives with the clean, cool air of autumn. Water now trickles through dehydrated creeks, and woody draws are vibrant in red and yellow hues. Bighorn rams join ewes in anticipation of the breeding season. The mule deer population swells as antlered bucks from the surrounding countryside seek refuge from bullets outside the park's boundaries. Snow will soon brighten the Black Hills and drift slowly eastward toward the Badlands before it descends to linger for months.

3.3 Methods

The Two Bison Lineages

Ancestral Sources.

Two types of bison are found in the Badlands: those descended from animals at the Fort Niobrara National Wildlife Refuge near Valentine,

PHOTO 3.3. Adult female and male bison of Nebraska (NL) descent

Nebraska, established in 1913, and those derived from Colorado National Monument near Grand Junction, Colorado. The national monument bison were descendants of three animals (two females and a male) held in a park in Denver, Colorado, around 1925 (McClenaghan, Berger, and Truesdale 1990). The population at Fort Niobrara began with six animals and increased over a forty-year period, when a small founding population was transplanted from Nebraska to Theodore Roosevelt National Historic Park in North Dakota. From these animals twenty-five were introduced into the Badlands in 1963. Three additional animals from Fort Niobrara were transplanted to the Badlands at about the same time, raising the initial founding population size of animals of Fort Niobrara descent to twenty-eight. The animals of Colorado descent were introduced to Badlands in 1984; both lineages were (and continue to be) sympatric and experience opportunities to mate with one another. We refer to the animals as the Nebraska (NL) and Colorado (CL) lineages. Additional details about the sources of the lineages are given in section 10.1.

Identification.

Animals of the NL and CL differ morphologically, in color, and in mass, with the CL being shorter and somewhat "pig-faced," darker, and smaller (chapter 10; Berger and Peacock 1988) (see photos 3.3 and 3.4). All the CL received conspicuous red, numbered cattle ear tags before

PHOTO 3.4. Adult female (NL descent) and male of the Colorado line. Note the male's short (broken?) horn.

their release in Badlands, and males were freeze-branded with numbers on their hips. Some NL bison initially had cattle tags and others had small, numbered silver clips in their ears indicating that they had received brucellosis vaccinations several years earlier. By noting fur color, the presence or absence of tags (some attached during our study), and brands (for males only), an animal's ancestry was determined. Once we became familiar with distinguishing characteristics of individuals (see below), it was easy to determine identities and lineage.

Trapping, Immobilization, and Darting

The Park Service had an established bison corral and chute system situated just outside the northwest corner of Sage Creek WA to facilitate handling and cropping excess animals. Before our study, capture was unpredictable because motorized ground vehicles could not be used to direct movements of animals inside the wilderness area, and helicopters, horses, and humans on foot were ineffective at herding animals in the desired direction, especially across kilometers of rugged terrain. The park erected a series of drive fences outside the wilderness, and the V-shaped

PHOTO 3.5. Group of about one hundred female, juvenile, and young male bison captured in early fall 1986. Background is Buffalo Gap National Grasslands.

arrangement channeled animals past gates into completely fenced areas about 2.5 km^2 in size.

We regularly relied on the drive fences to funnel animals into the corrals, first with the cooperation of Park Service personnel and trucks, then by baiting animals with alfalfa. We later learned that bison would feed in areas beyond the gates if we left gates open and if the animals were not harassed. Because our tents (as well as a research trailer) were often located in this area, we simply left the gate open, closing it when it was essential to capture animals. We successfully captured more than fourteen hundred animals in these ways (see photos 3.5 and 3.6).

Although some animals were prone to wander out of the wilderness area where they could be trapped, adult males were not. Bulls that emigrated did so in areas where it was not possible to trap them. Even those males that entered the corrals were often difficult and dangerous to handle. Therefore we immobilized males with carfentanil, a potent narcotic drug, in conjunction with xylazine (see photo 3.7). Twenty-five animals were darted (Kock and Berger 1987), ear-tagged, and measured, and blood samples were gathered. Tranquilized bison survived as well as

PHOTO 3.6. Bison in corrals after capture

nonhandled animals, suggesting the drug had no detrimental effect (Berger and Kock 1988, 1989).

Individual Recognition and Ages

Bison are individually recognizable because of conspicuous and subtle variation in their horn sizes, head hair, and bodies, differences that persist for years (see photo 3.8). Many individuals break horns, some of which grow back (see photos 3.9 and 3.10). Others have anomalous horns. We also tried to identify animals using pantaloons (thick fur covering the forelegs), capes, and penile tufts, but these were unreliable traits. During the first year, we used bleach, but the marks were not permanent. Therefore we attached more than 125 permanent numbered cattle ear tags (blue, yellow, orange, and white) to difficult-to-identify animals (see photo 3.11). Under ideal conditions we could recognize some individuals from

PHOTO 3.7. An immobilized adult, prime-aged male. Blood and body measurements being taken by, Michael Kock (left) and Joel Berger.

PHOTO 3.8. An adult male bison we called Musk Ox; the abnormal horn probably resulted from breakage at an early age.

PHOTO 3.9. *Left*, Bladerunner, an adult female, in 1985

PHOTO 3.10. Bladerunner with a broken horn in 1987

PHOTO   3.11.   Old spike (tag number 3) and adult female (tag Z)

as far away as 2.5 km; we had to be much closer to read numbered ear
tags. Overall, more than 200 animals were known individually.

Age was evaluated in three ways. First, information on exact birthdates
or year of birth was available for some individuals. Second, ages were
estimated categorically; that is, as calves, yearlings, two-year olds (also
called juveniles), and adults. Third, ages were determined by backdating
the number of years that elapsed since animals were marked with silver
tags by the Park Service during their irregular brucellosis testing.

Females could be nulliparous, primiparous, multiparous, or barren,
the latter referring to adult females that did not give birth in a given year
(Berger 1989). For males, two categories existed: (1) Animals with
upturned horns have been referred to as "spikes" for more than one
hundred years (Hornaday 1889) and they can be young, medium, or old
(Fuller 1959), classes that clearly overlap because of differences in
growth rates. Generally, young spikes are two to three years of age,
medium three to four years, and old four to five years (see photo 3.12).
(2) Bulls are typically larger males with horns curving tightly around the
head or worn short. We grouped them as young (five to six), prime
(seven to twelve), and old (thirteen-plus).

Not all animals were tagged by the Park Service, even when they were
captured. But those that were marked proved valuable. Their teeth served

PHOTO 3.12. A young female with a deformed horn bounded by two young spikes

as a standard by which the ages of animals of unknown age could be estimated. In trying to determine the most essential dental characteristics, several options were available. In African buffalo, reindeer, white-tailed deer, and other ungulates, a good relationship exists between age and some measure of premolar height (Skogland 1988; Spinage and Brown 1988; Taylor 1988). In northern bison the metaconid on the third premolar is inversely correlated with age (Haynes 1984). However, most studies of this sort are based on measures derived from dead animals. Sampling from live bison, even when they were restrained (though not immobilized in chutes), was dangerous. And bison were reluctant to open their mouths (see photo 3.13). When they did, it was difficult to see the premolars clearly, let alone measure their height accurately.

As an alternative, we examined whether a relationship existed between the height of the first incisor and age (see photo 3.14 and fig. 3.3). Because males are larger than females, we expected male incisors to be bigger and possibly, because the sexes inhabit different home ranges (see chapter 5), to wear at different rates. Although analyses revealed a statistically significant inverse relationship between age and incisor height ($p < 0.001$), the slopes of the regressions for males and females did not differ ($t = 0.44$; df $= 60$; NS). Given possible biases such as uneven tooth

PHOTO 3.13. Old spike, restrained in chute. Blood is taken from the jugular and incisors are measured. (Photo by Michael Kock)

wear among individuals, an angular or semicupped protrusion from the jaw, and some unevenness in the measurements from the gum line, so strong a relationship is surprising. Although between 83% to 88% of the variance in age was explained by incisor height, a measure of surface volume (area of tooth x height) might improve on the relationship (Jaarsveld, Henschel, and Skinner 1988), if surface area can be assessed accurately in live animals.

Rather than using only animals of known age, we attempted to further evaluate the validity of the relationship by checking the number of cementum annuli against age; in wisent, cementum annuli are reasonable predictors of age (Klevezal and Pucek 1987). Although the accuracy of this method has been questioned (Gasaway, Harkness, and Rausch 1978; Cooke and Hart 1979), it has been widely used and checked against animals of known age, producing reliable results in seasonably varied

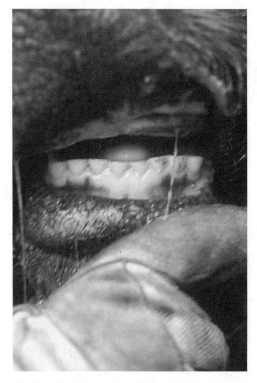

PHOTO 3.14. Old female, sixteen to eighteen years old, with well-worn incisors

climates (DeYoung 1989). We used only those incisors that we removed from animals found dead in the field, which restricted our sample to thirteen. (Numerous skulls were found, but because incisors become disarticulated rapidly, the sample could not be enlarged.) The pattern was similar to that found for known-aged animals, explaining 81% of the variance.

Assessment of Body Size, Mass, and Condition

The morphological measures taken on restrained or immobilized bison included head size (tip of nose to occipital condyle), head width (distance between the base of horns), body length (linear distance between tip of nose to anus), and chest girth. Mass was recorded directly from both manual and digital cattle scales set up in the bison chutes. Mass was also

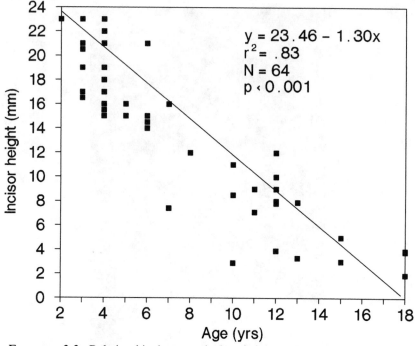

FIGURE 3.3. Relationship between incisor height and age, as described in the text.

estimated using single morphological characters and then by multiple regression (see chapter 6).

To determine body condition, we fitted the data to a multiple regression using body weight as the dependent variable, and head width, date of weighing, and parity as independent variables. A single morphological variable, head width, was then used since the exponential equation ($Y = AB^X$) explained the greatest amount of variance in weight ($r^2 = 0.76$; Berger and Peacock 1988). We had to rely on multiple regression to control for effects of weight change at different times of the year. For instance, the same-size females at winter's end weigh, on average, only about 80% of what they do the next July. Because head size and weight were known, points falling above or below the exponential regression with date controlled were assigned to an "above" or "below" average body condition category. Although this method is admittedly crude, it offers an alternative to evaluating breeding performances in relation to body mass per se; large animals may be in poor, and small animals in good, condition.

PHOTO 3.15. Photogrammetric device with digital calipers at 0.02 mm attached to a 300-mm telephoto lens

Determination of Growth Rates

Because it was not possible to handle animals at will, we relied on a photogrammetric device to assess changes in growth (see photo 3.15). Head and body sizes were measured using a Mitutoyo (500 Series) Digimatic Caliper, first developed by Jacobsen (1986) for evaluation of the size of killer whale fins. The procedure measures morphological features on photographs using actual distances between the object and photographer by scaling them with a Jandel Scientific Digitizer.

To determine distance to the object, the photogrammetric device is attached to a Nikon f4.5, 300-mm lens; it measures to the nearest mm the degree of ring extension on the focused lens. The relationship between distance and lens extension is $D = e^{(4.55 - \log L)}$, where D is distance and L is lens extension. When field tested on restrained bison and compared with masses computed from photogrammetric measures of head width, the amount of variation explained was 98.5% (see fig. 3.4). The device is accurate up to 37 m (Jacobsen 1986). However, care must be taken in darkroom procedures when photographs are prepared. Enlarger heights must be standardized, and all photos must be in crisp focus. The photogrammetric device enables determination of changes in young animals as they mature, comparison of growth trajectories between different classes

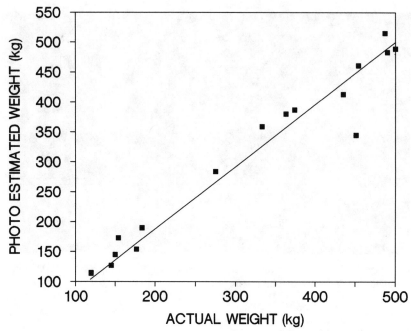

Figure 3.4. Relationship between actual summer body mass in sixteen non-pregnant, nonlactating females and weight estimated from a photogrammetric device (see photo 3.15). The regression equation is $Y = .99X + .3767$ ($r^2 = .99$; $p<0.001$).

of animals (e.g., male versus female, NL versus CL), and evaluation of body size.

Observations

The data are derived from about 8,750 hours of observation made throughout all months of the year. The field teams (six to eight people per year, including us) arrived in May or early June and remained until some time in August. One of our coworkers, Marj Glass—who lived at Pinnacles Ranger Station (see fig. 3.2)—gathered data from September until April each year, except for the summer months and other periods that we were at Badlands; these included March to May (1985), September (1985), March and September (1986), September (1987), April and September (1988), and April and October (1989).

   Two field camps were established, one just outside the northwestern edge of the Sage Creek WA, the other in a dilapidated cow barn about 30

PHOTO 3.16. Carol Cunningham approaches a mixed group in early morning in the southwestern section of Sage Creek Wilderness Area.

km to the southwest. Typically, we used spotting scopes to locate bison groups, some situated up to 10 km away. We then hiked to the site to begin detailed observation on known animals (see photo 3.16). Groups were usually closer than 10 km. If no animals were found or it was desirable to check on specific individuals, we searched larger areas, mostly on foot. Occasionally we drove up to 50 km to gain access to specific parts of the wilderness area (e.g., Tyree Basin) or to try to locate animals that had left the park.

We adhered to strict schedules. Half the field team conducted observations from sunrise to about 11:00 A.M., the other half from 2:00 P.M. to sunset. During the rut (from about 1 July until mid-August) first observations began at dawn and continued until 1:00 P.M. when the afternoon team arrived to observe the same individuals. General data that we recorded were total group composition, membership of known individuals, sex ratio and approximate age structure, locations, habitats, and weather.

Sampling methods of behaviors included focal animal (continuous) and instantaneous (point) techniques. The first of these offers reasonably systematic ways of gaining profiles of individuals (or events) for predetermined periods of time and provides unbiased estimates of activity budgets or interaction rates (Altmann 1974, 1980). During the rut, we worked on focal consorts where both members of a dyad were known. Observations continued until males either copulated or departed from the female. The number of males occurring within 15 m of the pair and their identities (when known) or age classes were noted, as was the frequency of threat and contact interactions, bellows, and displacements. In situations when only one member of a dyad was known, observations centered on known males because it was important to derive estimates of male copulation rates. Some data are included from unknown males that copulated, but these represent less than 20% of the total.

Our sampling scheme was not ideal, and undetected biases may have been introduced. For instance, when unknown males were observed, whether or not they copulated, we had no way to know whether the same individuals were sampled in subsequent years. In addition, not all animals were observed for the same periods of time. Although we attempted to minimize these potential problems by focusing as much as possible on known animals and by using rates of behaviors (e.g., bellowing or copulating; see chapter 8) in interindividual comparisons, some biases cannot be removed. Like many ungulates, bison females live in groups, and statistical problems may arise because the activities of some individuals may be affected by those of other group members. This is especially true when the gregarious nature of some species affects decisions about habitat use, thus violating assumptions about independence (Sokal and Rohlf 1981; Festa-Bianchet 1988a). The pooling of unknown individuals sighted on different days also poses a problem: the magnitude of contribution made by different individuals entering the data set is unknown. No simple way to circumvent this sampling problem exists, and it must be recognized.

Genetic Diversity

Our colleagues Lee McClenaghan and Ernie Vyse did most of the work to evaluate genetic diversity. Blood was obtained from tails, ears, or throats of immobilized or restrained animals, and placed on ice; plasma and red blood cells were separated four to six hours later. After being sent to the McClenaghan lab blood samples were stored at minus 70°C until processing, which included the absorption of hemolysates onto filter paper wicks, placement into 11% starch gels, and subsequent exposure to buffers of lithium hydroxide (pH 8.4; Selander et al. 1971), tris-citrate (pH 7.1; Selander et al. 1971), and JRP (pH 6.3; Ayala et al. 1972). Gels were also sliced and stained for catalase, superoxidase dimutase, lactate dehydrogenase, peptidase, hemoglobin, and hexokinase on lithium hydroxide gels; glutamate oxaloacetate transaminase, 6-phosphogluconate dehydrogenase, phosphoglucomutase, xanthine dehydrogenase, and mannosephosphatase isomerase on tris-citrate gels; and acid phosphatase, malate dehydrogenase, malic enzyme, and glucosephosphate isomerase on JRP gels (McClenaghan, Berger, and Truesdale 1990). Genic variability was estimated as the proportion of polymorphic loci (P), mean heterozygosity observed across loci via direct count (H_0), and mean heterozygosity expected from Hardy-Weinberg proportions (H_e). We considered loci to be polymorphic when the frequency of the most common allele was 0.99 (Selander 1976). The DNA methodology performed by Vyse and colleagues is described more fully in chapter 10.

Statistics

Because the information base was voluminous, not all data or analyses can be presented in their entirety. Where appropriate, both parametric and nonparametric tests were used (Siegel 1956; Siegel and Castellan 1988; Sokal and Rohlf 1981; Zar 1984). Data that were not normally distributed were transformed by logarithm, arcsine, or square root prior to analysis. For tests involving analysis of variance (ANOVA), a Student-Newman-Keuls multiple range test examined the location of potential interaction effects. Regression slopes were contrasted with analysis of covariance (ANCOVA) or with the t distribution. We also relied on multiple regression and partial correlation to hold constant the effects of one variable when examining for effects of another. In one case it was necessary to compare more than two proportions and we relied on the method outlined in Zar (1984). Briefly, the means of proportions used in a multisampling testing procedure investigating potential male mate choice (see chapter 8) were arcsine transformed and then standard errors in degrees contrasted. In multiple comparisons such as these, use of the normal approximation relative to the binomial may be acceptable, but we used critical values of the q distribution as recommended by Zar (1984).

For analyses involving nonparametric statistics, we relied on G-Tests with adjustments for small samples (Sokal and Rohlf 1981) and log linear models (Fienberg 1980). Point biserial correlation was also used when looking for possible effects of different factors on binary variables (e.g., calf produced or calf not produced). The more conventional rank-related tests (Mann-Whitney, Wilcoxon, Spearman rank correlation, Kruskal-Wallis [one-way] and Friedman's [two-way] analyses of variance) were employed when data were not normally distributed.

Computer programs we employed included Statistical Package for the Social Sciences (SPSS), Statpak, and Sigma Scan. Within each chapter, probability levels are given for specific statistical tests, which are numbered in brackets; corresponding analyses are provided at the end of respective chapters in the statistical notes. Levels of significance were accepted at the $p = 0.05$,, and unless designated otherwise, all tests are two-tailed. We use NS to designate nonsignificant difference in statistical tests when the probability of an event is less than one in twenty.

3.4 Ethogram

Bison employ a wide variety of behaviors when interacting. Those pertinent to this study are described below; further descriptions are in Fuller (1966), Lott (1974), Rothstein (1988) and Komers, Messier, and Gates (1992).

Behavior Patterns

Tail up (male). The elevation of the tail, when approaching animals of either sex, is a sign of aggression.

Tail up (female). Used aggressively in much the same manner as males do, except that females also elevate their tails for up to six hours after they have copulated (see chapter 6).

Flehman. This behavior, also known as a "lip-curl," is shown by both males and females, most often to assess reproductive status by smelling urine or the ano-genital region.

Paw. The scraping of the front hoof along the ground, usually displacing dirt.

Wallow. Whereas a wallow is a physical depression in the ground created by the action of rolling animals and hooking the ground with horns, wallowing is the rolling act itself.

Threat. Can assume numerous forms; males nod or swing the head, lunge, or approach in a straight-legged broadside manner. The repertoire for females is more limited, but involves a lowering of the head and a lunge.

Vigilance. The act of standing with head lifted and ears erect. Animals that are vigilant give the impression they are smelling or looking for potential predators or conspecifics, or attempting to ascertain the nature of a disturbance.

Vocalizations

Bellow. A deep roar given by males, most often during the rut, was described nearly 150 years ago as the "long continued roll of a hundred drums" (Audubon 1843, quoted in Cates 1986). Bellows are short (mean = 2.05 s), guttural, low frequency (mean = 230 Hz) exhalations (Gunderson and Mahan 1980).

Snort. An explosive breath of air through the nostrils. A variant on the snort is a "pfff" sound made by males, usually during the rut as they walk by other males or approach groups.

Social Groupings

A group. An assemblage of individuals that appear either clumped or cohesive in which members are aware of the actions of adjacent animals. (Although it was generally clear what constituted a group, in our detailed measures we omitted any case(s) in which uncertainty existed. Based on tests we ran with each new group of field assistants, agreement was reached on average more than 97% of the time.)

Mixed groups. Aggregations that contain females and males. Because bison aggregations almost always contain some yearling males, the most commonly observed groups were mixed, containing a high proportion of females and young, and some spikes.

Nursery groups. Associations that consist predominately of females and calves.

All male groups. Such associations usually involve young bulls and old spikes. Occasionally young spikes and old bulls also associate, but usually for not more than an hour or two.

Juvenile groups. These associations are infrequent, but may occur prior to the major pulse of births when young females and males (mostly one- and two-year olds) remain together. The largest juvenile group we observed was thirty-eight.

Solitary male. Ranging in age from six to twenty-one, solitary males are frequently referred to as "old bulls" (Meagher 1973), but this often is not the case.

Interactions

Butt. The act by which either males or females lower the head and engage in physical contact with a conspecific. Both sexes engage

in head butting (usually, but not always, with members of the
same sex), but fleeing animals and those in nonstylized fights may
be butted anywhere.

Kick. Kicks are rare; they are directed by both sexes toward coyotes and conspecifics.

Consorting. Previously called tending and guarding (Lott 1974;
Green and Berger 1990), consortships are close spatial associations (generally less than a body length apart) that occur between
a male and female most often during the breeding season. Males
guard females, bellow, and show other agonistic behavior toward
other males during the consortship, but if potential rival males are
not in close proximity, both members of a consort may feed
peacefully or even lie down.

Copulation. An animal with an erection that thrusts when mounted
upon a female, usually giving a short leap, with front legs being
lifted off the ground.

Fight. The engagement of two animals in a physical confrontation
that involves head butting and pushing with forward lunges; neither immediately retreats. Most fights last less than sixty seconds,
but some may be as long as fifteen minutes.

Fight Frenzy. The engagement of up to twenty animals in fights in
the same group at the same time.

3.5 Summary

1. Bison were inextricably linked to the ecology of the central prairies of North America. The largest shortgrass prairie ecosystem
   with bison occurs in South Dakota's Badlands National Park.
   The population was formed from a reintroduction in 1963, based
   on 28 founders descended from a source population in Nebraska. In 1984 20 bison from a Colorado lineage were added.
   During the five-year study (1985 to 1989), the population,
   which increased from 300 to 775 animals, was observed for
   about 8,750 hours.
2. Descriptions of the two lineages, trapping procedures, age and
   body condition determinations, observation schedules, sampling
   and statistical procedures, an ethogram, and other material pertinent to later findings are presented.

PART TWO

Behavioral Ecology of Females and Males

4. Social Spacing and Land Use Systems

The old bulls do undoubtedly leave the herd and wander off but I am disposed to believe this due . . . on the part of these old fellows, to whom female companionship no longer possesses its charm, rather than to their being driven out by the younger bulls as is generally believed. This habitual separation of the large herd into numerous smaller herds seems to be an instinctive act.

J. A. Allen 1875a:463

Group-living animals have long captivated the attention of naturalists. Two hundred years ago Thomas Bewick (1790:94) described immense springbok herds as "covering the plains as far as the eye can reach," a description not uncommon for bison on North American prairies until well into the last century. More than one hundred years ago Francis Galton (1871) asked how safety from lions might be gained by African cattle through associating with herdmates. We now know that group formation occurs for many reasons—such as to derive safety from predators (Hamilton 1971; Schaller 1972), to facilitate feeding (Caraco 1979), to minimize harassment from insects (Duncan and Vigne 1979), and to enhance social skills (Berger 1979, 1980). But group formation also entails costs, which may include increased aggression, feeding competition, and disease transmission (Rutberg 1986b). Ecological conditions may also mediate group sizes; for example bison form smaller groups in mountain meadows or boreal forests than they do on spacious prairies (Van Vuren 1983; Soper 1941; Fuller 1960). As Allen (1875a) indicated, male and female bison often segregate into distinct groups. Although the reasons why this occurs are unclear, it is of interest to know how a species uses the space available to it. In this chapter we consider the extent to which the sexes occur in different habitats and why. To help cast our bison data on social groups into a more complete framework, effects of body size on foraging are contrasted with those of other ungulates at Badlands and elsewhere. Finally, since our 250 km² study area is clearly not as large as the vast fenceless prairies where ancestral bison once roamed and predators other than humans are lacking, we question

PHOTO 4.1. Typical mixed group in early summer with at least sixteen calves present

the applicability of deductions about past selection pressures when they are based on present circumstances.

4.1 Ecology of Group Sizes

Habitat and Seasonal Effects

Huge herds were well known to early travelers of the prairies; solitary males and small groups of spikes were also regularly encountered (Allen 1875a; Hornaday 1889; Roe 1970). Such sights cannot be duplicated in today's fragmented world, but for a few hours we observed about five hundred animals together during the rut of summer 1988. Smaller groups were much more common (see photo 4.1), and in forested habitats near the northern limits of their range mean group size was about thirty to forty (Melton et al. 1989). Sex and age, as well as habitat, affect group sizes seasonally. [1; numbers in brackets correspond to statistical notes at end of chapter].

Sex and Age.

Bison females, like those of most temperate ungulates, formed larger groups than males. Irrespective of habitat, mixed groups were smallest during winter (November to March) and largest during summer (July and August). Bulls were the least gregarious. In April and May, their most social months, mean group size for bulls was still less than 3, with 1 being the median group size throughout all months of the year. Spikes, on the other hand, formed groups that approached 12 animals during April and May in the most favorable habitats. The overall lack of gregariousness in males at Badlands is similar to that reported for wood bison where the largest average group sizes were only 2.4 (Melton et al. 1989) (see fig. 4.1).

The qualitative pattern that emerges is that small mixed groups occur during winter and build progressively in size until the summer breeding season, after which they drop rapidly in size until winter. Group size changes are not nearly as dramatic for all-male groups. The largest we observed contained thirty-six bulls and large spikes during May 1988. Within two hours of the association, a fight frenzy erupted, and soon afterward about half the group dispersed into another area. Males are typically tolerant of one another, but rarely associate for longer than a few days, often drifting gradually away from one another. During the breeding season, bulls rarely associate with one another for more than a day, although spikes are a little more social (see fig. 4.1). Overall, males form small groups, and mixed groups containing more than an occasional bull or two are rare outside the summer months.

Habitats.

Three structural habitats were defined: nonundulating prairies (flat open regions from about 5 to 3,000 acres, which also included prairie dog towns); rolling hills and draws (regions of topographical relief associated with reduced visibility, which included woody ravines, valleys, and creek bottoms); and tabletops and breaks (steeply eroded sod tables, canyons, and washes) (see photos 4.2, 4.3, and 4.4). Cases in which habitats could not be demarcated clearly were omitted from analyses. The most dramatic effect of habitat on group size was for mixed groups (females and their young), where an approximate 50% reduction occurred from 157 (± 24; median = 133) on prairies to 79 (± 13; median = 67) in ravines or on rolling hills during July and August (see fig. 4.1). On average, group sizes at this time of the year were reduced by another 30 animals when occupying tabletops or breaks. Because bulls and spikes used the same tabletops as mixed groups, habitats per se were clearly not the reason for the smaller group sizes of males. Competition for mates, vulnerability to insects, the possibility of being preyed on, and body size—factors considered below—may all play a role.

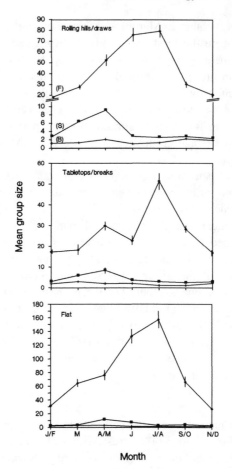

FIGURE 4.1. Mean group sizes and standard errors for *F*, females; *S*, spikes; and *B*, bulls in different habitats from *J/F*, January/February, to *N/D*, November/ December, in 1986 and 1987. The variation for spikes and bulls is too little to appear in some months.

Social Foraging in Bison and Other Badlands Ungulates

Group size is not the only conspicuous feature of bison. They are the largest terrestrial mammals of the new world, males attaining weights in excess of 1,000 kg (see chapter 6). Ecological implications of body size have been explored in numerous contexts. For instance, foraging is related to body size in at least three ways: (1) larger species require greater absolute amounts of food (Robbins 1983); (2) larger species tend to

PHOTO 4.2. Mixed group feeding on a prairie dog town in early morning. *Top center,* swift fox being approached by two calves.

PHOTO 4.3. Rolling hills and embankment eroded by Sage Creek. Three bison are above and to the left of the cut.

PHOTO 4.4. Breaks and tabletops

exploit open habitats (Geist 1971b, 1978; Jarman 1974); and (3) species
in open environments form large groups (Underwood 1982). Such trends
could result because large herbivores require more time to forage and
because nutritious food is abundant in open areas. However, large species
may form groups in open areas for reasons unrelated to food, such as
enhanced protection from predators. Small species also form groups,
sometimes in the absence of conspicuous predation pressures or rich food
patches. Moreover, small and large species (and even the sexes of the
same species) may differ in diets, habitats, vulnerability to predators,
reproductive demands, and other interrelated factors, thus making it difficult to separate the influence of one variable from another.

Among large mammals, feeding rates scale not only to body size
(Bunnell and Gillingham 1985), but to a variety of proximate ecological
factors including predators (see table 4.1). At Badlands many of the
potential sources of confusion could be minimized when assessing time

TABLE 4.1.

*Summary of selective examples of ecological variables that influence
vigilance and feeding rates of large herbivores*

Variable	Species	Reference
Sex	Red kangaroo	Short 1986
	Bison	Hudson and Frank 1986
Habitat	Several antelopes	Underwood 1983
	Reindeer	Trudell and White 1981
Food dispersion	Kudu	Owen-Smith 1979
	Many species	Bunnell and Gillingham 1985
Season	African buffalo	Sinclair 1977
	Horses	Duncan 1980
Food phenology	Elk	Hudson and Watkins 1986
	Moose	Belovsky 1981
Group size	Bighorn sheep	Berger 1978
	Ibex	Alados 1985
Predation	Pronghorn	Berger et al. 1983
Reproductive condition	Red deer	Clutton-Brock, Guinness, and Albon 1982
Position within a group	Pronghorn	Lipetz and Bekoff 1982
Insects	Horses	Hughes, Duncan, and Dawson 1981
	Reindeer	Espmark and Langvtan 1979

From Berger and Cunningham 1988

allocated to searching for predators and feeding. During a three- to four-week period in late winter/early spring, ungulates (especially pregnant females) are protein starved (Robbins 1983; Berger 1991a), and bighorn, pronghorn, mule deer, and bison congregate on the same plateaus to feed on the newly emergent and highly proteinaceous grasses (see photos 4.5 and 4.6). The four species differ in size and the resultant congregations offered unique opportunities to examine how body size influences feeding and searching times in the absence of contrasting ecological variables.

Effects of Feeding Location and Group Size on Vigilance.

To evaluate foraging and vigilance, we recorded the amount of time individuals spent feeding and vigilant per 180-s bouts in March and April. Data were gathered only from females, thus eliminating the greater variability found among males (Berger 1978; Risenhoover and Bailey 1985); group size categories were 1, 2 to 5, 6 to 10, and 11 +. We used the following mean female weights: pronghorn, 37 kg; mule deer, 46 kg; bighorn sheep, 51 kg (Jones et al. 1983); and bison, 400 kg.

PHOTO 4.5. *Left,* three bighorn sheep and, *right,* two bison in March

PHOTO 4.6. Four mule deer in the same habitat as bighorn and bison from photo 4.5

TABLE 4.2.

*Summary of percent time spent vigilant (per 180-s
observation period) by centrally foraging female ungulates
in Badlands National Park*

	Group size			
	1	2–5	6–10	11+
Pronghorn	95.5	9.4	7.8	4.4
Bighorn	62.2	38.3	21.1	17.2
Mule deer	64.4	27.2	8.8	8.3
Bison	38.8	4.4	1.1	1.1

Sample sizes in appendix 3

Animals at the periphery of groups tended to be more vigilant and variable in their behavior than those in the center, but species differences were evident (see appendix 3). Position effects occurred for pronghorn regardless of group size, but for bighorn sheep, central animals had higher feeding rates only in groups of six or more. Position effects were found in mule deer for all but the largest groups. Bison failed to conform to these trends. They rarely scanned their environment while foraging, and position within a group had no influence on vigilance.

Because vigilance rates for peripheral animals in all species except bison were consistently more variable, only data on centrally located individuals were used in evaluating group size effects. Vigilance rates declined with increased group size for all species although differences were consistently the most striking between solitary foragers and those in groups of 2 to 5 (see table 4.2). On average, solitary pronghorn spent 4.4% of each observation period feeding, whereas single bison cows fed about 61% of the time. Among all species, vigilance was lowest in the largest groups, but differences were not detectable between groups of 6 to 10 and 11 + [2]. Bison, on the other hand, spent little time vigilant once they were in groups of two or greater; more than 95.5% of their time was spent feeding.

Effects of Body Size.

If the above interspecific differences arose solely because smaller species were more vulnerable to predators than larger ones and, hence, allocated more time to searching for predators, then smaller species should be more vigilant (per unit body mass) than larger ones. This is the case when assuming a linear effect and simply dividing the vigilance times of each species (from table 4.2) by their mean masses. For instance, solitary pronghorn were about twenty-seven times as vigilant per unit body mass as solitary bison. However, rather than a proportional relationship between species mass and search time, vigilance may be related in other ways to body size. Therefore, we used multiple regression to examine effects of body and group size independently. While both factors had significant effects ($p<0.001$), group size had a stronger influence on vigilance than did body mass [3]. These results are important because they indicate that multiple factors should be examined in ascertaining how species allocate their time and that although interspecific differences in body size occur group size effects for bison are rather trivial once individuals are in groups of two or more.

Effects of Predation.

Despite their large body size, might bison vigilance rates be low simply because they live in an environment lacking natural predators? This idea is supported indirectly, as adult females and the young of the other Badlands ungulates (pronghorn, bighorn, mule deer) are subjected to predation by coyotes and bobcats. We examined this possibility directly by noting whether the presence of wolves affected vigilance differently in bison from Wood Buffalo National Park (WBNP). The WBNP data were gathered on centrally located females during late August and early September in both boreal and grassland habitats, sites where wolves are effective predators (Soper 1941; Fuller 1966; Oosenbrug and Carbyn 1985). As at Badlands, group size effects were evident, but the only difference was between group sizes of one and larger groups. No differences in vigilance existed between females from Wood Buffalo and Badlands national parks [4]. Hence, despite the presence of wolves, bison at Wood Buffalo Park were no more likely to scan their environment than were those in Badlands where wolves have been absent for more than sixty years.

Body Mass, Predation, and Possible Sources of Bias.

Although it is not surprising that group size exerted strong influences on vigilance in the three smaller ungulates that are still subject to predation at Badlands, bison females were notoriously nonvigilant even in areas where they still experience regular predation by wolves. The similarities between bison at Wood Buffalo and Badlands parks could result because (1) bison are large-bodied generalist herbivores that need to fulfill their energy and nutrient requirements by feeding often (Belovsky and Slade

1986; Hudson and Frank 1986), or (2) the northern bison that we observed had not been attacked by wolves when we gathered our data. Both explanations appear plausible; if predation had no influence on vigilance then results from the two study sites should not differ (as our findings show). However, bison become very attuned to wolves once attacked (Carbyn and Trottier 1987, 1988). The most obvious predation on northern bison occurs in winter when animals leave boreal forests and inhabit open plains. Had our data not been collected in late summer, different patterns of vigilance might have occurred. For example, bison have run as far as 86 km in a day after being pursued by wolves, and they leave forested areas to stand on roadway cuts where visibility is enhanced (Carbyn, Oosenbrug, and Anions 1993). Although some sources of bias can be controlled, either statistically or through experimental designs even in unstructured field settings, others cannot. Ideally, we would like to have compared bison from the two parks when females suffered identical gestational demands, inhabited the same environments, and fed upon the same food—but this was impossible. Further, it is likely that bison rely heavily on olfactory and auditory stimuli in detecting the presence of potential predators, neither of which would necessitate the shift from feeding to vigilance postures.

The extent to which vigilance is influenced by predation is not necessarily straightforward. Up to 90% of African buffalo at Lake Manyara may ultimately suffer predation (Prins and Iason 1989), yet central and peripheral individuals in a herd do not differ in vigilance during the day, but they do at night. Since lions are more active at night (Schaller 1972), this finding makes intuitive sense, but it is complicated to the extent that buffalo also shift into more thickly wooded areas where they feed. Males are also preyed on more than females and they are more vigilant; however, because predator attacks are not often witnessed, the size, composition, and location within a group remain unknown (Prins and Iason 1989). On the other hand, pronghorn in similar habitats varying in (human) predation pressure in the Great Basin Desert differ in vigilance, group sizes, and flight distances, suggesting sensitivity in their social responses to potential predation (Berger et al. 1983). These observations indicate that relationships among body size and vigilance are complicated by difficult-to-measure variables (which may include vegetation structure, predator densities, and the timing of predation) and that by reducing sources of potential variation to specific periods (e.g., emergence of new vegetation in late winter) and to the same habitats, antipredatory behaviors can be assessed in direct relation to body mass.

4.2 Sexual Segregation

The separation of groups by sex has been described for ungulates of temperate (McCullough 1979; Bowyer 1984; Shank 1982; Geist and Bayer 1988; Clutton-Brock et al. 1987) and tropical zones (Wirtz and Kaiser 1988), as well as for small mammals (Morris 1987), birds (Selander 1966), and even plants (Bierzychudek and Eckhart 1988). The bison that we studied afforded some opportunity to assess sexual segregation because altitudes did not vary, predation was absent, and the relative roles of different factors could, to some extent, be measured.

Habitat Differences

Not only did group sizes differ by sex and habitat (see fig. 4.1), but mixed groups were much more common on open prairies than all-male groups. Males, on the other hand, either in all male groups or when solitary, were more than one hundred times as common in breaks, woody draws, and ravines than were females. We were regularly startled by bulls in thickets, in the shade of tabletops, and at stream banks but never by females. In one exceptionally rugged 10 km² area, the Labyrinth (see photo 4.7), we never saw females although at least forty different males regularly used it. It had been inhabited by males since at least 1979. Overall, females used open areas whereas males were found in both open and fractured landscapes (see photo 4.2). Our findings parallel those reported for mixed groups of bison on the northern prairies including Wind Cave National Park (Coppock et al. 1983) and the Missouri River Breaks in North Dakota (Norland 1984).

Insect Harassment and Habitats

Numerous factors may promote the choice of specific habitats; the difficulty lies in ascertaining which ones are most important. Caribou often select open, windy sites for calving, but whether they do so to enhance the detection of predators, to feed at rich sites, to moderate body temperature, or to reduce insect harassment is uncertain (Downes, Theberge, and Smith 1986; Ion and Kershaw 1989). Although the northern prairies are not known for waves of insects, de Girardin (1849) described horrendous mosquito hordes in the Badlands—sights and sounds that we and our fieldworkers knew all too well. George A. Custer (1860:15) went so far as to claim "to such an extent do these pests to the animal kingdom exist,

PHOTO 4.7. Two bulls form a temporary association during late winter in the Labyrinth.

that to our thinly coated animals, such as the horse and mule, grazing is almost an impossibility, while the buffalo, with his huge shaggy coat can browse undisturbed.' Obviously, Custer did not know about impacts (i.e., "costs") that biting flies have on many large animals. Up to 500 cc of blood may be lost daily from cattle (Tashiro and Schwardt 1953), and calf weight gains may be reduced by up to 16% due to harassment of their foraging mothers (Haufe 1986). By avoiding or minimizing insect harassment large-bodied grazers may accrue benefits ultimately related to their fitness.

Two principal problems are inherent in examining habitat choice in bison. First, the quality of feeding sites must be approximated so that the importance of food can be weighed relative to other factors. Second, the sexes of bison, like most polygynous ungulates, differ in size and therefore they may differ in habitat requirements (Geist 1971a; Bowyer 1984).

One way to minimize the influence of food quality on microhabitat choice is to use areas where animals rest. For instance, bison at Badlands, Wind Cave, and Theodore Roosevelt national parks regularly move from high-quality food sites to prairie dog towns where they rest (Coppock et al. 1983; Krueger 1986; Norland 1984). Because prairie dog towns have less vegetation (Whicker and Detling 1988), they may serve as refuges with reduced insect harassment. If this hypothesis is true, then an explanation is needed for why males rarely rest on prairie dog towns. We examined these ideas using the data gathered by one of our coworkers, Linda Kerley. At Badlands the primary biting insects were stable flies, deerflies, and horseflies, all of which occurred both on and away from prairie dog towns (Kerley 1988).

If bison resting sites were affected by insects and other factors were equal, then refuge habitats should be characterized by lower insect densities than comparable adjacent areas. Kerley (1988) examined this idea by contrasting habitat use for males and females when ambient temperature, wind conditions, vegetation height, and visibility varied and controlling statistically for the different variables. She found: (1) although both sexes occupied open habitats with good visibility, females used these areas more than males (see fig. 4.2); (2) fly abundance was correlated with vegetation cover; and (3) selectivity for resting sites was inversely related to wind speed (flying insects are more abundant in the absence of wind; Lewis 1965). Despite differences in ambient temperature and insect abundance throughout the day, both sexes most often used sparsely vegetated microhabitats. However, females were much more likely to select habitats with greater visibility than males, presumably because the potential to detect predators was greater (Kerley 1988), an idea considered more fully in section 4.3. Based on these results, we conclude that bison (and especially females) designed their movements to enable them to rest in areas with good visibility and relatively low insect densities. For males, with their coincident small groups, insects may be less of a driving factor in habitat choice, or male habitat choice may be driven to a lesser extent by the need to detect potential predators. Irrespective of the causes, bison in northern environments are also affected by insect swarms (Melton et al. 1989), although the extent to which habitat shifts occur is uncertain.

Effects of Pregnancy and Neonates

Factors other than insects are likely to affect habitat choices. Because pre- or postnatal investment affects the vulnerability of females to predators in

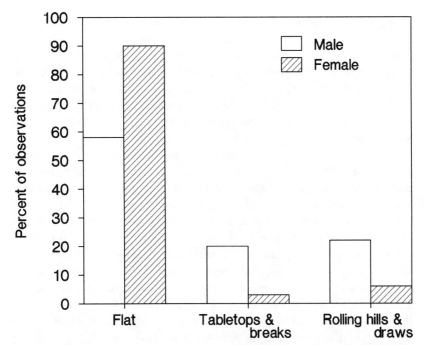

FIGURE 4.2. Comparison of the relative frequency that adult male and female bison were observed in different habitats on different days from May to August 1987. Modified from Kerley 1988.

several ungulates (Edwards 1983; Festa-Bianchet 1988b), habitat shifts may arise as a simple consequence of decreasing one's risk of predation. However, to minimize a loss of neonatal investment, pregnant or lactating females may avoid risky areas even though they forfeit access to nutritious food (Berger 1991a). Given that bison select habitats with open visibility even though effective predators are lacking at Badlands, we examined whether differences in habitat use existed between females that varied in energy requirements, contrasting barren females with those that were pregnant or lactating during different stages of plant phenology. If pregnancy or lactation had an effect on habitat choice, we predicted that nutrition should differ among habitats, and barren females should occur in habitats with the most nutritious food.

We knew which females were pregnant and which were not because individuals were followed throughout the year so that copulation and birthdates were known (see chapters 6, 7, and 8). Habitat use in relation to plant phenology, pregnancy, calving, and lactation was determined by noting the habitats used by twenty-nine pregnant and fourteen nonpregnant females. Data were recorded for three two-week periods—prior to parturition, the birth pulse, and after. Only the first location for each focal animal on any given day was used in the analyses to avoid the potential for autocorrelation between successive sightings in the same habitats. The topographical nature and presumptive visibility of habitats used by bison were evaluated by modification of a technique used to assess land surface ruggedness. Using topographical maps and a digitizer, we measured the lengths of contour lines for each one that intersected a 40-ha area within which a known female formed the center, and the mean number of contours was calculated per observation for each known animal. Because topographical diversity is highly correlated with contour line length per unit area, this technique offered a reasonably simple way to appraise habitat ruggedness (Beasom, Wiggers, and Giardino 1983). Not surprisingly, our quantitative results were in accord with our qualitative impression: relatively open areas and nonundulating prairie habitats were intersected with fewer contour lines (on average, less than 2 and 2.3) than were swales or valleys (3> contours) at 50, 100, and 150 m [5]. These findings allowed an approximation of the potential that existed for bison to detect predators in different habitats.

Does nutrition vary by habitat? On the northern prairies, the first green shoots of grass usually emerge in March, but not until late April or early May do the prairies become verdant. At other geographical locations, emergent grasses first appear on protected south-facing slopes, where soil temperatures are greater than those of open areas. Because nitrogen concentrations are highest in the meristematic tissues of emergent grasses preferred by both bison and cattle of shortgrass prairies of Colorado (Schwartz and Ellis 1981), we predicted that Badlands bison would maximize access to the most nutritious forage by feeding early in the year in protected areas and not on level, open prairies. For instance, range cattle in Colorado used south-facing slopes 250% more in March than adjacent regions in February or April (Senft, Rittenhouse, and Woodmansee 1985), presumably due to highly proteinaceous emergent vegetation. The food mosaic resulting from microgeographic variation in local soil, water, and temperature conditions creates not only heterogeneity in the distribution of protein but also spatial and temporal opportunities for habitat choice in pregnant and nonpregnant bison cows.

Since late gestation imposes greater nutrient requirements (Robbins 1983; Oftedal 1985) and may also impede locomotion, we expected habitat use to differ between pregnant and nonpregnant females. This

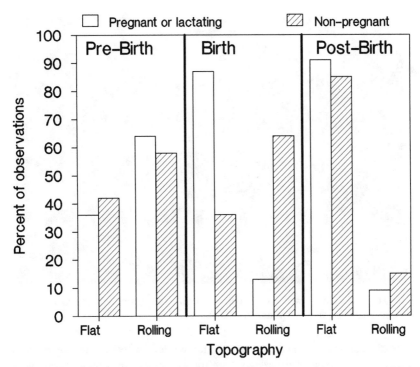

FIGURE 4.3. Relationship between time of the year with respect to birth season and the use of topographically based habitats in twenty-nine pregnant females that produced calves prior to 21 April and fourteen nonpregnant females. Prebirth (20 March to 4 April), birth (5 April to 20 April) and postbirth (21 April to 4 May); based on 414 total observations on different days.

prediction was unsupported by data (see fig. 4.3). During the period prior to parturition, late March to early April, pregnant and nonpregnant cows used rolling hills about 60% of the time and open, nonundulating areas about 40% of the time [6]. However, once the parturition season began, females differing in their reproductive status rapidly diverged in habitat use. Pregnant and lactating bison used flat, open topography almost 250% more than barren animals [6] (see fig. 4.3); mean group size of the former was also greater in such areas (91.1 versus 19.6, respectively) [7]. These striking contrasts between females of differing reproductive status disappeared during late April or early May (see fig. 4.3), when barren cows increased their reliance on flat open prairies from 36% to 85%, a value similar to that for pregnant or lactating females (91%) [6].

Two significant implications emerge from these results. First, irrespec-

Photo 4.8. Cows with two-week-old calves in open habitat; *foreground,* several yearlings and two-year olds

tive of reproductive status, during late winter, when bison are protein starved, animals shift to areas where they can feed on proteinaceous new grasses even though the food may be situated in habitats with reduced visibility. Second, once young are born, lactating mothers switch primarily to open sites with good visibility (see photo 4.8), but females without neonates make no such shifts, tending to remain in more rugged habitats with poorer visibility. However, within several weeks these differences vanish as barren females return to less undulating sites with better visibility; although we did not measure the rate of ''green-up'' directly in rolling hills and in flat, open areas, we suspect that barren females used the latter when the quality of nutrition in the two areas was similar, a prediction that needs to be tested.

Why do barren females, which have lower energy requirements than pregnant or lactating females, feed in swales or on hills when, under other conditions, they prefer visible sites? Two explanations, which are not mutually exclusive, are possible. If, by eating nutritious forage, barren females enhance their weight and body condition, they may further their reproduction in subsequent years. Data from our study site, Wind Cave, and the National Bison Range in Montana all suggest positive relationships between body condition and correlates of later reproduction.

We found that heavier animals experience estrus earlier in July and give birth earlier in the spring. We also found that early calves weigh more in September or October, possibly buffering them from overwinter mortality risks (see chapters 6, 7, and 8). Similar results have been reported for red deer and bighorn sheep (Clutton-Brock, Guinness, and Albon 1982; Festa-Bianchet 1988b). Green (1987) found that animals lactating in one year were lighter and gained less weight than those that had been barren during the same period, whereas nonlactating cows had more sons in the following season than those that had been lactating, the presumption being that females in better condition invested more heavily in the costlier sex (Rutberg 1986a). For Badlands females, those without young were clearly more tolerant of feeding in sites with low visibility but greater nutritional potential. Why this adjustment occurs was less obvious. Insects are rare at this time of the year, so pest avoidance is not a plausible alternative. Had effective predators occurred at Badlands, females might have been less likely to feed in putatively risky sites, but whether such avoidance would be due to the presence of vulnerable young or because the females themselves might beat risk is not clear. Alternatively, barren females at Badlands may have learned that such sites were not risky. Such scenarios must be examined in areas where bison are actively preyed upon.

4.3 Inferences About Indirect Effects of Predation

Predation obviously shapes a species' morphology and behavior, but it also has striking influences on community dynamics. The conspicuous effects—fewer sick, old, or injured animals—are demographic. But when active predation no longer occurs, as is the case for all North American bison populations except for those in reserves of northern Alberta and the Northwest Territories (Carbyn, Oosenbrug, and Anions 1993), effects on spacing and habitat use become subtle and can be ascertained only indirectly. For species such as elk or deer with an array of natural predators, assessing predation effects through comparison with control populations using similar habitats is possible. But comparing thickly wooded boreal forests inhabited by wolves to prairies without wolves is not feasible. Fortunately, observations of predator-bison interactions as well as archaeological and historical information allow inferences about how predation may have shaped habitat use and ranging patterns. The nature of this evidence is discussed below and summarized in table 4.3.

Sex and Age Structure

Although lions *(Panthera)* once preyed on the ancestors of bison, wolves have been the principal extant (nonhuman) predators of modern bison (Guthrie 1990). In northern Canada wolves may switch from male to female bison during different years (Haynes 1988), but at both the Slave River Lowlands and Wood Buffalo National Park, attacks appear to be preferentially directed toward female groups with young, and bulls are attacked or killed less than their abundance in the population might suggest (Carbyn and Trottier 1987; Van Camp 1987; Van Camp and Calef 1987). Gauging effects of past predation pressures on current behavior is impossible, but given the differing responses of the sexes, females may have been under stronger predation pressure than males. If so, bison group sizes, vigilance, habitat use, and the spacing between the sexes may all reasonably be expected to be affected by predation. We examine this tenet in the following sections.

Group Size

Females with young form large groups in areas with and without active predators (Rutberg 1984; Carbyn and Trottier 1987, 1988). These aggregations add credence to the idea that predation molded some patterns of habitat use and social groupings, even though wolves have been extirpated from most areas where bison now occur. Despite their smaller body size, females have larger home ranges than males, probably because they form larger groups (Larter and Gates 1990). It will be interesting to learn from future studies whether different size groups, controlling for sex, are exposed to varying predation pressure.

Vigilance

As our data from Wood Buffalo and Badlands parks show, bison are remarkably nonvigilant despite the presence and history of association with nonhuman predators, an idea consistent with the observations of Carbyn and Trottier (1987, 1988), who felt that bison become vigilant primarily when under the direct threat of attack. Therefore assessing vigilance within the context of foraging behavior may be a poor predictor of past (or even present) predation pressure for bison. This need not be the case when bison are hunted by humans (Van Vuren 1980) or for other ungulates (e.g., pronghorn, bighorn; see table 4.1, appendix 3).

TABLE 4.3.

Selective summary of studies with suggestions of indirect effects of predation on bison biology

Presumed effect	Evidence	Study site and predator	References
Sex/age structure modified	Sex and age of kills	Slave River Lowlands and Wood Buffalo National Park (wolves)	Van Camp 1987; Oosenbrug and Carbyn 1985
Group size changes	Increased association among females and cow/calf groups	Multiple sites and Wood Buffalo National Park (wolves); National Bison Range (none)	Geist and Karsten 1977; Carbyn and Trottier 1987, 1988; Rutberg 1984
Enhanced vigilance	Cows more alert than bulls; differences between females in various habitats *not* detectable; vigilance higher in both sexes after attack	Wood Buffalo (wolves) and Badlands (none) national parks; multiple sites (wolves)	Allen 1875; Berger and Cunningham 1988; Carbyn and Trottier 1987, 1988; Kerley 1988
Habitat use modified	Lactating and pregnant females shift to open habitats; sexes use areas differing in visibility; males have more freedom to use different habitats	Badlands (none) and Wood Buffalo (wolves) national parks; Alaska (several)	Lott and Galland 1985; Carbyn and Trottier 1987, 1988; Guthrie 1990; this study
Sexual segregation occurs			
Recent studies	Bulls in more rugged areas	Theodore Roosevelt (none) and Badlands (none) national parks	Norland 1984; this study
Historical records	Differential vulnerability of females with young to predation; adult males often separate from females	Central prairies (wolves)	Allen 1875a; Hornaday 1889
Archeological	Differential vulnerability of females by season; sex differences in habitat use due to food or predation pressure	Multiple sites (Paleo-Indians and wolves)	Reher 1974; Geist and Karsten 1977; Davis and Wilson 1978; Speth 1983; Guthrie 1990

Habitat Use

Our observations of female preferences for open nonundulating grass-lands with high visibility are consistent with the idea that predation has shaped habitat choice in females to a greater extent than in males (Lott and Galland 1985a). However, because females, by providing milk, invest more in their immediate offspring than do males, disentangling the proximate effect of offspring from ultimate pressures exerted by predation is difficult. Proximate events, such as the use of specific habitats, the number of calves present, or food sites containing greater amounts of nitrogen, can be measured directly, but assessment of ultimate factors like predation pressure relies on inference. If, for instance, barren females had consistently used habitats with better visibility than those of males, the hypothesis that cows chose such areas because of past evolutionary pressures cannot be discredited, because such pressures cannot be manip-ulated in the present. Nevertheless, the key issues are (1) males and females are found in different habitats (see fig. 4.1), and (2) although proximate factors may mediate differential reproduction, such events are influenced by natural selection. In the absence of information on mortality and reproduction of individuals in different habitats, the role of proximate influences on the current utility of behaviors remains unclear.

Sexual Segregation

The two sexes are generally segregated throughout most of the year because of differing preferences for visibility, variation in reproductive status, and abundant biting insects. We cannot say whether nutritional differences between habitats occurred because measurements were not taken. However, for other sexually dimorphic ungulates including moose and red, white-tailed, and mule deer (McCullough 1979; Bowyer 1984; Clutton-Brock, Iason, and Guinness 1987; Miquelle 1989) females often select areas of higher nutrient value. Thus numerous proximate factors in addition to predation pressure are likely to be important in explaining sex differences in habitat use.

Could habitat segregation be an artifact of the comparatively recent restriction of populations into confined areas, even when the reserves may allow animals to roam over hundreds of kilometers? We think not, for three principal reasons. First, comparative studies of populations at widely differing geographical locations point to sex differences in group size and habitat use (see table 4.3). Second, historical data from the nineteenth century indicate that although group sizes were much larger than those of today (Bamforth 1987), discrete mixed groups and male groups were common and may have been found in different habitats (Allen 1875a; Roe 1970). Third, archaeological reconstructions (Reher 1974; Speth 1983; Guthrie 1990) of seasonal trends in grouping and habitat use suggest that past patterns and evolutionary pressures (Geist and Karsten 1977) are reasonably similar to those occurring today. Given these disparate pieces of evidence (as well as those from table 4.3), the inference that sexual segregation has been a regular feature of bison biology for at least thirty-five thousand years seems reasonable.

4.4 Summary

1. Enormous variability characterized bison group sizes. Season, habitat, sex, and age all exerted independent effects on group size; the largest groups occurred during the summer mating season when up to five hundred animals congregated. Female groups were larger than male groups, presumably due to the potential to reduce vulnerability to predators.

2. Females were more selective in their choice of habitats than males although both sexes rested in areas with relatively lower densities of insect pests. Females preferred habitats with relatively better visibility and of presumed higher protein quality. Lactating females were more constrained in the range of habitats used than nonlactating females. The former relied primarily on flat open areas, probably the result of maternal strategies to reduce the susceptibility of their young to potential predators.

3. Vigilance among female prairie ungulates (pronghorn, bighorn sheep, mule deer, and bison) was influenced more by group size than by body size. In environments with natural predators, bison were no more vigilant than in areas without them.

4. Determining the extent to which patterns of habitat use today differ from those of former times is not easy. Sexual segregation, which is found in today's populations, is likely to have occurred in the past; records from the nineteenth century and archaeological data suggest that it has been a regular feature of bison biology for at least thirty-five thousand years. Although some bison characteristics, including the potential to migrate, have been altered by today's world, other traits may be less affected.

4.5 Statistical Notes

1. Comparison of effects of sex and age composition, habitat, and season on group size. Three-way Analysis of Variance (data normalized by log transformation): $F_{1,532}$ (Sex/Age) = 2922.36, $p<0.0001$; $F_{6,352}$ (month) = 6.78, $p<0.001$; $F_{6,352}$ (Habitat) = 24.47, $p<0.0001$: Sex x Month − F = 14.80, $p<0.001$; Sex x Habitat − F = 38.93, p <0.0001; Month x Habitat − F = 3.00, $p<0.001$; Sex x Month x Habitat − F = 2.65, $p<0.005$.

2. Comparison of the amount of time spent vigilant per foraging bout in groups of 1, 2 to 5, 6 to 10, and 11 + of four ungulates. One-way Analysis of Variance and Student-Newman-Keuls Test (SNK) values are for within-species contrasts. For all species, differences between groups 6 to 10 and 11 + were not significant (SNK).
   Pronghorn F = 105.44, $p<0.001$;
   Bighorn Sheep F = 23.20, $p<0.001$;
   Mule Deer F = 60.20, $p<0.001$;
   Bison F = 23.50, $p<0.001$.

3. Multiple regression of female group size (X_1) and mean body mass (X_2) on log (t + 1) vigilance rate (Y) (based on 426 180-s bouts) for four ungulates.
   $Y = 1.75 - 0.351X_1 - 0.001X_2$, $r^2 = 0.36$; partial correlation coefficients for $X_1 = -0.51$ ($p<0.001$), $X_2 = -0.36$ ($p<0.001$)

4. Comparison between vigilance and (a) group size for females in Wood Buffalo National Park and (b) study site (Badlands). Two-way Analysis of Variance:
   (a) $F_{3,184} = 25.36$, $p<0.001$; contrast between group size 1 and larger groups, $p<0.001$, but within-group contrasts for 2 to 5, 6 to 10, and 11 +, NS (SNK);
   (b) F = 0.053, NS

5. Comparison between mean visibility in one randomly chosen direction at (a) 50 m, (b) 100 m, and (c) 150 m in 20 areas of little and moderate topographical relief. T Test.
   (a) t = 3.60, $p<0.001$;
   (b) t = 2.08, $p<0.05$;
   (c) t = 2.99, $p<0.01$;

6. Comparison of the relative frequency that 29 pregnant and subsequently lactating females used habitats differing in topographical

characteristics (as described in text) in relation to those used by 14 barren females during three time periods. G Test.

(a) 20 March to 5 April : $G = 0.71$, NS

(b) 5 April to 20 April : $G = 14.98$, $p < 0.001$

(c) 21 April to 4 May : $G = 0.58$, NS

5.   Population Features

Under many conditions crowded animals not only do not grow but they die more readily and frequently reproduce less rapidly than when living in uncrowded populations.

W. C. Allee 1938:16

Bison today are exceptional survivors. They experience little natural mortality. In fact, we are not aware of any unsuccessful reintroductions into prairie environments. Although bison have been slow to reproduce after being introduced into areas of Alaska and Canada, numerous populations have been so successful that hunting and regular culls are now permitted (see table 2.2). This results, in part, from the lack of predators and an abundant food supply guaranteed by regular roundups. In this chapter we summarize data on the Badlands Park population, offer figures on rates of population increase and factors that affect them, and then present information on population density and on sources of mortality.

5.1 Population Changes at Badlands

The first reintroduced bison entered the Badlands in late 1963 when twenty-eight animals arrived, twenty-five from Theodore Roosevelt National Park and three from the Fort Niobrara Refuge. The National Park Service files after this date are a bit unclear, but it is also likely that "2 or 3 Yellowstone bulls [were] introduced" in 1965 (NPS files). The population doubled by 1966 (see fig. 5.1). The finite rate of increase, which is the ratio of change in population size per unit of time, averaged about 10.8% per year until 1972 when roundups to control population size began. It was not possible to calculate the rate of population growth in the absence of human intervention again until our research began.

During the four-year period from 1985 to 1988 when roundups were suspended, the population increased from fewer than 350 bison to more than 630, an 82% increase that is equivalent to a finite rate of increase of 20.4% per year. Although estimated from absolute numbers, this figure, like the 10.8% value from 1964 to 1972, is only an approximation

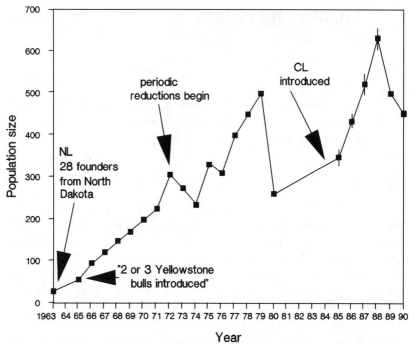

Year

FIGURE 5.1. Changes in size and chronology of major events in the bison population at Badlands National Park. *NL* and *CL* are animals whose lineages are of Nebraskan and Coloradan descent. Vertical lines are 95% confidence intervals.

because a greater proportion of young animals is recruited as the population grows. Only when the age structure stabilizes do rates of increase approximate growth over a several year period (Wilson and Bossert 1971; Caughley 1977). When the Badlands data are converted to an exponential rate of increase using the differential growth equation, $N = Noe^{rt}$ where N is the total population size, No is the initial size, e is the constant for the base of natural logs, r is the exponential rate of increase, and t is time in years. The value for r during our study period is 16.7% (see fig. 5.1).

Why the population sustained more rapid growth in the late 1980s than when first reintroduced is uncertain. We can discount harsh winters as a possible factor because records confirm winters were no worse during the early years than later. At least three possibilities exist. First, early growth may have been retarded if animals were unfamiliar with good foraging or watering locations. This scenario seems unlikely because, in the absence of prior heavy grazing, food should have been abundant. Second, population sizes during the late 1960s and early 1970s were estimated crudely, being based on incomplete counts; therefore they could have been minimum estimates. Finally, some animals could have been rounded up or killed, but the reports omitted from park files. Although we have no way of assessing which possibility is most realistic, we believe that bison population sizes were probably larger than estimated; obtaining accurate counts is difficult without a team of coworkers who are familiar with the terrain.

Although the growth of the Badlands population has been rapid during periods when uncontrolled, bison from other areas have sustained higher exponential growth rates and over longer time frames. In the Jackson herd that wanders into and out of Teton National Park, benefiting from food provisions on the National Elk Refuge each winter, the exponential growth is about 19.1% annually (Shelley and Anderson 1989). This herd began in 1969 when eight animals escaped from a private wildlife park near Jackson. The eighteen wood bison that founded the Mackenzie Sanctuary population near Great Slave Lake, Northwest Territories, experienced a 23.3% exponential growth rate from 1963 to 1979, a period during which wolves were apparently very rare (Calef 1984). These data suggest impressive growth rates for a large North American herbivore when not constrained by food, predation, or human control. Under modest hunting pressure in the Henry Mountains, Utah, bison had a 9.2% exponential increase over a seven-year period (Van Vuren and Bray 1986). These populations, however, are atypical because most are heavily managed (see table 2.2).

5.2 Dispersal and Its Restriction

Most bison populations are restricted in their movements, being confined to fenced parks where dispersal is not possible (see table 2.2). This was mainly the case at Badlands, although every year a few animals moved beyond park boundaries. Females left the park in only one of the five study years; a mixed group spent nearly thirty days feeding primarily on private lands adjacent to the park and a small amount of time on the Buffalo Gap National Grasslands. In four of our five study years, when the only animals to leave the park were adult males, the cumulative total was eighty-one. Whereas the mixed female group remained together, males often left the park as solitary individuals. When males left in small groups, these often splintered making it difficult to relocate the bulls (see table 5.1).

How do animals leave the park? Most move past fences that are down,

TABLE 5.1.

Sources and frequency of natural and human-related mortality and frequency of animals dispersing beyond park boundaries (ADBPB) at Badlands

	1985	1986	1987	1988	1989	Total
Total mortality						
Adult males[1]	1	4	3	7	3	18
Adult females	0 (0.5%)	0 (1.9%)	1 (1.8%)	2 (3.2%)	2	5
Juvenile males[2]	0	3	9	6	0	18
Juvenile females	0	3 (2.7%)	3 (4.2%)	3 (2.5%)	0	9
Natural[3]	0 (0%)	6 (1.4%)	8 (1.5%)	14 (2.2%)	4	32
Shot	1	4	8	4	0	17
Poached	0	0	1	0	1	2
Corral-related	2	2	3	4	1	12
ADBPB	11 males	19 males	39 males	9 males; 50+ mixed	12 males	140

[1] % of total adult population (males and females combined)
[2] % of juvenile population (calves included)
[3] % of total population
Total mortality = natural + animals killed outside the park (poaching and corral-related deaths excluded). Adults are 3+ (female) and 5+ (male) years. Juveniles include calves.

usually due to flooding in washes or heavy snow drifts. However, other avenues of departure exist. We once found a gate left open by a tourist; we saw four animals jump cattle guards; and more than twenty cases of bulls hurdling low fences at the north end of Sage Creek WA exist. Along the southern boundary bison were found on at least twelve occasions outside the park when all fences were intact. Because fences in this region are almost 2.5 m—a height that bison cannot leap—it is likely that they simply wandered through rugged unfenced areas until they passed beyond park boundaries. Because animals beyond the borders are often perceived as management problems, active attempts are made by Park Service rangers to move bison back into the park unless conflicts with humans or private property are unlikely. Attempts to return bison were made on foot, motorcycles, horses, and in trucks. Predictably, the success rate varied. Of ninety males that were out of the park during our five-year study, nearly 19% (N = 17) were killed (see table 5.1). Obviously, this figure ignores animals that left the park undetected and were killed.

Gauging how far animals would have moved in the absence of travel restrictions is difficult. Most animals that depart are located before they have traveled far from the park. In the late 1970s at least twelve bulls spent more than four months out of the park, somewhere between the Sage Creek drainage and the Cheyenne River to the west. During the winter of 1985–86, a twelve-year old (CL) male spent more than three months on the Pine Ridge Indian Reservation about 30 km south of the Sage Creek WA. He subsequently died in attempts to return him to the park in late February. In May 1987 three old spikes spent four days wandering south into Conata Basin on the Buffalo Gap National Grasslands south of the park. None could be trapped or returned to the park, and their fates were never known.

Excursions such as these are more well known in parks such as Yellowstone or the Tetons, although restricted dispersal and problems stemming from movements beyond the borders have taken place at virtually all locations where bison occur. Unconfirmed reports of bison nearly 50 km from Teton National Park were made after the 1988 fires in the Greater Yellowstone Ecosystem, and at least five bison spent the winter of 1988–89 in Shoshone National Forest to the east of Yellowstone. Perhaps the best-known movements of bison outside a park have occurred when animals have emigrated northward out of Yellowstone Park. During the four winters from 1985 to 1988, 57, 6, 36, and 569 animals were killed outside park boundaries in Montana (Yellowstone bison 1990). As with the active control programs in most parks, if animals cannot successfully be driven back into the safety of refuges, they are killed.

Only at sites in northern Canada, Alaska, and the Yukon can information on long distance movements be gathered. Unfortunately, there are few data. The best are from introduced populations. One unsuccessful transplant occurred in 1978 when wood bison reintroduced into Jasper National Park moved more than 160 km in thirty days. They were destroyed after conflicts arose when they entered areas of agricultural development (Reynolds 1982). A population of wood bison transplanted to Nahanni National Park in the Northwest Territories in 1980 splintered into several small groups with some remaining locally and others moving up to 350 km into British Columbia (Reynolds 1982).

5.3 The Potential for Density Dependence

Because of the lack of dispersal, population density increased over the study period. Excluding calves of the year, crude densities varied annually from 1.25 to 2.02 animals/km^2. Ecological densities (animals/available habitat; Eisenberg and Seidensticker 1976), which excluded gravel and other nonvegetated areas from calculations, increased from 1.87 to 3.01 bison/km^2 (see table 5.2).

Some of the most common effects associated with increased density in

TABLE 5.2.
Crude and ecological densities of Badlands population excluding calves
of the year

	1984	1985	1986	1987	1988
Crude	1.25	1.10	1.36	1.67	2.02
Ecological	1.87	1.64	2.03	2.49	3.01

Number/km²

large mammals are (1) decreased fecundity, (2) increased age at sexual maturity, (3) increased juvenile mortality, (4) increased adult mortality, and (5) increased dispersal distances (Sinclair 1977, 1989; Albon, Mitchell, and Staines 1983). We checked for potential relationships in the first four of these variables since emigration was rarely possible. Our fecundity measure was the number of calves per female three years of age or older. There was no statistically significant relationship for any of these variables [1; numbers in brackets correspond to statistical notes at end of chapter]. We also examined potential relationships of yearly density to other variables, including the total number of animals out of the park, total number of natural deaths, percentage of males that copulated at least once annually, calf recruitment, and the coefficient of variation for both male and female reproduction. Only the total number of animals out of the park and the total number of natural deaths were correlated to density ($p < 0.05$) [2]. However, evidence from other sexually dimorphic ungulates (McCullough 1979; Clutton-Brock, Guinness, and Albon 1982) suggests that it may not be prudent to compare total population size to factors suspected of being affected by density when females and males may be sexually segregated throughout much of the year. However, at our site, adult males and adult females contributed to the increase in population size and, since our analyses relied on rank-related statistics, the effects of separating the sample into males and females would have no bearing on the general conclusion that density had no effect.

To check for other possible influences, we compared yearly birth sex ratios to see whether they deviated from parity [3] or yearly with density; none did (see table 5.3). We also evaluated whether it was possible to extrapolate from our sample of known mothers by comparing it to the entire Badlands population when group sizes were largest (i.e., during the summer); at this time it was possible to determine the sex of almost all the calves. As with prior calculations, these did not deviate from a 50:50 ratio [4]. We even checked for additional potential effects of

TABLE 5.3.
Annual calf sex ratio at birth (males:females)

	1985	1986	1987	1988	1989
Total population	1.24 (74)	0.79 (93)	0.93 (104)	1.21 (126)	—
Known mothers	1.89 (26)	1.17 (39)	0.86 (69)	0.85 (65)	1.50 (15)*

*Does not include 12 calves of undetermined sex
Sample sizes in parentheses.

population density on birthdates. By calculating the median date of birth annually, which varied from 2 May to 8 May, the most compressed 75% of births, and the quartile deviation (see table 6.1), we examined whether density affected birth season chronology. None of these variables was influenced by population size [5 and 6].

Several explanations seem reasonable to account for the lack of clear concordance between population density and subsequent demographic performance. First, the five-year study duration may have been too short for a large, long-lived mammal (Sinclair 1989). In species like elephants (Laws and Parker 1968) or elk (Houston 1982; Boyce 1989), lag times in density dependence may be large. Density dependence must surely be reflected in populations without active control, as in Yellowstone, but this contention cannot be supported until the confounding effects of severe weather are separated from those of density (e.g., Meagher 1976). Second, although densities increased from 1.25 to 2.02 animal/km^2 at Badlands (see table 5.2), in the absence of ameliorating winters or drought these changes were probably too small to produce widespread demographic effects. Compared to other sites where bison densities have been estimated, such as Wichita Mountains in Oklahoma or the National Bison Range in Montana, densities at the Badlands were always the lowest. Nevertheless, our failure to detect density-dependence may have been affected by two additional factors. The contrasts between density and reproduction did not account for plant productivity, which surely varies among sites (see table 5.4). The only way for us to compare reproductive rates among sites was to standardize female age, which restricted our sample to three- to seven-year olds. Since evidence from some sites (but not Badlands; see chapter 7) suggests that this is the most fecund age cohort (Shaw and Carter 1989), any effect of density per se would probably be obscured by excluding older animals, even though it is this cohort that tends toward marginal body condition (Albon, Mitchell, and Staines 1983).

TABLE 5.4.

Summary of reproductive rates in 3- to 7-year-old bison at sites varying in average densities (bison/km²)

Location	Density	% females with calves	Reference
Badlands			
1985–89	1.25–2.02	64.3 (115)	This study
Witchita Mountains			
1981–89	2.30	71.0 (93)	Shaw and Carter 1989
1959–66	3.46	56.6 (198)	Halloran 1968
National Bison Range			
	4.33	82*	Rutberg 1986a

*For cows 3 years or older
Sample sizes in parentheses.

5.4 Sources of Mortality

Of sixty-three deaths at Badlands, 49% (31) were directly related to humans (see table 5.1). Seventeen animals were shot outside the park, two were poached in the park (photo 5.1), and twelve died due to goring- or trampling-related injuries that resulted from handling or trapping during roundups. The poaching-related deaths were acts of wanton destruction. Neither meat nor hide was taken, and their bodies were simply left rotting. Both deaths involved valuable (for us) old (15 + years) bulls that we had known since the beginning of the study.

Adult mortality on an annual basis varied from 0.5 to 3.2%; juvenile mortality (subadults + calves) ranged from 2.5 to 4.2% (see table 5.1). The maximum percentage that natural mortality accounted for was 2.2% in 1988. Overall, the samples were too small to detect whether sex differences in mortality occurred except for animals up to three years of age, in which mortality was twice as high for males as for females [7]. Young bison experience low mortality rates at other sites as well. For instance, only 1 of 153 calves born over a three-year period died at Wind Cave (Green and Rothstein 1991b).

Predation had no impact on the Badlands population. In the thirty-two coyote-bison interactions we observed, less than 25% involved more than a glance. On the four occasions that cows chased coyotes, each female had a calf less than five days old. In one of these instances we watched a coyote hiding behind bushes less than 40 m from a calf that was less than two hours old. The mother detected the coyote as it approached the calf, charged it, and then she and the calf ran over the hill and out of our view. In three other instances yearlings or juveniles chased coyotes.

PHOTO 5.1. A bull that was poached. The hide was worn raw by poachers, who dragged the animal about 6 km. Body measurements are being taken by Carol Cunningham.

Other mortality sources include sink holes, which are narrow, deep depressions (less than 2 m in diameter and as deep as 3 m). We discovered skeletons of one cow, two calves, and one bull in separate sink holes, and our coworkers found a live calf in a different one. Six animals died by drowning after they ventured onto a thinly frozen water hole partially concealed by a March snowdrift (see photo 5.2). Mass drownings have occurred at other sites. In Wood Buffalo National Park an estimated three thousand bison perished crossing a swollen river (Haynes 1982), and approximately two thousand drowned crossing the South Platte River in 1867:

Late in summer . . . a herd of probably four thousand buffaloes attempted to cross. . . . The river was rapidly subsiding, being nowhere over a foot

PHOTO 5.2. Three of six animals that broke through the ice and drowned. Photo was taken approximately two months after animals drowned.

or two in depth, and the channels in the bed were filled or filling with loose quicksand. The buffaloes in the front were hopelessly stuck. Those immediately behind, urged on by horns and pressure of those yet further in the rear, trampled over their struggling companions to be themselves engulfed in the devouring sand. This was continued until the bed of the river, nearly half a mile broad, was covered with dead or dying buffaloes. Only a comparatively few actually crossed the river, and these were soon driven back by hunters. It was estimated that considerably more than half the herd, or over two thousand buffaloes, paid for this attempt with their lives.

(Dodge quoted in Allen 1875a)

5.5 The Irony of Too Many Protected Animals

Conflicts with local landowners, quandaries about what constitutes natural ecosystems and how they should be regulated, and methods of population control are all fundamental issues that arise with the proliferation of protected populations. These issues are not limited to species introduced to new environments such as reindeer to South Georgia Island (Leader-Williams 1988), tahr and deer to New Zealand (Caughley 1977), or horses to the Great Basin (Berger 1986). Tigers eat cattle and occasionally kill villagers outside of Nepal's Chitwan National Park (Sunquist and Sunquist 1988); rhinos and elephants raid crops beyond park boundaries in Nepal and India (Sukumar 1986; Mishra, Wemmer, and Smith 1987). Lions *inside* Namibia's Etosha National Park have been implanted with contraception devices to slow population growth (Orford, Perrin, and Berry 1988), and sheep-eating grizzly bears are killed in buffer zones outside Yellowstone National Park but *within* the Greater Yellowstone Ecosystem. Additional examples abound (Jewell, Holt, and Hart 1981). Elk wintering in the Jackson Hole area of Wyoming are so numerous that they cause damage to fences and vegetation, and they may facilitate the spread of brucellosis (Boyce 1989).

Among the solutions to locally abundant populations, two stand out: harvesting and transplanting. The first entails active removal, a practice not uncommon in parks and nonprotected areas when habitats become overpopulated or vegetation is altered too dramatically (Owen-Smith 1988). Removals have included more than eight thousand African buffalo, twenty-five hundred elephants, and almost four hundred hippos in a five-year period from Kruger National Park, South Africa (Hanks 1981). The second, transplanting, involves moving animals from regions of high abundance in order to restock depleted areas or to supplement small populations. A third possibility, sterilization or contraception, has not gained wide acceptance in North America, although congressionally mandated research has resulted in studies of reproductive manipulations of feral horses.

For bison, however, neither killing nor transplanting have been viewed as palatable tactics by the public. Killing is viewed as cruel and unnecessary (Yellowstone bison 1990) and transplanting often produces inevitable conflicts with agriculture. In Canada transplants to reintroduce wood bison into former habitats in northern boreal forests have been viewed positively (Reynolds and Hawley 1987), but suggestions to repopulate Wood Buffalo National Park with wood bison, after removing the hybridized and diseased animals currently there, have been highly controversial (Geist 1990).

Except for the killings in the Greater Yellowstone Ecosystem (i.e., outside Yellowstone and Teton parks), few of the control measures in other populations, Badlands included, have stirred much public acrimony. At the Maxwell Refuge (Kansas), National Bison Range (Montana), Antelope Island State Park (Utah), Fort Niobrara National Wildlife Refuge and Niobrara Valley Preserve (Nebraska), and Wichita Mountains Wildlife Refuge (Oklahoma), animals are captured and auctioned to the public. Interestingly, the agencies involved have all adopted the same type of removal practice although they represent diverse constituents— the U.S. Fish and Wildlife Service, state fish and game departments, the Nature Conservancy (a nongovernment organization). Most roundups are annual events, employing helicopters and cowboys; at Wind Cave National Park they occur biannually and, at the Badlands, captures have been at unpredictable intervals, in part dependent on when animals leave the wilderness area. Except for the privately operated Niobrara Valley Preserve, the above cases involve bison on public lands. Nearly seventy-five thousand bison were on private ranches in 1985; they were marketed for beef, other products, and occasionally for hunting (Hawley 1989). Bison under the auspices of the National Park Service are given to various Native American tribes, fulfilling agreements with Indian reservations. The Pine Ridge and Rosebud Reservations, under the stewardship of the Lakota, accept animals from the Badlands and Wind Cave; bison in fenced herds are used in ceremonies, marketed for food and other products, and used to generate revenues derived from hunting by non-Indians.

5.6 Summary

1. During the first eight years after the reintroduction of bison in 1964, the finite rate of increase averaged 10.8%. Once population reductions begun, rates of increase over multiple year periods could not be calculated. However, during the years from 1985 to 1988 when no manipulations occurred, the finite rate of increase was 20.4%, or when converted to an exponential rate, 16.7%. Higher rates have been recorded for the Teton and Mackenzie Sanctuary populations and lower rates were found for animals at Yellowstone and in the Henry Mountains.

2. Dispersal beyond the park boundaries was prevented both by fences and human predation. Due to these restrictions, the potential for density dependence was exacerbated. However, none of the following variables were associated with population density: fecundity, age at sexual maturity, juvenile mortality, and adult mortality. Both the number of animals beyond park boundaries and natural deaths were correlated with density.

3. The total number of deaths during the study was sixty-three of which thirty-one were due to humans. Seventeen animals were shot outside the park, and two were poached within the park. Annual adult mortality varied from 0.5% to 3.2%, whereas an-

nual juvenile (subadult + calf) mortality ranged from 2.5% to 4.2%. Up to three years of age, mortality was about twice as high for males as for females; with regard to mortality among older animals no sex differences occurred.

5.7 Statistical Notes

1. Relationships between annual population density and (a) fecundity for 3-yr-old females, (b) fecundity for 4-yr-old females, (c) female age at puberty, (d) percent juvenile mortality, and (e) percent adult mortality. Spearman Rank Correlation.
   (a) $r_s = 0.60$; N = 5; NS
   (b) $r_s = 0.30$; N = 5; NS
   (c) $r_s = 0.00$; N = 4; NS
   (d) $r_s = 0.80$; N = 4; NS
   (e) $r_s = 0.80$; N = 4; NS

2. Relationships between population density and (a) total number of animals out of the park, (b) total number of known natural deaths, (c) percent of adult males copulating at least once annually, (d) coefficient of variation (CV) for adult male reproduction, and (e) CV for female reproduction.
   (a) $r_s = 1.0$; N = 4; $p < 0.05$
   (b) $r_s = 1.0$; N = 4; $p < 0.05$
   (c) $r_s = 0.60$; N = 4; NS
   (d) $r_s = 0.60$; N = 4; NS
   (e) $r_s = 0.70$; N = 5; NS

3. Comparison of frequencies of male and female offspring born (a) annually and (b) cumulatively. Chi Square Test.
   (a) 1985: $X^2 = 0.86$, N = 74, NS; 1986: $X^2 = 1.30$, N = 93, NS; 1987: $X^2 = 0.15$, N = 104, NS; 1988: $X^2 = 1.14$, N = 126, NS;
   (b) $X^2 = 0.06$, N = 397; NS

4. Comparison of birth sex ratios of calves of known mothers with that of the general population. Chi Square Test.
   1985: $X^2 = 1.41$, N = 100, NS; 1986: $X^2 = 1.05$, N = 132, NS; 1987: $X^2 = 0.05$, N = 173, NS; 1988: $X^2 = 1.12$, N = 171; NS

5. Comparison among median birthdates and year (data from table 6.1). Median Test.
   $X^2 = 1.01$, df = 4, NS

6. Comparison between annual population density and (a) quartile deviation/yr and (b) the most concentrated 75% of the births/yr. Spearman Rank Correlation.
   - (a) $r_s = 0.20$, NS
   - (b) $r_s = 0.50$, NS
7. Comparison of total mortality between juvenile males and females (corrected for total number of juveniles in the population during the 1985 to 1988 period). Chi Square Test.
   $X^2 = 3.97$, N = 1529, $p < 0.05$

6. Reproductive Synchrony and Breeding Biology

*One of the strange spectacles to be seen every recurring spring
soon after the grass had started were the thousands of circles trod-
den bare on the plains; which the early travelers, who did not di-
vine their cause, called "fairy rings." These were made during the
calving period of the buffalo, and as there were a great many gray
wolves that roamed singly and in great packs over the whole prairie region, the bulls in their great beats kept guard over the cows
and drove the wolves away, walking in a ring around the females
at a short distance and thus forming the curious circles.*

M. S. Garretson 1934:19

Reproductive synchrony, the birth of offspring at about the same
time, is a striking characteristic of both vertebrates and invertebrates
(Darling 1938; Ims 1990); for social ungulates like caribou and wildebeest
it can be a truly spectacular event with tightly clustered herdmates giving
birth to calves within days, hours, or minutes of one another (Lent 1966;
Estes 1976). Although both predation and plant phenology are major
factors that have shaped the degree of birth synchrony in ungulates
(Leuthold 1977; Rutberg 1984, 1987; Bowyer 1991), detection of the
magnitude of either, let alone sorting out the role of natural selection, has
been difficult. In species in which birth synchrony is not tightly constrained, the implication may be that either a low heritability in characters
associated with the timing of births exists or natural selection has not
been intense enough to mold it. Fortunately, evidence on variability in
births, especially the differential survival of neonates born at different
times of the year, is available, and it has been used to argue that selection
has honed parturition seasons to narrow windows of time in both feral
and native species (Guinness, Gibson, and Clutton-Brock 1978; Festa-
Bianchet 1988b).

In this chapter we deal with two somewhat different themes—the
common thread is that each ultimately deals with reproduction. First, we
present information on the timing of births in bison, paying attention to

synchronous breeding. We then investigate potential mechanisms that may facilitate this event, assessing possible costs and benefits. Our central tenet is that gestation length, within bounds guided by physical condition, is flexible and enables reproductive synchrony to occur. Because the relationships are not straightforward, we examine other factors that may explain reproductive synchrony. Second, we describe size-weight relationships for bison using data from both the Badlands and three populations managed at U.S. Fish and Wildlife Service refuges. Although we fail to determine why variation exists, we point out relationships between the sexes, among years, and among sites. Also, the general data on size and weight relationships form the bases for the two subsequent chapters in which we deal with the reproductive consequences of individual variation.

6.1 Parturition

Births and Number of Young

Bison are similar to cattle with regard to birth behavior. Signs of impending parturition begin when females become restless and carry their tails outstretched away from their body, rather than hanging. However, because yearlings and nonpregnant two-year olds assume similar postures, tail carriage is not an invariant characteristic of an imminent birth. Calves are remarkably precocial, rising, on average, eleven minutes after birth and becoming steady on their feet six minutes later (Lott and Galland 1985a) (see photo 6.1). The degree to which mothers remain in herds varies with social conditions. At the National Bison Range, nine of eleven births occurred in groups, whereas on Santa Catalina Island, where smaller groups occur and the topography is more rugged, five of six cows gave birth in isolation (Lott and Galland 1985a). Of thirteen births in the Badlands, ten occurred when cows were at the periphery of groups that varied in size from four to seventy-six animals. In three cases no other bison could be seen by the peripheral cow; one of these involved a mother that gave birth to a calf missing a rear hoof (see chapter 10). All birth locations involved topography that was rolling or bisected by ravines or draws.

Bison hardly ever give birth to more than a single calf. At Badlands we never saw twins. Neither did Meagher (1973) in Yellowstone from 1964 to 1968, nor Fuller (1966) who examined almost 475 uteri from Wood Buffalo National Park. McHugh (1972) and Halloran (1968) each

PHOTO 6.1. Female with twenty-minute-old calf. Note umbilical cord.

recorded a set of twins in Yellowstone and Wichita Mountain populations, respectively.

Annual Variation in Parturition

To measure the dispersion of births, we calculated five measures on an
annual basis: (1) median, (2) quartiles, (3) quartile deviation, which
offers a description of births in the central half of the distribution (Sokal
and Rohlf 1981), (4) number of days until 65%, and 80% of the births
occurred, and (5) most compressed 50% of the births. The quartile
deviation is $1/2(Q_3-Q_1)$ and it differs from the most compressed 50% of
births because it is sensitive to the tail ends of the birth distribution; the
compressed births will be a shorter time frame since it is based solely on
the most tightly clustered (see tables 6.1 and 6.2).

In any given year the earliest calves were first seen between 3 and 8
April and were soon followed by a flood of calf births. The first 25% of
calves born in a year occurred by 22 April and the median birth date over
the five-year study always fell between 2 and 8 May (see table 6.1).
Clearly, the dates of first calves as well as the median were highly
predictable. Averaged over the study, the quartile deviation for 50% of

TABLE 6.1.

Relationships among birth synchrony and year using three measures of dispersion of birthdates

Quartile	1985 (55) Dates	Time span	1986 (54) Dates	Time span	1987 (51) Dates	Time span	1988 (52) Dates	Time span	1989 (48) Dates	Time span
Q_1	7 to 20 April	13	8 to 22 April	14	8 to 24 April	16	3 to 22 April	19	6 to 17 April	11
Q_2	21 April to 2 May	12	23 April to 8 May	16	25 April to 5 May	19	23 April to 10 May	17	18 April to 2 May	15
Q_3	3 to 27 May	25	9 to 21 May	13	6 May to 5 June	31	14 May to 3 June	20	4 to 30 May	26
Q_4	28 May to ? Nov	—	22 May to ? Sept	—	6 June to ? Oct	—	5 June to ? Oct	—	2 June to ? Aug	—
$QD_{50\%}$		19		15		22		21½		22½
Median	May 2	25	May 8	30	May 6	27	May 5	31	May 2	25

Median for entire year; quartile deviation ($QD_{50\%}$) as described in text; sample sizes in parentheses; time span in days

TABLE 6.2.

Summary of parturition-related characteristics of bison in WCNP, NBR, and Badlands National Park

	WCNP[1]	NBR[2]	Badlands Park				
			1985	1986	1987	1988	1989
Mean gestation length (days)				292.5 (4.1)	286.2 (4.0)	277.8 (3.3)	276.6 (2.7)
Number of days from 1st birth to							
50% of births	32	14	25	30	27	31	25
65% of births	37	17	37	28	40	40	30
80% of births	49	23	60	41	61	69	44
Number of days for most compressed							
50% of births	21	13	27	22	21	26	20

[1] From Green and Berger 1990
[2] Interpolated from Rutberg 1984
Standard errors in parentheses
WCNP = Wind Cave National Park
NBR = National Bison Range

the births was least variable, ranging from 19 to 22.5 days, whereas the median varied from only 25 to 30 days (see table 6.1), and statistical differences among years were not detectable [1; numbers in brackets correspond to statistical notes at end of chapter].

The number of days that elapsed from the first birth until 50%, 65%, and 80% averaged (per year) twenty-eight, thirty-five, and fifty-five days, respectively; the most compressed 50% of births occurred within twenty-three days (see table 6.2). To what extent did interannual variation in these parameters exist? As with median birthdates, differences among all categories and for all years were not significant, except for the number of days from the first birth to the 50% point and the time span for these differed only between 1985 and 1986 [2]. The invariant nature of yearly birthdates was most conspicuous in a seven-year-old female (in 1985) that gave birth on the same date in two consecutive years, one day later the next, and within three days of this in the other two years.

The last detection of newborns was highly variable, with births being recorded sometime in November in 1985 and during August, October, and September in 1986, 1987, and 1988, respectively. The data on last births were less accurate than other births because neither we nor our assistants were in the field daily. During some winters, data were gathered only three to four times per month; if calves were born but died soon thereafter, their births might have been undetected.

Geographical Variation

How do our data on birth progression and synchrony compare to those from other sites? Precise dates are available from only two other sites, Wind Cave National Park (Green and Berger 1990; Green and Rothstein 1993a) and the National Bison Range (Rutberg 1984), making it impossible to compare precisely the dispersion of births for populations of the northern prairies with those from other sites. However, general information on birth seasonality is available. Sites like Yellowstone and Wood Buffalo parks, either situated at higher altitudes or at latitudes with longer more rigorous winters than those at Badlands, are characterized by births that usually commence in early May (Meagher 1973; Carbyn and Trottier 1987, 1988). However, calves born throughout the year have been suggested or documented at multiple sites, including Wind Cave, Theodore Roosevelt, and Wood Buffalo national parks (Soper 1941; Glass pers. comm. 1986; Green and Rothstein 1993a). The first births in Oklahoma occurred from 10 March to 7 April (Halloran 1968) making it likely that latitudinal variation occurs (Reynolds, Glaholt, and Hawley 1982).

At the northern prairie sites parturition was later. At both Badlands and Wind Cave parks, births began in early April and peaked by early May; Wind Cave's first birth dates were comparable to those at the Badlands, with first births beginning on 9 April in 1982 and 1983 and 5 April in 1984 (Green and Rothstein 1991b, 1993a). The population at the National Bison Range began a little later, but attained its peak more rapidly (Rutberg 1984). The degree of clustering for 50%, 65%, and 80% of the births was much greater at the Bison Range than at the two South Dakota sites). The most compressed 50% of the births occurred in only thirteen days; it took more than a week longer at Wind Cave; and at Badlands it ranged from twenty to twenty-seven days. Thus the maximum difference in the time for 50% of the most tightly clustered calves to be born was about two weeks (see table 6.2).

Numerous factors are likely to govern variation in birthdates both within and between populations, but the most obvious include plant productivity, winter weather, and population density. Together these would affect nutrition and, hence, body condition. Because data on these variables are not available, we can only speculate that the lesser degree of synchrony at Badlands was due to a poorer nutritional plane. The National Bison Range population is maintained at about 325 to 350 animals by annual fall roundups. And the population is rotated among pastures several times per year to prevent overgrazing. The contention that these animals were well nourished is supported by the fact that fecundity averages about 80% to 90% per year (Lott 1979; Rutberg 1986a, 1986b; Wolff 1988), whereas it is lower at the South Dakota sites (Green 1987; chapter 7). Data for bison [3] and other ungulates (Guinness, Lincoln, and Short 1971; Mitchell and Lincoln 1973; Mitchell, McCowan, and Nicholson 1976; Dyrmundsson 1978) demonstrate that animals in superior physical condition conceive earlier than those in poorer shape, and it is likely that the uniformly better nutrition available at the Bison Range helped to promote a higher degree of birth synchrony there relative to animals living under less favorable conditions elsewhere. If this hypothesis is true, then animals in places like Yellowstone (where nutritional limitations are severe [Meagher 1976]) should be characterized by a less constricted birth pulse.

6.2 Reproductive Synchrony and Gestation Adjustment

Although we suggest that a good food base promotes reproductive synchrony in bison, we have not rigorously examined the degree to which any factor affects the clumping of births. There is ample evidence that environmental, ecological, and physiological processes govern breeding seasonality (Sadlier 1969; McClintock 1983; Bronson 1989), but the individual costs and benefits of synchronous breeding remain unclear.

For gregarious ungulates of temperate regions, neonates born late in the season are at a serious disadvantage because they fail to accrue body reserves necessary to survive harsh winters (Clutton-Brock, Albon, and Harvey 1982; Festa-Bianchet 1988b); tropical savanna-dwelling ungulate calves deviating from the birth peak may experience greater predation (Estes 1976; Estes and Estes 1979; Sinclair 1977). Nevertheless, how synchrony is achieved remains obscure. Before estrus it may be facilitated by olfactory cues or other mechanisms (McClintock 1978); after conception, gestation adjustment may facilitate birth synchrony. Data to support or refute this idea are lacking, in part because most mammals are secretive, and copulation and birthdates are unknown. However, because intraspecific variation in gestation characterizes many mammals (Kiltie 1982), and body condition affects dates of estrus, we expected gestation to be a labile trait influenced both by body condition and social factors.

Are Gestation Lengths Adjustable?

To examine whether gestation lengths were adjustable, we first had to determine the extent to which they varied. We based analyses on data stemming from evidence of 261 copulations and exact birth dates or those estimated to within three days. Reproduction in males was evaluated by direct observation of copulations or when females erected their tails for up to six hours, a behavior characteristic of only mated females (Berger 1989) (see photo 6.2). In any given season about 95% of bison females copulate either once or, if more than once, with only one male (Lott 1979). To assess the extent to which other factors might influence gestation length and its consequences we determined maternal body weights, ages, skeletal dimensions, and body condition, and calf growth rates as described in chapter 3. Briefly, to control for effects of time of the year on female body mass, we used multiple regression [4]; to assess physical condition, body mass was scaled by power regression to a single morphological trait (head width) [5], and animals whose masses were below or above the line were then designated to be in relatively poor or good body condition, respectively; and a photogrammetric device was used to scale changes in body size with growth (see photo 3.15).

The mean gestation period varied from 277 to 293 days over the four

PHOTO 6.2. Female with tail lift and swollen vulva immediately after copulation

years for which data were available (see table 6.2) [6]. To demonstrate gestation length adjustments requires minimizing effects of potentially confounding variables. For instance, primiparous bison females exceeded multiparous females in mean gestation length, 287.96 [(SE) ± 3.64] vs 279.86 ± 1.82 [7], but calf gender had no effect (males: $\bar{X} = 281.45$ ± 3.00; females: $\bar{X} = 280.57$ ± 2.94) [8]. The extent to which other factors may have influenced gestation was investigated by excluding primiparous females and then partitioning the sample for multiparous females into the number of days that copulation and birth dates deviated from the median for that year, prior to examination of potential effects of different factors. While maternal mass had no effect on gestation length, both maternal condition and parturition season did, despite a significant interaction [9]. Females in good body condition that mated *before* the annual breeding median differed in gestation period from those in the same condition that mated *after* the peak (277.30 ± 4.15 vs 271.99 ± 3.15 days); those in poor condition that mated *after* the peak had the longest gestation lengths (294.16 ± 2.03 days), differing from females in good condition irrespective of when such females copulated [10]. Data from wild and captive red deer hinds are also suggestive of nutritionally determined effects on

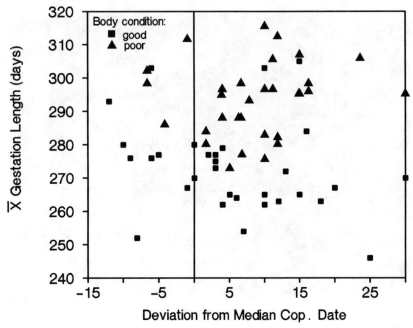

FIGURE 6.1. A comparison of gestation length and the number of days that copulations deviated from the annual median in multiparous mothers differing in body condition the summer before they conceived. From Berger 1992.

gestation length (Guinness, Gibson, and Clutton-Brock 1978) (see fig. 6.1).

The key point from the perspective of social facilitation of births, however, is not the effect of nutrition per se, but the extent to which compensation in gestation length occurs. If gestation length adjustments promoted synchronous births, females mating *after* the peak should be characterized by shorter gestation periods than those bred before, but cows in poor condition irrespective of breeding date had longer gestation periods. Had females in good condition modified their gestation lengths, effects should have been evident in the analyses in which gestation was contrasted between females in good condition and season [9 and 10]. However, because our analysis failed to account for variation in deviation *after* the mating peak, perhaps females bred well after the peak cannot afford an early in utero termination, whereas those bred nearer the peak can. Therefore we split females bred after the median into two groups based on copulatory date (1 to 14 and 15 to 30 days postmedian) and contrasted their gestation lengths with those for females mated prior to the median. Although the variance was greater for females bred from 15 to 30 days after the median [11], differences in mean gestation length were absent for females mated after the median [12], suggesting that some late-mated females could not, or in any case did not, adjust gestation. More striking, however, is that females bred within 14 days after the peak had significantly shorter gestation lengths than those mated before (271.36 vs 277.30 days) [13]. Hence, females in better than average condition reduced their gestation length an average of 5.9 days.

The differences between categories were not due to female age [14], nor is it likely they resulted from undetected copulations since about 95% of bison cows mate only once (Lott 1979). Nevertheless, our interpretation of gestation adjustment hinges on the assumption that copulations resulted in conception or, at the very least, that systematic biases against any particular category of animals were not evident. For instance, if cows failed to conceive in their first estrus, only to recycle and copulate later, then we would have overestimated gestation lengths on average by about three weeks, which is the approximate duration between cycles (Fuller 1966). We checked on this possibility in our daily censuses of group size and composition by noting which females were investigated or guarded by males and whether females that had copulated weeks before had raised tails or swollen vulvas, both indications of having been mated within several hours (Berger 1989). If our observations had been biased for or against females in good or poor condition, our estimations of gestation could probably have been off by weeks. Our sample of animals in different categories with both known copulations and birthdates was too small to permit robustness in minimizing the probability of a Type II error (i.e., accepting the null hypothesis of no effect when there is an effect), so we chose to compare females with known copulation dates only, increasing our sample size from 77 to 126. Of females in good condition, 4.4% recycled; 6.9% of those in poor condition did. The differences were not significant [15], suggesting that our results were not likely to bias erroneous gestation lengths in any particular direction. Hence, the data support the hypothesis that late-breeding females in good body condition shorten gestation, synchronizing births with other females, while no similar adjustments occur among poorly conditioned females. While comparable data are rare, well-fed dromedary camels experience gestation lengths from 359 to 423 days, but, like bison, females conceiving late in the season experience shorter pregnancy periods (Elias, Degen, and Kam 1991).

Benefits and Costs

Numerous social benefits may result from birth synchrony. Mothers might profit by (1) sharing feeding and vigilance (Iason and Guinness 1985), (2) reducing the probability of not being pregnant in the next year since late calving reduces subsequent pregnancy by 1% per day (Clutton-Brock, Guinness, and Albon 1983), (3) decreased interlitter competition (Schaller 1972; Bertram 1975; Packer and Pusey 1983a, 1983b), and (4) reduced predation on neonates, perhaps by predator glutting (Estes and Estes 1979; Sinclair 1977), a possibility we could not assess because prairie bison no longer coexist with wolves. In addition, early-born neonates are usually dominant, which may enhance later reproduction (Byers 1986), and animals born late can be disadvantaged because of a lack of accessibility to nutritious food (Festa-Bianchet 1988c) or heightened mortality risks (Hall and Hall 1988).

We examined one potential cost of gestation adjustment: by shortening gestation to give birth synchronously, females compromise the growth rates of their neonates. Diminished maturation rate can have serious reproductive costs because slow-growing animals may produce fewer offspring over their lifetimes (Le Boeuf and Reiter 1988; Green and Rothstein 1991b; Reiter and Le Boeuf 1991). We compared growth trajectories of calves gestated for different periods of time with maternal body condition categories; birth dates were standardized. The growth trajectory data were based on measures of juvenile head sizes (width and length) gathered photogrammetrically and then estimated by changes in skeletal size scaled to body mass [16]. At 180 days of age, a time when mothers still provide milk (Green 1986; Green, Griswold, and Rothstein 1989), calf body masses for (A), mothers in good condition mated *before* the median ($N = 5$), (B), mothers in good condition mated *after* the median ($N = 12$), and (C), mothers in poor condition mated *after* ($N = 6$) were estimated as 197.83, 179.66, and 179.21 kg. The regression slopes do not differ, but elevations do [17]. Therefore by 180 days calves of category (A) females maintain a mass advantage of about 10% over the calves of the other two categories, and other factors being equal, mothers trade synchronization by sacrificing 5.9 days of in utero growth, or approximately 18.17 kg at 180 days (the cost is $18.17/5.9 = 3.08$ kg/day for each additional day up to the mean not gestated). These values are conservative and underestimate the magnitude of biological difference because poorly conditioned mothers on average give birth 23.7 days after mothers in good condition. Since the analyses of growth trajectories

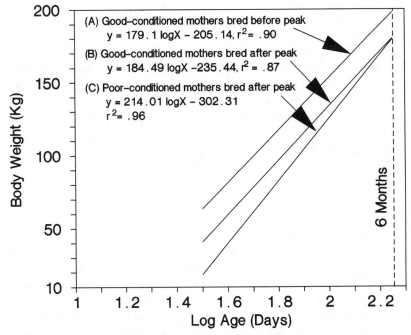

FIGURE 6.2. Relationship between growth rates (and sample sizes) for calves gestated for *(A)*, 277 days (5); *(B)*, 271 days (12); and *(C)*, 294 days (6). From Berger 1992.

compared neonates at the same age (i.e., beginning on their birthdays) even though they were born more than three weeks apart, calves of mothers in poor condition in the real world enter winter with three weeks of growth less than calves of mothers in good condition (see fig. 6.2).

In other species data suggest that extended gestation buffers against low birth weights. In cattle regressions of birth weight on the length of the gestation period indicate that for each day *not* gestated calves are almost 0.5 kg lighter (DeFries, Touchberry, and Hays (1959), whereas in horses gestation lengths of about 330 days are the threshold beyond which infant survival is not increased (Rossdale 1976).

Although differences in growth among bison neonates are associated with maternal condition and, presumably, tied to gestation-related variation, we do not know whether mothers that vary in physical condition also differ in the timing of implantation or intrauterine growth. Nevertheless, because high juvenile body mass is associated with superior survival among numerous temperate mammals, including rodents, lagomorphs, and pinnipeds (Calambokidis and Gentry 1985; Iason 1989; Murie and Boag 1984), mothers that shorten their gestation may trade synchronized births for diminished juvenile body masses and, hence, greater mortality.

Whether the adjustment of gestation lengths arose as a consequence of intense selection brought about by heavy predation is difficult to say. Some females may possess the ability to cue on proximate phenological triggers. If this is the case, it is difficult to imagine how the potential benefit of feeding on some nutrient-rich vegetation for a few extra days could outweigh the costs of terminating gestation early with its coincident diminution of subsequent neonatal growth.

Mechanisms That Facilitate Reproductive Synchrony

Might tactics less radical than gestation shortening be available for late-mating mothers in good condition to achieve parturition synchrony? For many species, sensory information about female reproductive status is obtained by ano-genital (A-G) investigations, although the major hypotheses to account for flehman in females have focused on dominance and neonate recognition (O'Brien 1982; Pfeifer 1985). Even so, it is possible that high-ranking females show greater reproductive synchrony, which may be accounted for by higher rates of flehman (Thompson 1991). Irrespective of dominance, if bison cows use olfactory cues to facilitate estrous synchrony, we predicted that (1) unmated females should investigate A-G regions of both mated and unmated females; (2) mated females should not be involved in A-G investigations because information on conspecific estrus would no longer be of importance; and (3) female-female A-G sniffing should be more pronounced before the breeding peak.

These predictions were supported. More than 93% of the A-G investigations by females of known reproductive status were initiated by unmated cows. Differences between the period before and after the peak were not detectable [18]. However, the distribution of A-G recipients changed, with unmated females predominating during the period *prior* to the median and mated females *after* [18]. Overall, flehman was about twice as frequent during the twenty-one-day period before the median than the same period after [19]. These results suggest that females use olfactory cues to explore the status of other females before their own estrus, but later rely on a different mechanism to facilitate synchronous reproduction–gestation shortening (see fig. 6.3).

Although evidence for gestation modification in other species is mea-

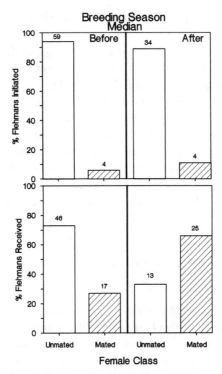

FIGURE 6.3. Relationship between female reproductive status (mated or un-mated), breeding season period (before or after annual median), and sender or recipients of A-G investigations that resulted in flehman. From Berger 1992.

ger, both eutherian and placental mammals exhibit remarkable intraspe-cific variation in gestation (Kiltie 1982; Lee and Cockburn 1985; Elias, Degen, and Kam 1991). Because factors such as social environment, body mass, and offspring's sex can explain up to 43% of the gestation variance in horses (Berger 1986), there is reason to suspect that gestation in other species could also be lengthened or shortened in response to environmental or social cues. For instance, springbok in the Namib Desert may shorten gestation to coincide with mild conditions (Skinner and van Jaarsveld 1987). Alternatively, gestation lengthening may occur in Dall sheep when unpredictable late spring snowstorms render neonatal survivorship questionable (Rachlow and Bowyer 1991). In other circum-stances, gestation shortening might be beneficial when diminished neona-tal growth is worth trading for improved survivorship (by minimizing predation). In at least two species, bison and squirrel monkeys, a similar mechanism may facilitate birth synchrony via gestation adjustment since females employ olfactory monitoring and A-G investigation around the time births begin (Boinski 1987). Although additional data will be necessary to confirm both the existence of and mechanisms responsible for such putatively adaptive behavior, our evidence suggests that some gregarious mammals have the option to employ gestation adjustments that facilitate birth synchrony. In the case of bison, the price for the "premature birth tactic" is steep. By trading synchronous parturition for smaller neonates, the offspring of such females are, on average, 20 kg lighter when six months old than offspring of those not making the trade. These data illustrate not only the existence of a mechanism differing from estrous synchrony but also the costs that gregarious females pay to compress their birth season.

6.3 Size-Weight-Age Relationships

In Males and Females at Badlands

Although we have presented data on some aspects of size-weight relationships in live females, for most ungulates information on such associations are based on dead animals. This is not always the case, as scales can be used to measure changes in growth in live wild animals (e.g., baboons; Altmann and Alberts 1987), but it usually is for large and dangerous species. This prevents study of the extent to which size may affect a number of life history characteristics, and it also obscures differences that may arise from changes within individuals rather than from differences among individuals. Here, we present information on general relationships in bison before considering, in the next chapters, how individual variation affects reproduction.

Bison are sexually dimorphic and the sexes differ in body proportions (Reynolds, Glaholt, and Hawley 1982); therefore males and females were analyzed separately. We examined relationships between size-related traits (body length, chest girth, head width, and head length), age, and body weight by multiple regression employing all variables, correlation matrices (to assess relationships between all single variables), and simple regressions using single independent variables. Multiple regression, explained about 96% and 69% of the variation in body weight of males and females, respectively. However, because several of the variables were not always available for all animals, simple regression was used to predict weight from single variables (see table 6.3).

TABLE 6.3.

Correlation matrix of morphological characters for 64 male and 56 female bison

Sex	Age	Body weight	Body length	Head length	Head width	Chest girth
Males						
Age	1.000					
Body weight	0.784	1.000				
Body length	0.670	0.849	1.000			
Head length	0.683	0.827	0.860	1.000		
Head width	0.750	0.861	0.821	0.862	1.000	
Chest girth	0.708	0.777	0.795	0.732	0.745	1.000
Females						
Age	1.000					
Body weight	0.714	1.000				
Body length	0.678	0.790	1.000			
Head length	0.711	0.864	0.756	1.000		
Head width	0.679	0.756	0.789	0.794	1.000	
Chest girth	0.434	0.585	0.656	0.545	0.533	1.000

From Berger and Peacock 1988

We also used four regression equations, linear, exponential, natural log transformation, and power to determine which variable in a simple regression was the best predictor of body weight. The fit for any of the equations was about the same; for males, the r^2 value was best for body length (0.81) and, for females, head length gave the best fit (0.76). Cannon bone length was the poorest predictor, explaining no variance in either sex, whereas chest girth accounted for 64% of the variance in males and 33% in females (see table 6.4).

Cranial measurements have only rarely been used to estimate body weight. This is not surprising given the availability of other ways, some of which give superior relationships between chest girth and body weight than ours (Rideout and Worthen 1975; Seip and Bunnell 1984). For instance, in one study of carcass weight, chest girth explained about 82% and 61% of the variance in male and female weight, a considerably higher proportion than we could (Kelsall, Telfer, and Kingsley 1978). This difference is not unexpected when considering that our measures were probably not as accurate because handling live animals, even when restrained in chutes, is dangerous; bison kick and rotate back forth, making chest measures precarious. Because chest measures are more sensitive to seasonal fluctuations in weight (Franzmann et al. 1978), they would undoubtedly be the superior variable to gauge weight if ways of obtaining such data were easily available. An alternative method when individuals cannot be regularly handled is to use head length, head width, or body length, all variables for which data can be obtained using the photogrammetric device modified by Jacobsen (1986).

In Males and Females from Other Populations

At the U.S. Fish and Wildlife Service refuges at the National Bison Range (Montana), Fort Niobrara (Nebraska), and Wichita Mountains (Oklahoma), bison weights have been recorded on a regular basis at annual roundups. The degree to which mean weights varied annually at both the National Bison Range and Fort Niobrara sites, and average weights at the Wichita Mountains (over an eight-year period; Halloran 1961) are illustrated in figures 6.4 and 6.5. In bison at both the National Bison Range and Fort Niobrara, year had an effect on mean body mass, but differences were not evident between sites [20]. The variation is undoubtedly caused by many factors.

TABLE 6.4.

Coefficients of determination (R^2) for regression equations used to predict body weight from morphological characters, and Y-intercepts and regression coefficients for the power relationships

Sex	Linear $Y = A + BX$	Exponential $Y = A^{BX}$	Logarithmic $Y = A + B \log X$	Power $Y = AB^X$	Y-Intercept	Regression coefficient
Males						
Body length	0.72	0.81	0.68	0.81	$1.67\ 10^{-4}$	2.78
Head length	0.68	0.78	0.66	0.80	$2.09\ 10^{-2}$	2.42
Head width	0.74	0.76	0.71	0.79	2.00	1.52
Chest girth	0.60	0.64	0.57	0.64	$1.57\ 10^{-4}$	2.72
Females						
Body length	0.62	0.65	0.61	0.66	$1.48\ 10^{-4}$	2.80
Head length	0.74	0.75	0.74	0.76	0.025	2.39
Head width	0.57	0.60	0.58	0.62	0.78	1.87
Chest girth	0.34	0.34	0.33	0.33	$5.45\ 10^{-4}$	2.46

From Berger and Peacock 1988.

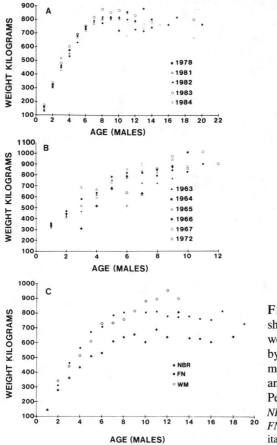

FIGURE 6.4. Relationship between age and body weights in males: *A,* NBR, by year; *B,* FN, by year; *C,* mean weights at NBR, FN, and WM From Berger and Peacock 1988.

NBR, National Bison Range; *FN,* Fort Niobrara; *WM,* Wichita Mountains

6.4 Age-related Reproduction

Fecundity and Puberty at Badlands

Because bison at Badlands have high reproductive rates that are not counterbalanced by much mortality, the annual increase in population size has been controlled on a regular basis (see fig. 5.1). How fecund are females and to what extent is reproduction affected by age?

By adding the total number of offspring per year that survived to 6 months and dividing this value by the total number of known females within an age cohort, we calculated the number of calves expected by age. Although bison may produce their first calves as 2-year olds, few do (4.1%). Given the 288-day gestation length of primiparous females, that means that at least one of twenty-four 2-year-old animals conceived as a

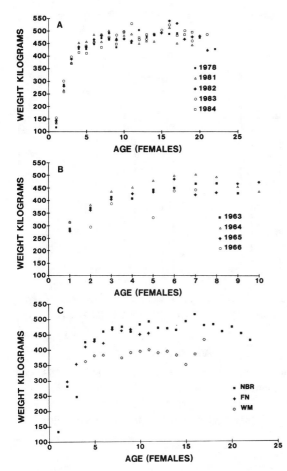

FIGURE 6.5. Relationship between age and body weights in females: *A*, NBR, by year; *B*, FN, by year; *C*, mean weights at NBR, FN, and WM From Berger and Peacock 1988. *NBR*, National Bison Range; *FN*, Fort Niobrara; *WM*, Wichita Mountains

yearling. Although conception rates were probably higher than this in the 2-year-old cohort, among mammals, young and small individuals generally do not have sufficient reserves to carry a fetus to term. At Badlands 2-year olds were approximately 25% lighter than 3-year olds, with the mean age of first birth for thirty cows being 3.4 years. Both age and weight (estimated for the month the first calf was born) varied annually: 1985, 3 yrs ($\pm$ 0[SE]), 389 kg (N = 2); 1986, 3.13 yrs ($\pm$ .21), 407 kg (N = 7); 1987, 3.45 yrs ($\pm$ .15), 432 kg (N = 10); 1988, 3.50 ($\pm$ .25), 355 kg. (N = 3); 1989, 4.0 ($\pm$ .47), 387 kg (N = 3). Nearly 58% of the three-year olds produced calves. Animals in the 10- to 11-year-old cohort were the most fecund, averaging 0.75 calves per year. Once animals reached 14 to 15 years of age, their fecundity decreased, with the chances

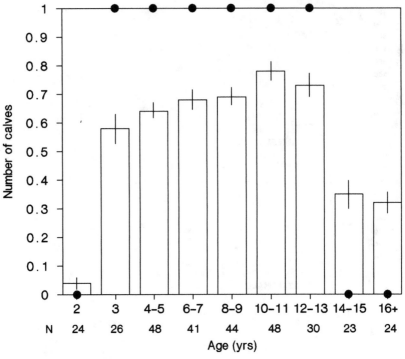

FIGURE 6.6. Mean fecundity (calves per female) from 1985 to 1989 with standard errors. Dots are medians for that cohort.

of producing a calf being slightly better than half that of 3-year olds (see fig. 6.6).

Fecundity and Puberty in Other Populations

Information on age-specific calf production generally is not available from most other populations, but some comparable data exist. At Wood Buffalo and Wind Cave national parks, about 5% of the two-year olds produced calves (Fuller 1966; Green 1990); 13% of the yearlings from the Wichita Mountains conceived (Halloran 1968), although the number that would have actually produced calves was unknown; and about 6% of a combined sample from Fort Niobrara, Wind Cave, and Custer State Park had corpus lutea (Haugen 1974). For two-year olds, Fuller (1966) found that pregnancy rates for two different areas of Wood Buffalo National Park varied from 38% to 59%; 73% from the Wichita Mountains conceived (Halloran 1968); and 87% of the northern plains sample were carrying embryos (Haugen 1974). About 80% of the three-year olds at Wind Cave had calves (Green and Rothstein 1991a). Conception rates of three-year olds tend to be lower at Yellowstone (Meagher 1973).

The figures for the U.S. reserves tend to be higher than those reported for Badlands. This is not surprising. The refuges have been more managed, and most of the data were gathered from culled animals, in which pregnancy rates will exceed the percentages of calves actually born. At Wind Cave National Park, however, age-specific fecundity (Green 1990) is also higher than that for Badlands animals, probably because of differences in management. Wind Cave bison are rounded up biannually, whereas Badlands animals were allowed to proliferate during the first four years of our study. Thus, although density dependence was not detectable at Badlands (see chapter 5), food limitation, perhaps in conjunction with other factors, may have been responsible for the lower fecundity and less synchronized breeding seasons observed relative to those at Wind Cave.

6.5 Summary

1. Annual differences in the birth peak median were slight, ranging from 2 May to 8 May. Fifty percent of the births occurred within nineteen to twenty-three days, a range comparable to another prairie population, but nearly a week longer than bison in Montana.
2. Gestation lengths were highly variable, with reproductive synchrony being achieved by gestation adjustment. Females in good body condition that mated after the breeding peak shortened gestation by about six days; similar adjustments were not evident in females in poor condition. Cows that shortened their gestation length incurred a cost; their neonates were, on average, 20 kg lighter when six months old.
3. Body mass was related to body length, head length, head width, and chest girth. The best single predictor of mass was head length in females and body length in males. When used in a power regression, it explained between 76% and 81% of the variation, respectively. Although body mass was consistently related to age in different populations, slight variations occurred among sites.
4. Calf production was highest in females five to thirteen years of age, with 75% of the ten- to eleven-year olds producing calves

annually. Fewer than 30% of the cows fourteen years or older had calves; only 4% of the two-year olds produced young. Reserves more managed than the Badlands experience higher levels of calf production, with some averaging 0.8 to 0.9 calves per adult.

6.6 Statistical Notes

1. Comparison among median birthdates and year. Median Test: $X^2 = 1.01$; df = 4; NS
2. Comparisons of interyear variation and 4 birth parameters, number of days of first births to (a) 50%, (b) 65%, and (c) 80% points and (d) the most compressed 50% of the births. Kolomorov-Smirnoff Tests:
   (a) 1985 vs 1986, $p < 0.05$, all other pair-wise contrasts NS
   (b) all pair-wise contrasts NS
   (c) all pair-wise contrasts NS
   (d) all pair-wise contrasts NS
3. Correlation between late-winter body mass (X) and estrous date (Y) in 14 female bison 3 years or older at Badlands National Park (1985). Pearson Product-Moment Correlation Coefficient:
   $r = 0.81$, $p < 0.01$, $Y = 49.53 - 0.065X$
4. Multiple regression of head length (X_1) and date of weighing (X_2) on body mass (Y) in (a) 33 nonparous and (b) 55 lactating females.
   (a) $Y = 11.66X_1 + .18X_2 + 3.04$, $r^2 = .56$; second order partial regression coefficients for $X_1 = 0.60$ ($p < 0.001$) and for $X_2 = 0.23$ ($p < 0.05$)
   (b) $Y = 7.39X_1 + .22X_2 - 224.96$, $r^2 = .48$; second order partial regression coefficients for $X_1 = 0.72$ ($p < 0.001$) and for $X_2 = 0.27$ ($p < 0.05$)
5. Relationship between head width and body mass in 56 females: $Y = .025(2.39)^{X_i}$ $r^2 = .76$
6. Comparison of (a) annual differences in mean gestation length and (b) the difference between number of females classified in good vs poor condition by year.
   (a) One-way Analysis of Variance: $F_{3,48} = 4.53$, $p < 0.02$;
   (b) Binomial Probability: 1986 (N = 17, $p < 0.025$), 1987 (N = 17, NS), 1988 (N = 17, NS), 1989 (N = 17, NS)

7. Comparison between gestation length in primiparous and multiparous females.

T Test: $t = 2.29$, $df = 77$, $p < 0.05$

8. Comparison between gestation length of male and female offspring in multiparous females. (The sexes of several 1989 calves were unknown.)

T Test: $t = 0.22$, $df = 60$, NS

9. Comparison of effects (a) maternal mass, (b) maternal condition, and (c) parturition period on gestation length. Three-way Analysis of Variance:

(a) $F_{1,41} = 1.62$, NS
(b) $F = 9.73$, $p < 0.001$;
(c) $F = 122.12$, $p < 0.001$; interaction [between b) and c)]
$F = 4.22$, $p < 0.05$

10. Comparison of interaction of effects of birth period (before or after median) and body condition (above or below mean) (from statistic 9) on gestation length.

Student-Newman-Keuls Test:

body condition above, early births vs body condition below, late births- $p < 0.01$;

body condition above, early births vs body condition above, late births- $p < 0.01$;

body condition above, late births vs body condition below, late births- NS

(for the category, body condition below, early births, the sample size was too small for comparison)

11. Comparison of variance in gestation length between females bred from 1 to 14 days and 15 to 30 days after the median. Test for Homogeneity of Independent Variances.

$F_{10,10} = 5.37$, $p < 0.02$

12. Comparison of gestation lengths between females bred from 1 to 14 days and 15 to 30 days after the median. Mann-Whitney U Test:

$U' = 56$, NS

13. Comparison of gestation lengths between females bred before the median and those mated from 1 to 14 days after it. T Test:

$t = 2.94$, $df = 19$, $p < 0.01$ (the variances were similar; $F = 2.53$, NS)

14. Comparison of mean ages between females bred before the median and those mated from 1 to 14 days after it. T Test:

$t = 0.09$, $df = 19$, NS

15. Comparison of the frequency that 68 females in good condition and 58 in poor condition recycled. G Test:

$G = 0.37$, NS

16. Multiple regression of head width (X_1) and length (X_2) on body mass (Y) in (a) 14 juvenile male and (b) 15 juvenile female bison.

(a) $Y = 4.19X_1 + 5.84X_2 - 105.24$, $r^2 = .87$;

(b) $Y = 4.03X_1 + 6.86X_2 - 171.95$, $r^2 = .84$;

17. Comparison of the (a) slopes and (b) elevation of regressions in figure 6.2.

Analysis of Covariance:

(a) $F_{2,17} = 0.89$, NS;

(b) $F = 9.13$, $p < 0.02$; (difference between regressions A [from figure] and B is significant [$p < 0.01$], but regressions B and C do not differ from each other) (Scheffe's Test)

18. Comparison of the frequency of ano-genital investigations (a) initiated and (b) received by females differing in reproductive (mated or unmated) status in relation to the breeding season median. G Test:

(a) $G_{adj} = 0.51$, $N = 101$, NS

(b) $G = 14.84$, $p < 0.001$

19. Comparison of the distribution of female-female flehmans between three-week periods before and after the breeding season median. Chi Square Test: $X^2 = 17.31$, $N = 212$, $p < 0.001$

20. Comparison of effects of year on mean (a) male and (b) female weight at the National Bison Range (NBR) and Fort Niobrara National Wildlife Refuge (FN) and (c) between each area. Weight was regressed on the natural-log transformation of age ($r^2 = 0.94$ for males; 0.76 for females) and the natural-log transformation of age, then used as one factor in a two-factor completely randomized analysis of variance.

(a) males (NBR) $F_{4,562} = 5.03$, $p < 0.01$, (FN) $F_{3,129} = 5.39$, $p < 0.01$;

(b) females (NBR) $F_{4,627} = 7.12$, $p < 0.01$; (FN) $F_{1,81} = 9.70$, $p < 0.01$

(c) males $F_{1,42} = 3.75$, NS, females $F_{1,43} = 1.20$, NS

21. Comparison between the spring body weights of 3- and 4-year-old ($N = 78$) and 5- to 13-year-old ($N = 191$) females. T Test:

$t = 2.66$, $p < 0.01$

7. Female Mating and Reproductive Success

To dominate is to possess priority of access to the necessities of life and reproduction. This is not a circular definition; it is a statement of a strong correlation observed in nature.

E. O. Wilson 1975:287

Although behavioral biologists have paid much attention to dominance relationships in natural populations, what is of ultimate importance is the differential propagation of genes from one generation to the next. If all individuals contribute equally or if differences between generations exist but representations from the same family lines are subsequently equalized, then differences among the various future genotypes will be minimal, and opportunities for selection will be negated. Therefore, it is critical to account for possible age effects on reproduction.

Most studies of variation in reproductive success have concentrated on species in which natural mortality is significant. For instance, in elephant seals, lions, and red deer survivorship in the first year of life is precarious, with approximately 40% (Le Boeuf and Reiter 1988), 67% (Packer et al. 1988), and from 30% to 90% (Clutton-Brock, Albon, and Guinness 1988) of the neonates perishing, respectively. In species such as wild horses or bison, juvenile mortality averages less than 9% (Berger 1986; chapter 5), and variation in reproduction among individual mothers is dramatically less than that observed in lions, vervet monkeys, red deer, or elephant seals (see fig. 7.1). Because selection can be more intense in populations whose matrilines are characterized by higher variances in juvenile survivorship, it is important to specify not only the degree of differences among individual mothers (if they are slight, short-term projections of potential effects of selection will not be possible) but also potential correlates of reproduction that may mediate individual differences.

For locally abundant species in which most individuals survive and reproduce, natural selection will be less intense. Issues of these sorts can be examined only with data on the degree of variation that exists within and between the sexes. This chapter's theme is concerned with the repro-

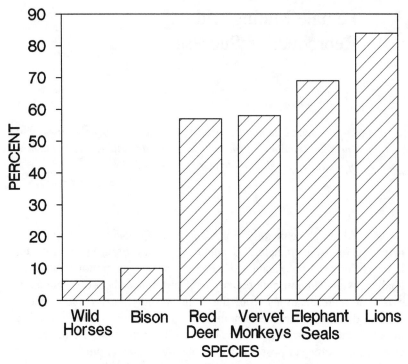

FIGURE 7.1. The percent contribution of neonatal survivorship to variation in lifetime reproductive success in red deer (Clutton-Brock, Albon, and Guinness 1988), vervet monkeys (Cheney et al. 1988), elephant seals (Le Boeuf and Reiter 1988), and lions (Packer et al. 1988); the bison and horse (Berger 1986) data reflect total neonate mortality uncorrected for differences between individuals.

duction of individual females. We describe copulations and courtship, the effects of various factors on reproduction, and reasons why dominance has only a small effect on differences in calf production among females that vary in social status. The final section compares our findings to those of other studies.

7.1 Courtship and Copulation

Male Approaches to Females

Adult male and female bison remain in sexually segregated groups throughout most of the year (see chapter 5), but when males encounter groups with females, they often approach and smell the ano-genital (A-G) regions of females. This behavior, which we call A-G investiga-

PHOTO 7.1. Adult male smells the ano-genital region of a female as a subordinate male feeds nearby.

tions, often involved males performing flehman (see photo 7.1). Such approaches were highly skewed temporal events; on average we noted that males sniffed the A-G regions of females about 80 times in May, 260 in June, 960 in July, 110 in August, and 12 in September. The mean frequency of female-female investigations during the same months was 12, 38, 66, 6, and 2. Although these data were based on ad lib sampling and do not account for the prevalence of different age and sex classes, they suggest males were much more likely than females to investigate a female's A-G region. In July, when most conceptions occurred (see chapter 6), the mean frequency of male A-G investigations of females was nearly 15 times more common than that of females. Since males of a wide variety of vertebrates, including ungulates, gather information on female reproductive condition using the vomeronasal organ (Estes 1972; Hart, Hart, and Maina 1989), it was not surprising that males regularly approached and investigated females.

Once males had investigated a female, they either moved on to a different female or remained next to the first. If males remained with a female, they bellowed or stood by the female's side, often preventing her from leaving. Such associations have been termed "tending" (Lott 1974), but we refer to consortships as guarding because males actively

PHOTO 7.2. A bull prepares to copulate with a receptive female.

thwart the advances of rivals either through increased bellowing or by agonistic interactions (Berger and Cunningham 1991).

Copulations in bison are similar to those in cattle; the female remains in place although she may move once the bull mounts her (see photo 7.2). Copulations are brief. The total time from the first intention movements, when males mount females, to dismount is less than 8 seconds while the actual time elapsing between intromission and dismount is less than 4 seconds (Lott 1981). After copulating, a female releases a milky flow of urine and holds her tail out for 15 to 360 minutes (our longest observation time). Even on the second and occasionally third day after copulation the tail of a recently mated female may be extended away from the body. Usually the labia of the vulva are swollen or distended (photo 6.2), but this is not a reliable characteristic for assessing whether females have been recently mated.

Female Approaches to Males and Evidence of Choice

We expected female bison to exercise some degree of preference for certain males since a substantial body of literature suggests mate choice. According to theory, females should display selectivity for males when the latter vary in quality and such differences affect female reproduction

(Darwin 1871; Geist 1971b; Bateson 1983; Gibson and Bradbury 1985). For instance, in many species of birds, males provide care for the young through territorial defense or against predators, and it may be that females base their choice of males on their ability to provide for young. However, this would not be a relevant criteria in bison since males are polygynous; they typically abandon females soon after mating to seek additional cows (see chapter 8). Three lines of evidence, of which we examined two, would support the idea of female choice in bison.

First, choice might be demonstrated if females were more apt to flee when courted by less preferable males. If this were the case, then females would remain for longer periods of time while being investigated by males with preferable traits. For instance, bighorn sheep females run from smaller males (Geist 1971a), or they are blocked more by them than they are by larger males (Hogg 1984, 1988). Elephant seal cows protest vocally more often when associated with subordinate males (Cox and Le Boeuf 1977). And of twenty-four copulations observed in Sri Lankan Axis deer, three cases (12.5%) involved choices by females (Barrette 1987). Nevertheless, to show active choice one must demonstrate that preferences exist within age classes of males, not between them, and for wild populations ages are often unknown. Although we knew bison ages, the possibility of female choice based on their behavior toward courting males could not be evaluated directly because data on female behavior in the presence of two or more males were not recorded systematically. However, because estrous females sometimes burst into swift runs, eliciting pursuit by up to nineteen males, and traversing up to 10 km in less than thirty minutes, it is possible that females employ active mate-avoidance. If so, the males who eventually mate may emerge as the result of male-male competition, a process that may be facilitated by passive female choice for, or rejection of, specific males (Hogg 1987).

Second, rather than waiting for males to establish dominance, females may choose males, perhaps by moving toward them when in estrus or approaching estrus. The frequency that females showed any movements toward males (rather than simply standing) was compared on the day of estrus and on each of the three days before estrus (see table 7.1). The lack of significant relationships in male-directed approaches among females that differed in reproductive category irrespective of their timing of estrus suggests not only that sexual consortships were not instigated by females but also that females showed little overt interest in males [1; numbers in brackets correspond to statistical notes at end of chapter].

Nevertheless, females might be attracted to males who differ in charac-

TABLE 7.1.

Mean (± SE) frequency/3-hr observation period that different females approached to within 5 m of different males

Female reproductive status	Days before estrus			
	3	2	1	0
Barren	.20 ± .20 (5)	.40 ± .40 (5)	.38 ± .18 (16)	.50 ± .27 (24)
Lactating	.40 ± .13 (10)	0 (9)	.42 ± .25 (12)	.14 ± .08 (37)
Nulliparous	0 (5)	.25 ± .22 (4)	.60 ± .36 (5)	.21 ± .12 (19)

From Berger 1989
Three cases in which females moved to the same male multiple times were counted as only one approach per female; sample sizes in parentheses

teristics such as bellowing. For bison, bellowing might be a sign of prowess. If this were the case, females might have moved toward males that bellowed more conspicuously, but females did not differ in their approaches (see table 7.1). In fact, the bellowing rates of males when guarding females varied only slightly once the effects of other factors were removed (see chapter 8). An additional possibility exists; perhaps females "copy" the performance of other females and simply mate with the same male that they observed breeding with another female. Our sample size is too small to evaluate this possibility. In two different years we saw a male copulate with a female, and then another female move to the same male and copulate. In both instances the second female had been tended by a smaller male; so she may have moved to a larger male or copied the first female. Lott (1981) described two instances in which females were unusually receptive to specific males. We had evidence of 261 copulations, but so few involved female movements to males, it appears that if copying occurs it must be rare.

7.2 Variation Among Females

Rationale and Assumptions

Reproductive success was relatively easy to evaluate in females. Distended or baggy udders indicated that a female was lactating (see photo 7.3). We counted a female as being reproductively successful only when she was accompanied by a calf who suckled from her and who lived for at least three months. This procedure seemed reasonable since calf mortality is generally low (less than 2.5%; see chapter 5), and mothers usually nurse only their own offspring (Green 1986). The total number of calves produced by mothers known during the study was examined during a five-year (1985 to 1989) and four-year (1986 to 1989) period, the latter because it allowed us to increase our sample of potential mothers from twenty-three to fifty-eight (i.e., more individuals were identified in 1986 than in 1985).

Number of Offspring by Individual Females

The maximum number of offspring expected for any female over the five-year study was five since twinning is exceedingly rare (see chapter 6). However, because not all females in the population had calves annually, variation among individuals would be expected unless such differences

PHOTO 7.3. A lactating female with a distended udder

were equalized during the study. The number of progeny among individual females varied. From 1985 to 1989, 17% of the females produced no offspring; almost one-third of all females had four or five calves. Six of twenty-three females (26%) produced calves each year. When only the four-year (1986 to 1989) span is considered, 7% of the cows never produced surviving calves, whereas 24% produced four, the maximum number possible. Hence, regardless of the time frame, some individuals were more successful than others (see fig. 7.2).

What factors might have contributed to these differences? Clearly, the variation could not be attributed to differences that might accrue over an individual's lifetime because the study did not cover the lives of most animals, and any consideration of lifetime differences would have biased the sample toward animals dying early. Was it likely that the reproductive variation resulted from differences in the ages of animals considered? In other words, might all females be expected to breed equally? If so, then the observed variation could be a consequence of individuals in the population having dissimilar ages (see Rowell 1974). Alternatively, if individuals within the same age class differed in the number of calves they produced over the same period of time, then age differences per se would not account for the variance (Gibson and Guinness 1980a), and it

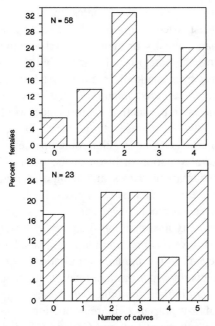

FIGURE 7.2. Variation in total number of calves produced over four-year (1986–89; upper histogram) and five-year (1985–89; lower histogram) periods by females three years or older.

is possible that during the five-year study period differences in offspring production over one's lifetime could be accrued.

As expected, age affected female reproduction (see fig. 6.6). A strong age-graded relationship exists when calf production per year is compared among different age categories [2]. Females fourteen years or older had lower reproductive rates than any other age class, except for two-year olds, a relationship not too dissimilar from that reported at Wind Cave National Park where the decline in reproduction began at about fifteen years of age (Green 1990). From the ages of five to thirteen years, females at Badlands were essentially invariant in their individual reproductive performances [2]. However, other factors were also likely to affect reproduction, some in subtle ways that might have important consequences on lifetime reproductive success. These include dominance, body weight, horn size, birthdates, and calf growth rates, all of which might interact with each other.

The data based on Badlands females are from a population in which management has a potentially significant effect on reproductive contributions to the population. All of the females on which our data are based were captured at least twice during roundups. Had the Park Service been rounding up animals annually or biennially and had they not been interested in preserving the integrity of our study, the sample of known animals would have been markedly reduced. At least 20% of the identified individuals were captured annually. Had they been removed, the variance in individual reproductive performance would have been increased, skewing potential representation toward the remaining mothers. Although the scenario favoring regular roundups certainly does not approximate the natural situation of bison of the past, today's populations lack effective nonhuman predators and habitat is limited. Most bison populations today are managed more intensively than those at the Badlands. Hence, skewed reproductive performance with a high degree of variance may be more typical than the situation we observed at Badlands. Nevertheless, we believe it is important to establish a baseline of information in the absence of active human perturbations before attempting to understand the effects roundups or other manipulations have on the degree to which females vary in their reproductive success.

Our findings of low variance in reproduction in Badlands females agree with the observations of Lott and Galland (1985b), who studied the bison population introduced on Santa Catalina Island west of Los Angeles. Based on the reproductive performances of ten known animals followed for four to five years, they reported individual variation in reproductive rates: two females produced only two calves throughout their study while others had more.

7.3 Factors Affecting Reproductive Success

Dominance

It seemed reasonable to expect an association between dominance and reproduction in bison given the number of studies of other organisms that have found socially mediated effects. For female bison, prior work on social rank has differed with respect to the potential importance of dominance. Researchers have found: (1) structured dominance hierarchies (McHugh 1972) were present and associated with age but not weight (Rutberg 1983, 1986b); (2) weight affected dominance when animals were artificially confined (Lott and Galland 1985b); and (3) dominance was related to reproductive success once the effects of age were removed (Green 1987).

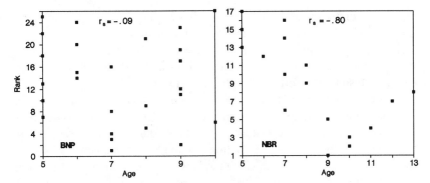

FIGURE 7.3. Relationship between dominance rank and age in five- to thirteen-year-old females at BNP and NBR (from Rutberg 1983). The BNP data are mean rank from 1986 to 1989; nine-year olds are twelve years old in 1989. Sixteen of the seventeen NBR females produced calves.
BNP, Badlands National Park; *NBR*, National Bison Range.

We restricted our analyses to females from five to thirteen years old in view of the influence age has on reproductive success. This is the cohort in which we failed to detect age-related effects on reproduction [2]. Three- and four-year-old animals were excluded from these analyses because their body mass was significantly less than animals in the five- to thirteen-year-old cohort [3]. Rank was assessed by the construction of dominance matrixes in which an individual was scored as a winner when, by threatening or approaching another animal, it elicited avoidance. Individuals were ranked higher when their win-loss ratio exceeded that of others (see appendix 5). Only females involved in ten or more interactions in a year were included, a criterion that allowed inclusion of at least 90% of our known individuals in any given year.

No evidence of a relationship between age and dominance was found. However, we also examined data from the National Bison Range, restricting the sample to the same age cohorts employed in the analyses for Badlands bison. The relationship there is highly significant, with age being inversely associated with rank (see fig. 7.3). Surprisingly, we failed to find a relationship between age and dominance at Badlands when one has been noted at both Wind Cave (Green 1987) and the National Bison Range (Rutberg 1983). The lack of association at Badlands may be due to more mobile groups with greater interchange among individuals, promoted perhaps by wider ranging movements than occurs at Wind Cave or the National Bison Range, where bison occur in smaller areas. Individuals at the other sites may encounter each other more often and develop stronger hierarchies than those that we found. Moreover, at Wind Cave, a high frequency of aggressive interactions occurs at rich but localized sites of high mineralization (Green 1987), a situation that might well parallel the situation described by Lott and Galland (1987), where enclosed bison cows formed a clear hierarchy.

An additional factor is worthy of comment in analyses of this sort. We restricted our sample to prime-aged animals, those in the five- to thirteen-year cohort, and then used this age class in our survey of dominance relationships reported from the National Bison Range (Rutberg 1983). We assumed this was reasonable given the lack of significant size variation in animals five years or older and the lack of reproductive differences recorded at the Bison Range (nearly 90% give birth annually; Lott and Galland 1985b). However, it may be that restricting age cohorts to those similar in reproduction obscures the possibility that other factors may be more important in determining fitness consequences for cows. Perhaps the quality of offspring is important, a factor we assess through changes in the body masses of calves of mothers differing phenotypically.

Horn Loss

It is plausible that horns are currently (or have in the past been) functional in bison (Rutberg 1986b) and other horned female bovids (Kiltie 1985; Packer 1986), although the relation between horn size and reproduction in female ungulates remains unknown. We were able to assess the hypothesis that female horns serve an intrasexual function because bison females lost their horns through natural breakage and by banging them in chutes. Females with at least one broken horn could be compared to those with intact horns in two ways. Ideally, we would like to have assessed body weight and physiological changes in response to horn loss, but this was not possible. We determined that age affected horn growth and regrowth rates; therefore it was important to account for female age prior to contrasts. For instance, females with intact and broken horns between the ages of four and nine had higher horn growth and regrowth rates ($\bar{X} = 15.7$, 12.4 mm/yr, respectively) than older females ($\bar{X} = 2.8$, 1.5 mm/yr respectively); horn growth rates of broken-horned four- to nine-year olds were more variable [4] and slower than those of intact four- to nine-year olds [5].

The first functional comparison tested the idea that offspring of broken-horned mothers experienced slower growth rates than offspring of intact mothers. The underlying assumption here is that hornless mothers have

TABLE 7.2

Comparison of changes in interaction rates (adjusted for hours of observation) and ratio of initiations (I) to recipients (R) of aggressive acts for 4- to 9-year-old females over two successive years (1987–88)

	Dehorned			Intact		
	Initiations	Recipients	I:R	Initiations	Recipients	I:R
% Change	−39.3 (67)	+288.5 (101)	—	−28.5 (160)	−37.3 (121)	—
p	<0.05	<0.01	<0.01	NS	NS	NS
N	8	9	10	10	9	10

N = number of different animals in the sample; discrepancies occur because individuals not changing in I or R were discounted from sample (see Zar 1984)
For dehorned animals, data reflect changes the year after horn loss; sample sizes for total number of interactions in parentheses.
Wilcoxon Paired-Sample Test

diminished access to resources and are lower in social rank, thereby producing less milk for their neonates. To test the idea, we first controlled for body condition and then regressed offspring age against body mass for horned and hornless mothers. When slopes and elevations of the two regressions were compared, no differences existed [6]. Growth trajectories of calves from mothers with broken and intact horns did not differ.

The second functional comparison was designed to explore if females with broken horns were disadvantaged in some other way. Using horned animals as a control group, we evaluated whether these animals were recipients of more agonistic interactions than intact cows. The ratio of initiations of agonistic encounters to those received in the control group was contrasted in two successive years with that of broken-horned females during a year when horns were intact (year one) and broken in the subsequent year. Although the percentage of initiations and recipients decreased from one year to the next for the intact females, the changes were not significant. For broken-horned females, initiations declined significantly and there was an almost 300% increase in the frequency of aggressive encounters received. Horn loss can evidently have serious consequences that include a diminished capacity to instigate agonistic encounters and an increase in the rate of receiving them (see table 7.2). Whether these changes were sufficient to result in reproductive losses is questionable as there were no differences in calf growth rates or the production of calves between dehorned and intact females. Seven of ten females in each horn category had calves.

The assessment of horn function in females is difficult. Although our data do not support an intrasexual function, horns may serve as traits for individual recognition or signs of status. If so, horn loss might have rendered individuals more likely to challenge by conspecifics, a scenario in line with the data on the frequency of types of interactions, although it still does not explain why horns evolved (see table 7.2). Bison horns and, indeed, those for other bovids could have evolved as defensive weapons to thwart predators (Geist 1966; Packer 1986) or they could be products of pleiotropy (Kiltie 1985).

Horns, Body Mass, and Age

The above analyses considered individuals who lost or broke their horns. The sample was expanded by including females with different size horns, to determine whether relative horn size or factors such as dominance or body mass were associated with calf production in a given year. As in the prior analyses, our sample was restricted to prime-aged females, but we tested for an age effect within the five- to thirteen-year range (see table 7.3).

By considering interactions between both known and unknown females, irrespective of age, we found a positive relationship between dominance and reproduction in each year of study [7]. However, pooling data by including interactions of both known and unknown animals for all ages biases the sample because interactions with young animals can carry undue weight. For example, we witnessed a nine-year-old female dominate two-, three-, and four-year olds in forty-nine interactions in a single year. The inclusion of these data inflated that female's win-loss ratio and her total number of interactions well above that of another nine-year-old female who had won six interactions and lost two with prime-aged females. Therefore we included only those interactions between known prime-aged animals with the result that in no year was there a relationship between dominance and calf production. Likewise, age had no effect, and in three of four years, neither horn size nor body mass had any influence on reproduction (see table 7.3). These analyses examined the effects of each variable separately; however, when the potential effects of other variables were removed statistically, no factor was correlated with offspring production [8]. We conclude that if horn size or body mass had a direct effect on calf production, the effects must have been subtle.

TABLE 7.3.
Relationships among annual offspring production and age, morphological, and dominance characteristics for prime-aged (5 to 13 yr old) females

	1986				1987				1988				1989			
	Age	Weight	Horns	Dom	Age	Weight	Horns	Dom	Age	Weight	Horns	Dom	Age	Weight	Horns	Dom
r_{pb}	.14	.33	.38	.03	−.17	.05	.06	.03	.08	.16	.13	.11	.01	.21	.28	.05
p	NS	<0.05	<0.01	NS	NS	NS	NS	NS	NS	NS	NS	NS	NS	NS	NS	NS
N	46	45	45	41	32	21	21	34	32	22	22	29	24	17	17	27

Dominance described in text; N = number of different individuals; r_{pb} = point biserial correlation coefficient

TABLE 7.4.

Effects of body condition and mass (kg) on calf production in the next year for prime-aged females

Body	Good		Condition G[1]	Poor	
Mass	%	N		%	N
≤435	67.8	28	0.82	55.0	20
436 to 480	65.4	26	0.02	65.2	23
≥481	67.7	31	0.00	68.8	16
Total[2]	G = 0.03			G = 0.80	

[1] Pair-wise contrasts between condition categories
[2] Effects of mass class
% is proportion producing calves; data for 1986–89

Body Condition and Mass

Although evidence shows that subordinate bison cows may forage less efficiently (Rutberg 1986b), we failed to detect reproductive debits in such females at our study site. However, lower feeding efficiency may involve less obvious effects and result in poor body condition independent of body mass. Thus we examined relationships between body mass, condition (see chapter 6), and calf production, using a heterogeneity G Test (Sokal and Rohlf 1981) in which the contribution of a single category to the total variance can be examined. Body masses were classified as light ($<$ 435 kg), medium (436 to 480 kg), and heavy ($>$ 481 kg) to assure approximately equal numbers of females in each category. Reproductive performance in relation to annual body condition was examined (see table 7.4).

Body mass had an imperceptible effect on the proportion of cows that reproduced; a 13% difference between females in the light category in good condition and those in poor condition was observed, but this difference was not significant (see table 7.4). An effect of mass is evident only when the reproductive performances of medium and heavy females are contrasted with light, poorly conditioned cows [9], although this effect is negated when the sample consists of females of medium weight in poor condition [10]. In other words, the detection of weight-related influences on calf production was sensitive to sample size effects; only after combining data from different age classes was robustness gained.

Nevertheless factors other than offspring production might vary as a function of female mass. Red deer hinds that gave birth after the peak experienced a reduction in the probability of subsequent pregnancy of 1% per day (Clutton-Brock, Guinness, and Albon 1983). For bison the combination of reproductive status (lactating or barren), body mass, and body condition explained 39% of the variance in offspring birthdate [11]. Body condition had the strongest influence; given two females of the same weight but differing in condition, the animal in better condition would give birth twenty-three days earlier. To accelerate birth by one day requires 10.7 kg of additional weight above 341 kg, the estimated minimum female weight in the summer before giving birth [11]. A female in poor body condition would have to weigh 246 kg (10.7 x 23) more than a conspecific in good condition to give birth on the same day. Clearly, body condition is a more important determinant of birthdate than body weight per se.

7.4 Dominance, Reproduction, and Scramble Competition

Contests and Expanding Populations

Our inability to detect a direct relationship between dominance and reproduction was not unanticipated because the Badlands population was rapidly expanding and density dependent influences were few (see chapter 5). In populations that approach or exceed carrying capacity, or in those where resources are defensible, effects of dominance might be more noticeable. Nevertheless, dominance, size, and maternal experience were all important correlates of reproduction in an expanding elephant seal population (Le Boeuf and Reiter 1988), indicating that factors other than resource limitations also influence reproduction. Ralls (1976) suggested that bigger females are more likely to be better or more fecund mothers and some evidence supports this contention for humans: "Women who are genetically short, whose growth has not been stunted, are on the whole less efficient at reproduction than women who are genetically tall" (Thomson quoted in Ralls 1976). Also, females who were small at birth have more problem pregnancies than larger females (Hackman et al. 1983), and women with more fat may be more fecund (Caro and Sellen 1989). In species such as chamois large size may be associated with dominance (Locati and Lovari 1991), but this is not always so. Neither body mass nor horn length was consistently correlated with elevated social status in captive bighorn sheep ewes or Dama gazelle females, nor did dominant individuals have superior productivity (Eccles and Shackleton 1986; Alados and Escos 1992). And in wild bighorn females, once the effects of age were removed, no relationship existed between dominance and reproductive success (Festa-Bianchet 1991). Nevertheless, at least two other variables may obscure direct reproduction-related effects of dominance.

The first is body condition, which is difficult to assess in live animals. The measures we employed were admittedly crude, but our findings are in line with those of several others: body condition per se has more dramatic influences on potential reproduction than do factors such as body mass (Clutton-Brock, Guinness, and Albon 1982; Petrie 1983; Green and Rothstein 1991a). Although size and body condition were interactive (at least in bison [see table 7.4], red deer [Albon et al. 1986] and probably other species) and the expectation that females can maximize their reproductive potential by being large seems reasonable, the failure to estimate condition may make it difficult to detect more subtle reproductive correlates of dominance.

Second, the influence of different factors on dominance may be confounded. Age may be among the most obvious, but to assess how dominance affects mating success requires information on possible correlates of reproduction. Green and Rothstein (1993b) reported the most direct evidence. They found that female bison calves who were born earlier in the year became dominant and may therefore be buffered against mortality during harsh winters. In addition, heavier juvenile females reproduced earlier and had greater fecundity over the eight-year period during which they were studied by Green and Rothstein (1991a). Evidence concerning the relationship between early puberty and lifetime reproductive success in other species is mixed. In Columbian ground squirrels, Murie and Dobson (1987) found that early reproducers had more total offspring but shorter life spans. When a nine-year data set was examined, however, age at first breeding had no influence on lifetime reproductive success (King, Festa-Bianchet, and Hatfield 1991). And in northern elephant seals, females that produced young as three-year olds had poorer adult survivorship than did females that deferred pupping until they were four (Reiter and Le Boeuf 1991).

Obviously, the ecological and social conditions in which species live can have dramatic influences on the behavior of individuals. For this reason the importance of dominance has received equivocal support. Besides problems associated with the measurement of hierarchies in captive populations, the resources available to wild animals vary, and these will certainly affect dominance relationships. Populations without abundant food should be characterized by more intense resource-related competition than those with no limitations (Sinclair 1977; Houston 1982;

Clutton-Brock, Guinness, and Albon 1982). For example, aggressive interactions in caribou were more common at snow craters than elsewhere (Barrette and Vandal 1985), and drought exacerbated mortality among subordinate Toque macaques (Dittus 1977, 1979). Among bison, some of the major effects of varying levels of food abundance (at dissimilar study sites) were differences in fecundity, birthdates, and reproductive synchrony.

Accrual of Benefits During Periods of Scarcity

Perhaps the most critically important issue in understanding relationships between dominance and reproduction is that species that vary in morphology and trophic levels will amass different types of benefits under contrasting ecological situations. In large-bodied herbivores, each morsel consumed is an infinitesimally small portion of the diet. Because food is generally of low value and resources are widespread, food is usually not worthy of contests (Geist 1974), and any direct effects of contests over food may be difficult to detect. The idea that animals compete by "scrambling" to consume rather than contesting resources has received support from studies of free-ranging ungulates (Nicholson 1957). In an expanding wild horse population, where intraband food competition might have been expected to exacerbate agonistic interactions among females of low-quality home ranges, scramble competition played a more prominent role in reproduction than did dominance contests (Berger 1986). Among red deer hinds, interactions over food were generally passive (Thoules 1990), but the possibility that dominance was unimportant cannot be ruled out. Scramble competition may also prove to be a more important process than previously reported for primate societies (Van Schaik and Van Noordwijk 1988).

The foregoing identifies an alternative explanation for why effects of dominance may not be conspicuous—because in many species contests over resources may be more costly than simply maximizing feeding rates. However, environments vary, and potentially subtle effects of dominance may become heightened only during or after periods of resource scarcity. If this is true, then expectations of conspicuous dominance-related effects in bison populations where food is not limited may be naive. In fact, it is only with the study of fine details, such as birthdates in relation to dominance or differences in body weight relative to body condition, that such effects could have been noticed.

However, such detail ignores the more general issue of the circum-

stances in which effects of superior body condition, perhaps due to
dominance, might arise. At least three scenarios come to mind. First,
resources such as natural mineral licks are often in short supply and can
be sites of high rates of interaction. Green (1987) noted this for bison at
her Black Hills study site. But mineral licks do not occur at Badlands,
and the ecological differences between sites might account for the lack of
dominance effects between these two areas. Second, during "ecological
crunches" dominant females may be buffered against the effects of severe
conditions such as excessively hot weather, droughts, or harsh winters.
Three pieces of evidence support this idea. Female horses on Sable Island
experienced greater mortality than males during hard winters (Welsh
1975). Similar situations existed during a drought in the Namib Desert,
where more female than male gemsbok died (Hamilton, Buskirk, and
Buskirk 1977), and during a blizzard on the Tibetan plateau, where chiru
females incurred higher mortality than males (Schaller and Junrang
1988). Determining whether survivorship advantages accrue to dominant
females must await the study of who survives and who does not during
periods of resource bottlenecks when social status is known. Third, the
costs of reproduction may be intensified during years of pathogen outbreaks. For example, although reproductive costs were not detected in
female bighorn sheep whether they produced sons or daughters, after a
pneumonic epizootic, ewes that reproduced at an early age were more
likely to die (Festa-Bianchet 1989). Although the bison we studied did
not show dramatic dominance-related effects, we found that condition
and size affect the timing of births; under extreme conditions influences
of social rank might have been more severe.

7.5 Summary

1. Current ideas about mate choice by females were examined. Evidence indicated that females rarely approached males.
2. Adult females varied in their ability to produce young; 7% produced none, whereas 24% had calves every year. Age affected
   offspring production, with animals between the ages of five and
   thirteen being the most fecund. Within this cohort, dominance
   was not associated with calf production, nor was horn size or
   body mass.
3. Females with lost or broken horns produced as many offspring
   as those with intact horns, and no differences in neonatal growth
   rates between classes of mothers were detected. However, fe-

males with broken or lost horns were recipients of nearly 300% more aggressive interactions than those with intact horns.

4. Although body mass did not affect offspring production, when body mass and condition were considered together, an effect was detectable. This was noticeable only after medium and heavy females in poor body condition were combined and their reproductive performances contrasted with those of light females in poor condition. The reproductive rates of light females in good condition were 13% higher than those in poor condition, but the differences were not significant.

5. Body condition had a stronger effect on birthdate than mass. Given two females of the same weight but differing in body condition, the animal in better condition would give birth twenty-three days earlier. An effect of body mass was also evident. For every 10.7 kg above 341 kg, a female accelerated her estrous date by one day. Because early-born animals weighed more at the beginning of winter, their chances of survival would be improved. By being heavier and in good condition, a mother may increase the chances for her offspring's survival.

7.6 Statistical Notes

1. Comparison of frequency of approaches per 3-h observation period that barren, lactating, and nulliparous females made toward males (a) 1 to 3 days prior to estrus and (b) at estrus. Analysis of Variance (data normalized by log transformation):
   (a) $F = 1.15$; NS
   (b) $F = 1.16$; NS

2. Comparison between female reproductive success and age per year for the five-year period 1985 to 1989. Analysis of variance and between cohort contrasts with Student-Newman-Keuls Test (SNK). (data normalized by square root transformation)
   $F_{8,299} = 198.13$; $p < 0.0001$.
   $p < 0.05$ (SNK) for the following age cohorts: 2 vs 3; 2 vs 4 to 5; 2 vs 14 to 15; 2 vs 16$^+$; 3 vs 4 to 5; 3 vs 14 to 15; 3 vs 16 +; all others not significant

3. Comparison between spring body weights of 3- and 4-year-old (N = 78) and 5- to 13-year-old (N = 191) females. T Test:
   $t = 2.66$; $p < 0.01$

4. Comparison of variation in horn growth rates between 10 randomly chosen intact and 10 broken-horned 4- to 9-year-old females. F-Max Test for Homogeneity of Variance:
   $F = 3.50$; $p < 0.05$

5. Comparison between growth rates in 10 randomly chosen intact and 10 broken-horned 4- to 9-year-old females (all from statistic 4). Mann-Whitney U Test:
   $U = 70$, $U' = 30$; $p < 0.05$

6. Comparison of (a) slopes and (b) elevations of regressions of calf growth (age vs mass) between 10 broken-horned and 10 intact cows.
   (a) $t = 0.48$; NS
   (b) $t = 0.76$; NS

7. Comparison between calf production in 1 yr and the proportion of social interactions won in the prior year (analyses based on all interactions irrespective of age and identities of all participants). Point Bi-Serial Correlation.
   1986, $r_{pb} = 0.83$, $t = 9.29$, $p < 0.001$; 1987, $r_{pb} = 0.88$, $t = 10.47$, $p < 0.001$; 1988, $r_{pb} = 0.92$, $t = 12.22$, $p < 0.001$, 1989, $r_{pb} = 0.74$, $t = 5.50$, $p < 0.001$;

8. Comparison of effects of single variables on calf production in prime-aged females during 1986 after removing the effects of other factors. Kendall Rank Order Correlation Coefficient.
   Dominance$_{Tau}$0.09, NS; Weight$_{Tau}$0.03, NS; Horn Size$_{Tau} = 0.02$, NS

9. Comparison of calf production between 20 poorly conditioned, light females and 39 poorly conditioned, medium and heavy females (combined weight categories). G Test:
   $G = 193.94$, $p < 0.001$

10. Comparison of calf production between 20 poorly conditioned, light females and 23 poorly conditioned, medium females. G Test:
    $G = 0.46$, NS

11. Multiple regression of body condition (X_1), body mass (X_2), and parity (X_3) on birthdate in 59 females 4 to 16 years old.
    $Y = 23.45X_1 - 0.093X_2 - 16.16X_3 + 137.61$; $r^2 = .39$; partial correlation coefficients: $X_1 = .44$; $X_2 = -.23$; $X_3 = -.33$

8. Male Mating and Reproductive Success

*Does the female prefer any particular male, either before or after
the males may have fought together for supremacy; or does the
male, when not a polygamist, select any particular female?*

Darwin 1871:544

As pointed out in the last chapter, females are often expected to
be the prudent sex even though our findings for bison gave no strong
indication of this. However, the evidence for female mate choice is
diverse, ranging from the preferences shown by Kipsigis women in Kenya
for wealthy men (Borgerhoff Mulder 1990) to female wrasse who mate
with males in territories situated in deep water (Jones 1981). Nevertheless, among nonhuman mammals little direct evidence for mate choice by
either sex has been presented, and under certain conditions it may be that
males, rather than females, do the choosing—a scenario first alluded to
by Darwin. This possibility is but one of the concerns of this chapter. We
also consider how male breeding behavior changes with age, whether
bulls advertise by bellowing, and the extent to which males vary in their
reproductive performances. This latter topic is important because of the
common claim that dominant males sire more offspring than subordinate
ones; if this were true, then selection on characteristics associated with
dominance should be intense, assuming such traits are strongly heritable.
Although our samples are not adequate to examine selection intensities
per se, it is possible to determine the degree of association between
phenotypic variables and reproductive success, a topic forming the final
section of the chapter. We use the terms mating success and copulatory
success interchangeably. Numerous authors have distinguished correctly
between them, defining mating success as "the number of mates that bear
progeny given survival of the mating organism to sexual maturity" (Arnold and Wade 1984:720). For bison this distinction is unnecessary
because females generally mate once per year (see chapter 7) and neonatal
survival to puberty exceeds 90% (see chapter 5).

8.1 Reproductive Effort and Age

Male bison change in mass and morphologically as they age. The greatest masses are attained at around ten to thirteen years (see fig. 6.6), with the heaviest male ever recorded at Badlands weighing 1,270 kg in the 1970s. The mean weight for ten- to thirteen-year-old males in late September (about eight weeks after the rut) was 821 kg, which was both heavier and less variable than those for older males ($\bar{X} = 762$) [1; numbers in brackets correspond to statistical notes at end of chapter]. Horn length shortens as bulls grow older. Theory generally dictates that reproductive effort increases with age, as residual reproductive value declines (Williams 1966; Gadgil and Bossert 1970) where reproductive effort is the proportion of an individual's budget (usually energy) allocated to current reproduction (Pianka and Parker 1975). Older individuals are considered to have fewer reproductive opportunities ahead; therefore, they may reap greater benefits by fighting for mates immediately rather than waiting for future opportunities. Nevertheless the choice of accepting greater risks depends on several factors, not the least of which include physical condition, fighting abilities, age, and the tactics adopted by others in the population.

Time at the Rut and Feeding Tradeoffs

A potential problem in examining questions about reproductive effort in bison, at least at Badlands, is that not all males arrive at the rut and associate with females for the same amounts of time. For instance, in 1985 three- to five-year-old males were in association with groups containing females during the rut nearly 80% longer than older males (6+ years of age). Of thirty-one older males, only 13% were in mixed groups for longer than fifteen days, and less than half of these were present for fewer than ten days. Conversely, nearly two-thirds of the sample of males less than six years old were at the rut longer than fifteen days (see fig. 8.1). These data suggest that males that vary in age opt for differing ways to prolong associations with mixed groups. To clarify these putative associations, we refined our classification, designating bulls as *young* (4 to 6 yrs), *prime* (7 to 12 yrs), and *old* (13+ yrs). Age classes differed significantly in their rut tenure with the mean number of days ($\pm$ SE) for each age class being young, 12.6 ($\pm$ 0.9); prime, 8.9 ($\pm$ 3.8); and old, 6.2 ($\pm$ 0.9) [2].

To check the extent to which age affected feeding, we recorded the proportion of time that focal animals spent feeding/2-h period in mixed

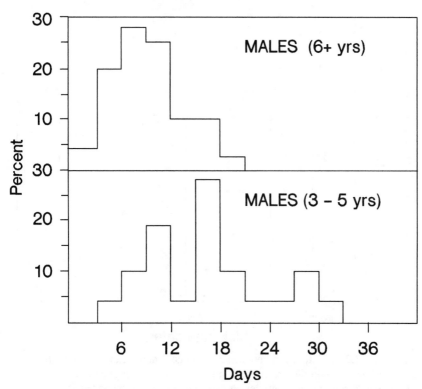

FIGURE 8.1. Frequency distribution of the percentage of known three- to five- and six-plus-year-old males that spent differing numbers of days at the 1985 rut.

groups, both when they guarded females and when they did not. To minimize annual variation, only data from the same year were used. Male feeding time was affected to a greater extent by female presence than male age (see fig. 8.2), but both factors exerted significant effects [3]. When guarding females, male feeding time decreased, on average, by 370% for young, 580% for prime, and 335% for old bulls, and in the presence of females, prime males were affected more strongly than bulls of the other age cohorts, as they fed about 80% less than the others [4]. We also assessed whether bull feeding times varied before and after the median of the rut but detected no differences [3].

These data show some age-related variation, but the differences were slight and it is difficult to attribute biological meaning to them. And these findings are not new. Maher and Byers (1987) have shown age-related variation in bulls from a Nebraskan population where eight- to eleven-year-old males fed less than younger bulls during the rut. However, since

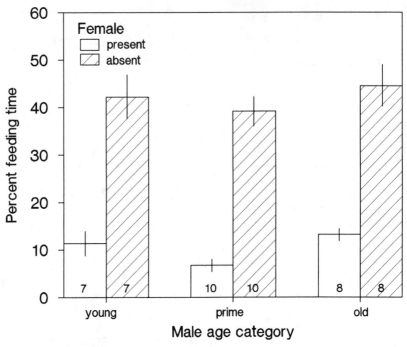

FIGURE 8.2. Relationship between age category and mean time spent feeding by the same males in the presence of females (i.e., guarding) and in the absence of females during the rut. Samples and standard errors are indicated.

males older than twelve were culled from the population, if a decrease due to old age (such as we found) occurred at their study site, it would have been impossible to detect. In wood bison, Komers, Messier, and Gates (1992) reported that rutting bulls fed less in mixed groups than when alone. These findings are in line with the precipitous declines in feeding reported for many ungulates, including red deer and moose, which form consortships with females during the rut (Clutton-Brock, Guinness, and Albon 1982; Miquelle 1989). But in at least one primate, olive baboons, feeding rates did not decline during associations with females (Bercovitch 1983). Additional information is needed to clarify the extent to which age and potential mates affect feeding and, more importantly, any relationship with later reproduction.

Mate Searching and Travel Distances

Variables other than changes in feeding time may be more reflective of reproductive effort. Among numerous mammals, females may be widely dispersed, and rather than competing directly for females by fighting, males may travel great distances to search for females. In thirteen-lined ground squirrels, for instance, highly successful males traveled more widely than less successful ones (Schwagmeyer 1988). At Badlands the greatest twenty-four-hour movement by a male bison exceeded 42 km; a different male moved more than 30 km despite ambient temperatures exceeding 39°C (102°F). These relatively broad coursing movements by solitary bulls occurred only during the rut. We frequently observed a male approach a group of females from many kilometers away, smell the ano-genital regions of three to ten females in rapid succession, remain in a group for periods varying from ten minutes to several days, and then vanish into the distant prairie, only to turn up at another group kilometers away and repeat the entire procedure. To what extent are these travels related to mating success?

To address this question, we contrasted data on minimum (linear) travel distances for males who mated and those who did not during randomly selected twenty-four-hour periods. Further, because our central interest was in assessing the prediction that old bulls expend more in reproductive effort, we compared travel distances of males according to the age categories identified in the above analyses of feeding times.

Prime bulls traveled the furthest, averaging 13 km/day; old bulls traveled slightly less (12.2 km/day); and young males moved the least per day (9.6 km). The effects of age were stronger than those of mated status [5]. For all age categories, mated males moved less than those who did not mate, but the differences were significant only for mated and unmated prime males (see fig. 8.3) [6]. Old unmated bulls were the most variable in their daily searches, with individuals ranging from 3 to 17 km/day [7].

These data are difficult to reconcile with theory. We expected searching to change with age, with old males traveling more than younger males. Although males who failed to mate moved more, presumably because breeding opportunities at a given site were restricted, it is still unclear why differences in travel between mated and unmated old bulls did not occur and why old bulls did not move as far as prime bulls. One possibility is that by being lighter and possessing body frames similar to prime males [1], old bulls did not have the body reserves necessary to travel the distances that prime males did. The fact that old bulls were at the rut for fewer days is also indicative of reduced total reproductive effort [2].

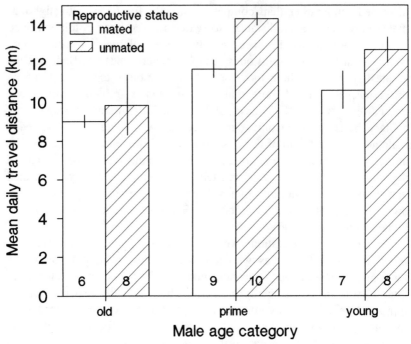

FIGURE 8.3. Relationship between age category, mean travel distances, and reproductive status (mated or unmated during a 24-h period) during the 1987 and 1988 (combined) rut. Sample sizes and standard errors as indicated.

Escalation of Aggression

We have reported some statistical differences in parameters associated with age, but the variables (feeding time, travel distances) are subtle. One of the most overt ways in which different aged males might vary is in their propensity to interact agonistically (see photos 8.1, 8.2, and 8.3). In bison at the Fort Niobrara refuge, bulls between the ages of eight and eleven were involved in more dangerous fighting than bulls in other age categories. But as Maher and Byers (1987) have pointed out, males older than twelve were removed from the population, thereby preventing further consideration of age effects. However, because resource holding potential is important in determining when and how much to escalate (Parker 1974), both age and relationships with females must be considered when predictions are made about reproductive effort. For example, in wild horses, old males not in possession of harems escalated aggression

PHOTO 8.1. Adult male spraying urine and kicking up dirt in response to a potential rival (not shown)

PHOTO 8.2. Two bulls pause from displaying to one another as a younger bull approaches.

PHOTO 8.3. Two bulls engage in head-to-head combat.

more than 400% above that of equivalently aged stallions who associated with females (Berger 1986).

In our analyses of bison escalation, our sample included only males with erect tails (see Komers, Roth, and Zimmerli 1993) that were involved in at least ten social interactions (per year) during the rut. An encounter was considered to be escalated when threats were followed by charges, or contact occurred, followed by a charge. Data on sequential patterns of aggression were gathered in 1986 and 1988. In both years young bulls escalated a smaller proportion of encounters regardless of whether females were guarded. Both female presence and male age affected the escalation tendencies of bulls [8]. Because yearly differences were not evident, data were combined. Unlike the previous analyses, where differences generally were subtle, variation among prime and old bulls was substantial. Escalation occurred when males guarded females, but if females were absent the escalation rates of prime and old bulls were similar. When old bulls guarded females, however, aggression rose nearly 25% over that of prime bulls (see fig. 8.4).[8]

These data on intrapopulation variation are important for two principal reasons. First, they indicate that age has strong effects, some of which may not be obvious in one year, but will be in another. Second, they

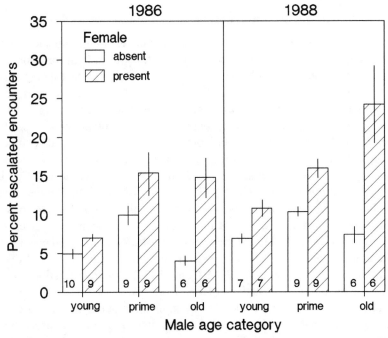

FIGURE 8.4. Relationship between age category and the percent of escalated encounters (as described in text) in males in the presence and absence of females during the rut in two different years. Sample sizes and standard errors as indicated.

suggest that in populations in which older individuals are removed prematurely, a full range of behaviors may not be displayed by males. Our data on feeding, mate searching, and fighting were all in accord with the idea that old age affects behavior even though the magnitude of differences was generally quite small (see figs. 8.2, 8.3, and 8.4).

Understanding why age-graded differences in reproductive effort may vary interspecifically is a difficult issue, but the very different escalation tendencies of old wild horse males and old bison bulls seems worthy of note. Because female horses live in harems year-round, guarded usually by one stallion (Berger 1986), and bison cows are individually guarded by single bulls for brief periods, the reproductive rewards are likely to be quite different. For an old bachelor horse, the chances of recovering an entire harem may outweigh the benefits to be accrued by an old bull who might copulate with only a single cow.

8.2 Vocal Advertisements: Messages to Females or Males?

Darwin (1871) proposed that when male ungulates are ornamented they usually employ their secondary sexual characteristics to fight for females. He also suggested in 1872 that "the sexes of many animals incessantly call for each other during the breeding season; and in not a few cases, the male endeavors thus to charm or excite the female" (Darwin 1872:84). His hypothesis has not been rigorously examined in mammals, partly because of difficulties in separating potential effects of male-male competition from those of female choice. Evidence exists to show that breeding season vocalizations by male ruminants may accelerate estrus (McComb 1987), discourage rivals (Clutton-Brock and Albon 1979; Bowyer and Kitchen 1987), deter predators, and maintain spatial proximity to mates (Tilson and Norton 1981). Vocal communication among ungulates is widespread (Kiley 1972), and the sounds of cattle have received considerable study (Hall et al. 1988). However, except for studies on red deer (Clutton-Brock and Albon 1979; McComb 1987), few investigations have been conducted on the functions of vocalizations.

The males of sexually dimorphic mammals are polygynous, and after mating they would not be expected to maintain prolonged consortships with females (Kleiman 1977) unless sperm competition occurs (Hogg 1988; Ginsberg and Huck 1989). Because males of non-harem-holding species often terminate their guarding of females after copulating (Lott 1979), it should be possible to make inferences about functions of male displays by contrasting their behavior before and after mating. For instance, if male calls are advertisements to females, then males should vocalize to females before mating, but not after, regardless of whether conspecific rivals are present. Mammals have been particularly problematic for investigations of this sort because most species are nocturnal, small, and difficult to observe. The visible species that copulate in the open, such as fallow deer or wild horses (Apollonio, Festa-Bianchet, and Mari 1989; Berger 1986), are not prone to conspicuous vocal episodes. Bison, however, bellow vigorously, copulate in the open, and differences in male pre- and postcopulatory behavior are relatively easy to quantify.

Because males bellow when guarding females and when confronting rival males, it is important to specify the conditions in which bellowing might support or reject a female advertisement or a male-male competition hypothesis, although both could ultimately be responsible for male bellowing. The female advertisement hypothesis predicts that males should bellow prior to copulating, but not after, and that bellowing should be independent of the presence of rival males. The male deterrence hypothesis predicts that bellowing should occur only in the presence of rivals, irrespective of the timing of copulations. We assess these predictions using breeding season vocalizations in relation to the presence of rival males and the timing of copulation to evaluate for whom males bellow.

Our observations, which focused on consortships where both members of a dyad were known, continued until males either copulated or departed from the female. The number of males located within 15 m of the pair and their identities (when known) were noted as were frequencies of threat, contact interactions, and displacements. When only one member of a dyad was identifiable, observations centered on known males. The reproductive status of females was determined by noting whether they were nulliparous, barren, or lactating, the latter by the presence of a distended, swollen udder (see photo 7.3). Bellowing frequency of focal males was recorded with mechanical counters both before and after mating. We adopted standard thirty-minute periods, but because animals occasionally moved out of view or consorted for shorter amounts of time, bellowing frequency was averaged per thirty minutes, a value we designated "bellowing rate." The analyses were based on bellowing data for focal males (both those who copulated and those who did not) and included bellowing rates for breeding males subdivided into periods before and after copulation. Postcopulation data were omitted if males did not remain for at least ten minutes. For males who did not copulate, but remained in consort with females during observation periods, data were used to contrast bellowing rates of breeders versus nonbreeders.

We adopted the following definitions.

Attendant male group size. Males within 15 m of the consort pair. Because the number of attendees varied during observation periods, we recorded the number of males present at five-minute intervals, and then computed an average per thirty minutes before and after copulation.

Copulatory status. Mated and unmated males.

Female reproductive potential. The probability that a female will produce a viable calf in the following year. These data were based on retrospective analyses of a female's actual reproductive performance over a multiple year period. For instance, lactating females had a lower probability of producing offspring during the next year than did females that were barren in a given year (Berger 1989).

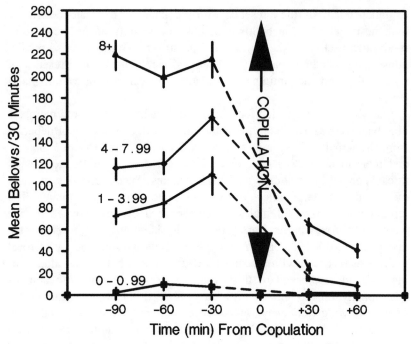

FIGURE 8.5. Relationship between time before and after copulations and mean number of bellows per 30 min for each of four average group sizes (as indicated on graph) of attendant males. Bars are standard errors. Sample sizes for attendant male groups at -90, -60, -30, 30, and 60 min are: *0–0.99*, 7, 7, 9, 7, 3; *1–3.99*, 18, 17, 15, 18, 9; *4–7.99*, 9, 18, 26, 16, 11; *8+*, 4, 5, 10, 7. Modified from Berger and Cunningham 1991.

Interval to mating. One of several thirty-minute time periods prior to copulation. Time at copulation is zero, and periods before are indicated by a negative value (e.g., minus thirty minutes is thirty minutes before mating); postcopulatory periods have positive values (see fig. 8.5).

Days at rut. The number of days that males associated with female groups.

Ecological and Social Factors Affecting Bellowing

Bellowing frequency varied among individuals from 0 to 956/h and up to 3,272 for a 4-h period. Interval to mating, attendant male group size, and copulatory status all affected bellowing rates (see fig. 8.5). The single most important variable affecting bellowing rate was copulatory status. Postcopulatory rates were only 16.1% of precopulatory rates [9]. Attendant male group size also had strong effects, and when groups of eight or more males were present, bellowing rates were approximately 60% higher than when male group size was four to seven. When males consorted with females away from others, bellowing rates dropped. For instance, of nine observed copulations when females were sequestered (i.e., not in view and at least 1 km from other males), bellows averaged less than 7.7 per thirty minutes, in contrast to 110 per thirty minutes when one to four males were present [10]. Bellowing dropped precipitously within two minutes after attendant males left a consorting pair [11]. As time to mating decreased, bellowing rates of males with attendant males of intermediate group size increased, presumably because precopulatory guarding entailed thwarting advances of potential rivals, partly accomplished by increased bellowing rates. Evidence in support of this is the inverse relationship between bellowing rate and the number of social interactions per minute per male, whereas the absence of a relationship between bellowing rate and duration of precopulatory consortships suggests that males do not necessarily enhance their associations with females by increased vocalizations [12]. The overall effect of interval to mating was highly significant [9]; it remained significant when effects of increased male attendance were removed [13].

At least three additional factors may affect bellow rates. First, adult males enter the rut at different periods during the summer, participating for different lengths of time (see fig. 8.1). If some males had participated in the rut for twelve days and others for only two or three, direct comparison might confound interpretation because bellow rates may have been reduced in the former as a result of fatigue. Second, because females vary in their probability of bearing a calf in the next season (Berger 1989), consort males might bellow more in defense of those females with a greater chance of giving birth. Third, bellow rate may vary seasonally, independent of other factors. We explored these possibilities with multiple regression, explaining 60% of the variance in precopulatory bellowing rates [14]. Female reproductive potential had no effect.

If, however, males competed more for estrous females than they did for females regardless of estrus state, then bellowing should be greater on days when females were in estrus. Less than 10% (N = 121) of fourteen hundred consortships led to copulations (Green and Berger 1990), although more than 75% involved bellowing. However, both estrous state and attendant male group size independently affected bellowing rates

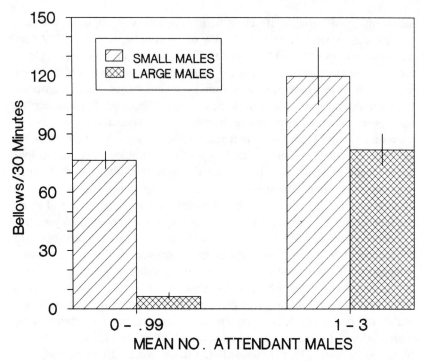

FIGURE 8.6. Relationship between mean bellowing rate/30 min and same-age small and large males with different number of attendant males on days when females were not in estrus. Bars are standard errors. The sample consisted of three males (5, 7, 9 years old) in each size class with 2 and 4 replicates for each in the 0 to 0.99 and 1 to 3 attendant male categories, respectively. Modified from Berger and Cunningham 1991.

[15], indicating that males did not bellow as intensively when females were not in peak estrus.

In addition, because males of many species employ alternative tactics to enhance chances of mating (Howard 1988; Sherman 1989), some of which are related to body size, we questioned whether body mass influenced bellowing and compared small- and larger-bodied males. Age, seasonal (i.e., date), and copulatory status effects were controlled by contrasting evenly matched, same-aged but different-sized males during a nine-day period in mid-July 1988 when none had copulated. The mean body mass of three large males (797 kg) was significantly greater than that of three smaller males (705 kg) [16]. Bellow rates for the smaller males were about 185% higher , with body size exerting a stronger effect on bellowing than the number of attendant males (see fig. 8.6) [17].

Body Size, Bellowing, and Intrasexual Competition

The data are inconsistent with the idea that males advertise to females; they rarely vocalized when other males were absent (see fig. 8.5). Had bellowing occurred when females were sequestered from other males, an epigamic function for bellowing might seem reasonable But the positive relationship between bellowing rate and male group size favors the tenet that the male vocalizations served an intrasexual function. Nevertheless, difficulty remains in separating potential intrasexual and intersexual roles. Perhaps males bellow when other males are present simply to provide females with a more direct *and* simultaneous choice, an unlikely scenario since males bellowed to one another even when females were absent. In addition, the strikingly abrupt cessation of bellowing after copulation irrespective of the number of attendant males (see fig. 8.5) indicates a strong effect of the copulation itself, although it remains unclear why postcopulatory bellowing drops to only 16% of precopulatory rates. If sperm competition occurred, there is no reason to expect dramatic differences between pre- and postcopulatory bellowing rates, assuming that rivals do not depart and bellowing coupled with active aggression by mated males deters the advances of rivals. Although our methods of data collection accounted for the number of attendant males present both before and after copulation, we did not gather data on the bellowing rates of attendant rivals. It is possible that rival males changed components of their behavior (including a reduction in bellowing) because of the copulation. If so, then the males who copulated may have altered their vocal behavior in response to an undetected or unmeasured variable that rendered rivals less competitive. Alternatively, the drop in bellowing rate after copulation may have occurred simply because rivals posed a reduced threat.

Why small males bellow more is unclear. If diminished breeding opportunities were compensated for by increased vocalizations and smaller males successfully copulated, support for an epigamic function might be gained simply because small males advertised more. Although none of the smaller males copulated in 1988, perhaps their high vocal rates served to intimidate (future) rivals. Conversely, high vocal rates in nonbreeding subordinate males may be a nonadaptive consequence of small size.

A unique feature of the data reported here is that predictions about vocal functions were examined within the pre- versus postcopulatory framework while controlling for effects of potentially confounding proximate variables. The evidence offers a reasonably sound refutation of a potential epigamic function for breeding season bellows in bison. Other studies of ungulate vocalizations have generally been descriptive (e.g., Kiley 1972; Gunderson and Mahan 1980), neither placing their findings in a hypothesis testing mode nor examining them in the context of sexual selection. While the pre- versus postcopulatory framework has not been used before, principally because data on mating in other mammals in relation to vocalizations have been lacking, it cannot by itself refute all possible scenarios. For instance, although we demonstrate that attendant male group size affects the bellowing rates of males guarding estrous females, males may still need to vocalize when females are sequestered from other males because the females remain unconvinced about the prowess of their male consorts. Additionally, the infrequent bellowing rates we reported for sequestered pairs may be sufficient to provide females with the necessary information to make a choice, perhaps through characteristics of the bellows themselves rather than bellowing rate per se. Finally, we do not rule out the possibility that male bison impress females through scent urination involving urine metabolites (Coblentz 1976) or other olfactory processes (Blaustein 1981) or fighting. Nevertheless, our data on the rate of bellowing episodes are inconsistent with the notion that breeding season vocalizations serve as advertisements to females, a suggestion with indirect support based on song data of several primates (Mitani 1988; Sekulnic 1982), and suggest that female bison do not evaluate their fellows' bellows, at least not on the basis of repetitive bellowing.

8.3 Evidence for Male Mate Choice

What Criteria Support a Choosy Male Model?

Data have not substantiated the idea of female mate choice, but there is no reason to expect that male mammals will be nonselective for mates. Mate choice should occur if potential fecundity varies as it does in some female invertebrates (Snead and Alcock 1985), fish (Sargent, Gross, and Van Den Berghe 1986), anurans (Ryan 1985), urodeles (Verrell 1985) and birds (Burley 1981). In essence, each sex may benefit by identifying the reproductive potential of possible sexual partners. If so, male mammals should also judge female reproductive potential and maximize opportunities to mate with the most fertile females and breed as often as possible.

Although several investigators, particularly of primates, claim to demonstrate that males discriminate among females (Anderson 1986; Conaway and Koford 1965; Galdikas 1985), data are either anecdotal or equivocal. To show that male mammals distinguish among potential partners has proved challenging because of difficulties in demonstrating four conditions at the same study area:

1. Females vary in their probability of producing progeny (i.e., their reproductive potential).
2. Females varying in reproductive potential are differentially available so that discrimination by males is possible.
3. Males do not copulate randomly. Although male and female behavior might jointly influence nonrandom mating because females may make themselves differentially available to some males, it must be shown that nonrandom breeding is, at least in part, a consequence of male, and not exclusively female, behavior.
4. When given simultaneous presentations, males selectively mate with females that promote higher fitness (i.e., females of higher reproductive potential).

The data we gathered allowed us to address all but the last point for bison. To some extent the lack of data on fitness can be overcome by assuming that males who mate with fecund females gain a reproductive advantage over those who do not because the former have greater possibilities of producing offspring in each year and there is a high degree of concordance among annual breeders (see section 8.5).

Variability in Estrus and Female Reproductive Potential

To determine whether females were differentially available to males, the distribution of 164 estrous females was noted (see fig. 8.7). Median estrous date was 27 July, although when females were segregated according to their reproductive performances in that year an orderly progression from early to late estrous was as follows: barren females, mothers with daughters, mothers with sons, and nulliparous females. A similar progression has been noted for bison at a Montana site although nulliparous individuals were not the last female class (Wolff 1988), and at Wind Cave mothers with sons did not lose more weight than those with daughters (Green and Rothstein 1991b), so cows there may not have conceived

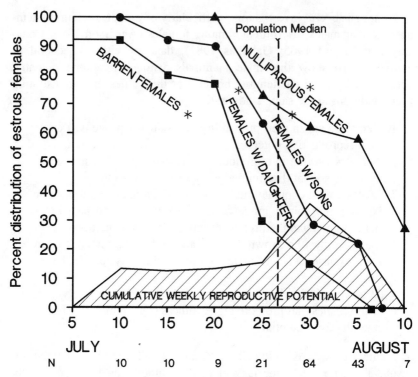

FIGURE 8.7. Distribution of estrous dates of females in relation to reproductive status during 1985. Asterisks are median estrous dates for each class of female. Cumulative weekly reproductive potential is the product of the frequency of estrous females and their reproductive potential. Percent distribution of estrous females is obtained by dividing the number of estrous cows of different reproductive status by the total number of estrous females per five-day period. From Berger 1989.

at different times. At Badlands the females who attained estrus early in the season were typically large and in good condition (see chapter 7), as also reported for wild and domestic ungulates (Guinness, Lincoln, and Short 1971; Mitchell and Lincoln 1973; Gunn and Doney 1975). Although these data indicate differential estrus times for females varying by prior reproduction, they say little about potential fecundity.

Reproductive potential was estimated by comparing the proportion of females with young in each class to those without young. In one year 90% of barren females were likely to produce calves in the next (N = 30),

whereas 38% of lactating females produced calves in the next year
(N = 81) Calf sex had no effect [18]. For nulliparous cows only 15% of
females produced calves in the next year (N = 20). These findings agree
well with those on other female ungulates (Mitchell, McCowan, and
Nicholson 1976; Robinette and Olsen 1944) that also show marked differences in fecundity stemming from breeding performances in the prior
year (Clutton-Brock, Guinness, and Albon 1982). Equally important is
that females bearing offspring early in the season are likely to have
heavier calves with coincident greater survival probabilities than late-
born calves (Albon, Clutton-Brock, and Guinness 1987); thus, with other
factors being equal, early-breeding females should be a more valuable
resource for males than late-breeding females.

Male Options and Tests of the Discrimination Hypothesis

Under ideal conditions, males should be present during the entire rut to
maximize mating opportunities. Given that not all males associated with
females throughout the rut, we assumed costs of attendance were incurred
by males, an idea borne out by the relationship between male age and
time spent at the rut (see fig. 8.1) and the loss of about 100 kg in male
body weight (see below). Because factors associated with individual
males, including arrival times, were known, it was possible to determine
three ways in which males might choose females: (1) arriving at the rut
during periods that coincide with the estrous females of highest reproductive potential (a correlational approach), (2) investing more in defense of
females with relatively higher reproductive potential (a different correlational approach), or (3) selecting females with higher reproductive potential when simultaneous choices between females of differing reproductive
classes are possible (a direct test).

Male Arrivals and Investigations of Females.

It was possible to test whether breeding efforts by males were skewed
toward more fecund females or toward as many as possible. If males
concentrated breeding efforts on the most fecund females, more males
should have been present early in the rut because twenty-three of twenty-
seven (85%) estrous females during the first quartile of the breeding
season were barren (see fig. 8.7). That is, the females with the highest
probability of bearing offspring were in estrus early during the rut. If,
however, males enhanced reproductive success by maximizing the num-

ber of mates, more males should have been present near or at the end of the rut, the period when the greatest number of females became estrus (see fig. 8.7).

To examine the distribution of estrous females in relation to reproductive potential and absolute availability, we calculated female "cumulative weekly reproductive potential," the product of the sum of each female category multiplied by respective reproductive potential values. This measure was skewed toward the end of the rut (see fig. 8.7). In essence, given that males restricted participation in the rut to a few short weeks (see fig. 8.1), it is important to know whether they arrived early when females of relatively high reproductive potential were more available or later when the cumulative weekly reproductive potential was greatest. To determine the period when males (medium spikes to old bulls) were most frequent, the distribution of 1,847 cumulative sightings (only 1 sighting/ male per day was counted) of bulls visiting groups of females was divided into those occurring before and after the median date of cumulative weekly reproductive potential; 64% occurred before 26 July [19]. Hence, an association between male arrival and the estrous cycles of predominately barren females occurred.

These data, by themselves, do not support the hypothesis that males select females of high reproductive potential for mating. If males discriminate among female reproductive categories, such behavior should be reflected by the frequency with which individual cows were investigated by males. We examined this possibility by noting the frequency that males six years or older sniffed the A-G regions of females during standardized three-hour observation periods. A-G investigations were influenced both by female reproductive status and time during the breeding season [20]. Barren anestrous females were selected most frequently during the first quartile and nulliparous anestrous females most often during the last; during the two middle quartiles lactating anestrous females were investigated the most. These data, while somewhat generic, indicate that males directed approaches toward females in a nonrandom manner selecting females with the greatest reproductive potential in each breeding season quartile (see fig. 8.8).

Male Defense of Females Differing in Reproductive Potential.

We did not evaluate whether males were more or less likely to escalate aggression when guarding females that differed in reproductive status. However, we reasoned that males would bellow more when defending females of high reproductive potential, but when the effects of potential

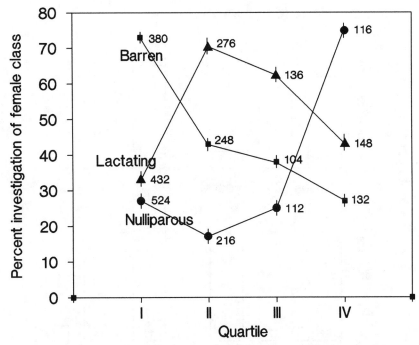

FIGURE 8.8. Relationship between breeding season quartile and the mean percentage of male ano-genital investigations of three classes of females. Data were corrected for percent availability for each female class. Sample sizes are the number of marked females censused for at least 3 h per quartile. Vertical bars are standard errors. Modified from Berger 1989.

confounding factors were removed by multiple regression [14], none of the variance in bellowing rate was accounted for by female reproductive status. If males expend more effort in defense of high-quality females, it was not evident based on our considerations of bellowing rates.

A direct test.

Much of the prior information offers only indirect support for the notion that males evaluate female breeding potential. Fortunately, a direct test was available: estrous females that differed in reproductive potential occurred in the same groups simultaneously. Thus opportunities for males to choose between females that differed in the probability of calf production existed. From 22 July to 3 August 1985, males differentially approached 120 estrous females from different categories of reproductive potential; on any given day females from at least two different reproduc-

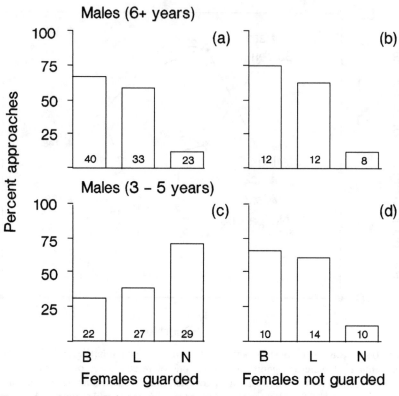

FIGURE 8.9. Comparison of percent approaches by two categories of males to estrous females guarded by males or unguarded. Sample sizes indicated for *B*, barren; *L*, lactating; and *N*, nulliparous females. From Berger 1989.

tive categories had to be present, experiencing estrus, and within 100 m of each other for data on male choice to be recorded. We scored choices by males if they approached to within 15 m of a cow. Although males discriminated, their choices depended on their age (see fig. 8.9). When females were already guarded, males six years or older more often moved to females of higher reproductive potential. But in the same circumstances, younger males moved to nulliparous females [21]. When females were unguarded, males of all ages moved toward cows with the greatest reproductive potential (see fig. 8.9). Although the cues on which males based their choices are unknown, the data suggest that males evaluated females. They were differentially attracted to females that were more likely to produce offspring in the next season. These data coupled with those on lack of female approaches to males (see table 7.1) reinforce the idea that males, not females, were more actively involved in mate choice and that their mating patterns were adaptive.

Possible Confounding Variables.

Interpreting mate-choice data may be difficult because of problems in sorting out cause from effect. Perhaps older males that bred nulliparous females had less sperm with which to impregnate females. Or perhaps females of all categories were equally likely to conceive, but nulliparous females were more likely than barren females to suffer prenatal deaths. Should this latter point be true, the arguments we developed about male mate discrimination would still pertain because males were attracted differentially to potentially more fecund females independent of the proximate mechanisms governing fertility. But if older males had less sperm, then the reproductive potential of females would be dictated by the interaction of physiological constraints and behavior of males, not from the reproductive history of females. Unfortunately, little is known about sperm quality or depletion in bison. For domestic bulls the effects of age are unclear because spermatazoal concentration and total sperm per ejaculate are affected by numerous factors, including copulation frequency, testes size, and hormonal status (Amann 1991). Nevertheless, female reproduction obviously will hinge on the fertility of males with whom she mates. Field studies cannot account for the possibility that sperm depletion or variation in male fertilization abilities occurs and that these factors might cause differences in fecundity among females. Fortunately, other studies (Mitchell, McCowan, and Nicholson 1976; Clutton-Brock, Guinness, and Albon 1982; Green 1990) in addition to ours offer an equally plausible explanation for variation in female reproductive potential—the differential costs of rearing prior offspring. Hence, a basis for male evaluation of females exists.

Male Choice in Other Mammals

Theory generally predicts that females ought to be the more selective sex when males are adorned with secondary sexual characteristics, Fisher (1958), however, indicated that either sex should be discriminating if its reproductive success will be affected. This appears to be true only when mating costs are involved (Dewsbury 1982). For instance, if male bison incurred no mating costs, selection for females of different reproductive potential should not occur because indiscriminate mating would have no bearing on later reproductive success. Conversely, choice might still be favored if net benefits were derived from breeding with females of different classes and if, because of time limitations, males could not breed with every female in the population. That older males spend less time at the rut than younger males [2] (see fig. 8.1), even though females capable of being fertilized are still available, suggests that mating costs are involved; included among these are substantial losses of body mass. At the National Bison Range, four males older than five years lost an average of 101 kg/individual between 17 July and 8 October, and three younger males lost an average of 45 kg over the same period. Further, in other ungulates, energy expenditures by males increase with the number of females guarded (Berger 1986), and wounds and death are not uncommon costs of rutting activities (Geist 1971a; Clutton-Brock, Guinness, and Albon 1982).

Despite the fact that sexual relationships and consortships have been studied in many nonungulate mammals, demonstrations of male discrimination among potential mates have rarely been described. It seems unlikely that, except for bison and thirteen-lined ground squirrels (where males avoid copulating with previously mated females [Schwagmeyer and Parker 1990]), males of other species are incapable of being choosy. Three disparate lines of evidence, in fact, suggest male mate choice in other taxa. First, males of numerous species identify and follow estrous females (Eisenberg 1981), indicating that males distinguish between categories of females at different times of the year. Second, females vary in their reproductive potential in primates, ungulates, carnivores, rodents, and pinnipeds (Altmann 1980; Armitage 1984; Clutton-Brock, Guinness, and Albon 1982; Reiter, Panken, and Le Boeuf 1981; Rood 1980). Third, males may distinguish among reproductive categories and choose the most fertile class of females (Anderson 1986; Smuts 1986). Nevertheless, to demonstrate choice per se will require detailed study of estrous dates, subsequent reproduction, and availability of females differing in status.

8.4 Reproductive Variation Among Males

Rationale and Assumptions

We evaluated reproductive success (RS) directly by counting the number of copulations individual males had with different females. This method suffers from several potential biases, which we attempted to account for.

1. Copulations might occur at night. If this were primarily the
   case, we might miss a high proportion of the matings. To check

this possibility, we compared over ten-day periods in 1986, 1987, and 1988 the change in proportion of cows with fully erect "tail up" postures (a sign of being recently copulated with) at two periods, 8:00 A.M. to 8:00 P.M. and 8:00 P.M. to 8:00 A.M. We reasoned that if more copulations occurred during the night than during the day, then the relative number of cows with new tail ups should be higher early in the morning. For these analyses, we used only data gathered on groups with more than two hundred animals that did not move more than 1 km during the night or day, thus assuring us of approximately the same group composition. Differences between night and day were not detectable [22]. In fact, our analyses were conservative, as daily observations began at first light and extended to dusk.

2. Copulations might not equate to RS per se because males may mate with females more than once, and more than one male may copulate with the same female. The proportion of females mating with different males has generally been assumed to be less than 5% (Lott 1981). Because data from our study suggest that this value may be closer to 10% and we did not know which male may have actually fertilized a female, we assigned each copulating male a proportion of the putative offspring fathered. Thus if two males copulated with the same female each was assigned 0.50 offspring. In only 2 of 261 (0.8%) cases did more than two males copulate with the same female. Finally, we assumed that the males we observed copulating more often with different females had relatively higher putative reproductive success although genetic data on paternity were not gathered. Recent DNA fingerprinting analyses have shown that behavioral estimates accurately assess the relative success of individual males, although they may overestimate absolute success (Pemberton et al. 1992).

3. Because individuals were observed for different periods of time, it was possible that whoever was watched the most could have had the highest RS. To standardize comparisons across males, we restricted analyses to focal animals and expressed the number of copulations observed on an hourly basis. Otherwise, without sampling animals for every active hour throughout the breeding season, it would be impossible to derive a reasonable expectation for the total frequency of copulations achieved by individuals over the entire rut. In attempting to circumvent this

problem, we relied on data gathered in two areas. First, we evaluated on a yearly basis the relationship between copulations and observation time, using males that had copulated at least once. The point (asymptote) at which copulations no longer increased with total observations was then used to mark the period at which copulations per hour would no longer scale to total hours observed. Second, because we knew how long (in days) animals associated with females, we considered the total time an animal participated in the rut. By taking into account participation time and knowing the asymptote, we could estimate total copulations per male during a given season. For instance, in 1986 no relationship was found between copulation frequency and observation hours beyond twenty-seven. Therefore an individual that was observed for thirty hours and that mated 6 times during the 1986 season would be credited with a total of 6 copulations. In contrast, an individual that was observed for twenty hours and copulated 3 times (0.15/h) would receive a seasonal total of 3 (actual copulations) + 7(0.15) (prorated copulations) or 4.05 copulations. In cases where individuals exceeded the asymptote, their actual copulation frequency was counted. In cases where individuals fell below the asymptote, we estimated the number of days they participated in the rut and then, based on fifteen hours per day (the amount of time data were gathered daily), multiplied this value by their copulation rate.

Two additional points are worthy of mention. Although we initially tried to sample all known individuals for equal periods of time, it soon became obvious that some individuals had a much greater probability of mating than others. Therefore we deliberately oversampled males from both extremes (i.e., high probability of mating, low probability of mating) at about the same rate. We felt that this was important, especially in contrasts between animals of the two lineages since males of the Colorado Line tended to be wimpy males; that is, they lost most encounters and had low probabilities of breeding (see chapter 9). Also, a question arises as to whether males who were sampled for only a few hours and did not breed would have eventually done so had our sampling for such males been longer. Following Pruett-Jones and Pruett-Jones (1990), we compared sampling efforts for nonmated males with the number of hours that elapsed until the first mating of breeding males (matched by age) was detected, the latter being indicative of the sampling effort needed to

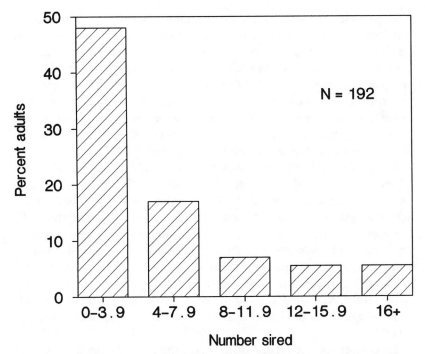

FIGURE 8.10. Variation in estimated number of calves sired (based on copulatory success) from 1985 to 1988 by adult males.

observe at least one mating. In three of four years, no differences existed; in the other, the time to first copulation was less than the observation hours of nonmated males [23]; these data indicate our sampling efforts should have been sufficient to detect breeding in the unmated males had they been able to copulate.

Number of Offspring by Individual Males

In estimating RS, we first considered only males four years or older; males younger than this rarely guarded females. Among males the number of copulations with different females varied considerably (see fig. 8.10). Of 54 males, 6 (11% of the total), whose ages at the study's end ranged from 9 to 15 years, accounted for 48% of the matings (92 of 192).

What factors might account for the differences in mating success? Clearly, the variation could not arise as a result of lifetime performances because so few animals died during the study. Although we removed some possible age biases by initially restricting the analyses to individuals four years or older (see fig. 8.10), age was likely to exert some effect on breeding performance, as it does in virtually all ungulates studied to date (Lott 1979; Gibson and Guinness 1980a; Hogg 1987). Because males gain weight progressively until they are about ten years old, it should not be surprising that body mass, age, or some combination affects breeding success. At Wind Cave National Park, play partners are chosen on the basis of sex, not size (Rothstein and Griswold 1991), and early experience is likely to influence later reproduction (Byers 1986).

At our Badlands site age had a pronounced affect on the number of calves putatively sired [24], with bulls in the 7- to 12-year-old class being the most successful). The 13- to 14-, 15-plus-, and 6-year-old cohorts were the next most fecund, but they did not differ from each other [24]. The most successful male in a given year copulated with a minimum of nine different females, four of them in twenty-four hours, and was estimated to have mated with twelve females. However, large interindividual differences existed, and in six of the seven age cohorts, the median number of calves sired was estimated at zero; only in the 11- to 12-year-old age class did more than 50% of the bulls copulate (see fig. 8.11).

To control for age-related differences, the breeding performances of seven males (between the ages of seven to nine in 1985) were contrasted over the study duration; the most successful mated with 28 females, the least successful with none. Intermediate values were 1.5, 3, 7, 8, and 13. The variation among individuals was great [25] and would likely result in lifelong reproductive differences; the one unmated male died, another suffered a broken pelvis, and there was no indication that the individual who reproduced more was exposed to greater mortality risks (see below). The evidence also indicates that the greatest differences in reproduction arise once individuals reach prime age. The within-cohort variance in RS was highest relative to old males [26], and interindividual differences in RS were not detectable for six old males more than thirteen years old in 1985 [27], but such variation occurred among prime males [25].

8.5 Factors Affecting Reproductive Success

Changes in Dominance and Year-to-Year Concordance

In a variety of mammals, dominance has marked effects on male mating (Packer 1979; Gibson and Guinness 1980b; Le Boeuf and Reiter 1988),

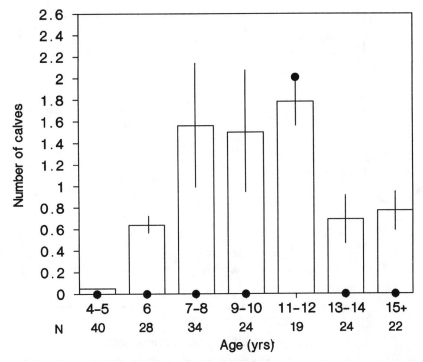

FIGURE 8.11. Age-specific fecundity (copulations with different females per male) from 1985 to 1988 and standard errors. Dots are medians for that cohort.

but whether body size is related to dominance (Berger 1986) reproductive activity (Bercovitch 1989), or territorial defense (Byers and Kitchen 1988) is uncertain. Among bison bulls in Montana neither age nor weight was related to copulation rates (Lott 1979). However, because bison males participate in the rut for only short periods of time, it is possible that body condition deteriorates rapidly and breeding males are successful for only a portion of the time they are at the rut. In addition, individuals that breed in one year may be less successful during the next because of the costs of successful reproduction, although this was found not to be the case for red deer stags (Clutton-Brock, Guinness, and Albon 1982) or for bison (see below).

The capture of males to obtain information on changes in body mass would have been too disruptive during the rut, but it was possible to evaluate behavioral changes associated with reproduction. We expected an association between mating frequency and the proportion of fights won during a season but no such relationship was found. Only when we

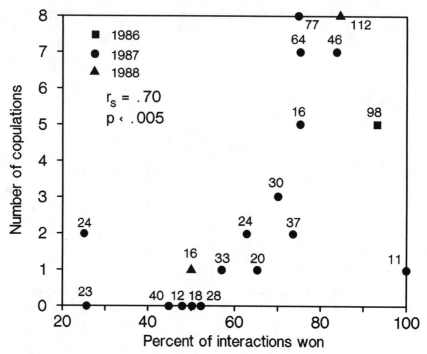

FIGURE 8.12. Relationship between proportion of interactions won by prime-aged males and their copulatory success during the first half of their rut tenure. Numbers indicate frequency of social interactions.

divided the period of participation into halves did we detect significant relationships between the proportion of fights won and copulation success (see fig. 8.12); these associations were consistent across age cohorts and held true for prime males whether years were combined or examined separately. The percentage of total number of interactions won was also associated with copulation frequency in old males and for young and prime males from 1986 to 1988 (see table 8.1).

The above analyses consistently demonstrate that success in agonistic interactions during the first period of an individual's participation in the rut is related to reproduction. However, they did not indicate whether individuals who were successful in one year fared well in the next. Despite data on consistent interannual performances in red deer stags (Clutton-Brock, Guinness, and Albon 1982), the evidence is that the rut is costly to prime-aged bison males who may lose on average at least 100 kg (see section 8.3). Because males who were successful at mating in a

TABLE 8.1.
Rank correlations between male copulation frequency and percentage of aggressive interactions won during two periods of the rut

Age	Total interactions	First half	Second half	Year
Young[1] r_s	.80***	.84***	.23	1986–88
N	14	14	14	
Prime r_s	.34	.76**	−.16	1988
N	14	14	14	
Prime r_s	.47*	.70**	−.23	1986–88
N	19	19	19	
Old[2] r_s	.86*	.84*	.86*	1987–88
N	6	6	6	

[1]Greatest number of different males in yearly sample was 6
[2]Greatest number of different males in yearly sample was 4; no data were available for old males in 1986
*$p<0.05$; **$p<0.01$; ***$p<0.001$

given year generally won a greater proportion of aggressive interactions, they may also have suffered from early "burn-out" and reproduced less well in subsequent years. We evaluated this supposition in several ways.

First, we contrasted the reproductive performances of seven prime bulls from 1985 to 1988 and found concordance among mating success. Individuals that were successful in a given year tended to be successful over the entire period, although for old males there was no such relationship [28]. Because most bulls did not reproduce, perhaps the reduced variability [26] did not allow for consistently high performances among individuals. In any case, the cumulative data for prime males demonstrated consistent performances over the study period. Nevertheless, it is possible that strong year-to-year differences existed based on prior reproductive performances. To examine this possibility, the subsequent breeding of males who mated more than three times in a year was contrasted with that of bulls who copulated less, to assess whether mating frequencies changed. Of ten prime males who bred two or fewer times, 40% experienced reductions in mating activity in the next year, whereas 87% of those (N = 16) breeding three or more times bred less in the next year; hence, the chances were much greater that there would be reductions in subsequent breeding by males who copulated more than three times annually [29].

TABLE 8.2.

Correlations between annual copulation frequency (adjusted for hours of observation) and morphological and ecological variables

	All males				Prime males			
	Body mass	Head size	Rut tenure	Travel distance	Body mass	Head size	Rut tenure	Travel distance
1986 r_s	.66*	.31	.41	.38	.66	.61	.41	—
N	.10	.16	.15	.13	.07	.05	.05	—
1987 r_s	.34[a]	.24	.03	.10	.29	.24	.19	−.40[a]
N	.23	.25	.32	.31	.10	.16	.15	15
1988 r_s	.58**	.40*	.31[a]	.24	.61[a]	.31	.16	−.17
N	.28	.30	.30	.30	.10	.16	.22	15

*$p<0.05$; **$p<0.01$
[a]$0.05<p<0.10$

Size, Rut Tenure, and Travel Distances

Because the data set was reasonably complete, we evaluated the extent to which other variables potentially influenced annual reproductive performances. The sample sizes for old and young males were generally too small to permit separation of these age classes, so two analyses were performed, one combining all males and the other with just prime males. Not surprisingly, body mass affected mating frequency when all ages were combined since young bulls are smaller and generally precluded from mating by larger animals. Using head size as a single variable, the relationship with RS was significant in 1988, but not in other years. Although data on head size are easier to gather than those on body mass, and an association exists between head size and body mass, mass should be a more sensitive predictor of RS than head size because rutting males lose weight but head size remains constant. Nevertheless, in only one of three years did a relationship between RS and body mass approach significance for prime males. Similarly, travel distance and mating frequency appeared to be inversely related but the associations were not statistically significant (see table 8.2).

These data generally reaffirm the results of several studies in which male size per se was not the most salient variable related to reproduction (Bercovitch 1989; Berger 1986; Feh 1990), but they also differ in several important respects. The evidence in favor of the idea that fighting success in males determines reproduction is mixed, receiving support from work on red deer (Gibson and Guinness 1980b; Clutton-Brock, Guinness, and Albon 1982), but not fallow deer (Apollonio, Festa-Bianchet, and Mari

1989); our data show that an individual's fighting ability is important only during the first half of its tenure at the rut. The possibility exists that dominance rank may be inherited, as in some primates (Smith and Smith 1988), but this seems unlikely in highly dimorphic species where intense aggressive interactions for females occur during short periods. Clearly, early social interactions help in the development of fighting skills in bison (Rothstein and Griswold 1991) and other species (Bekoff 1977; Byers 1980; Fagen 1981), but relationships between ontogenetic history, subsequent body size, and reproduction are generally unclear (Berger 1986). What seems most reasonable for bison is that a threshold size is necessary for successful reproduction (Lott 1979), but fighting skills, at least early in the rut, are also critical if males are to dominate rivals and then guard females from them.

8.6 Summary

1. Theory generally predicts that older males should take more risks than younger animals in obtaining mates because future reproductive opportunities will be more limited in the former. The prediction was examined by contrasting males of three age categories (young, prime, old) with respect to parameters associated with reproductive competition. Old males were at the rut for fewer days and were more variable in the daily distances that they traveled than prime males. However, neither feeding times nor travel distances differed between males of respective age categories when they mated successfully. In one of two years, older males escalated aggression more often when guarding females, but in the other year differences between prime and old males did not occur.

2. Males bellowed incessantly during the rut. Whether these vocalizations were advertisements to females or threats to other males was examined by contrasting the timing and frequency of bellowing with respect to female estrus and the number of potential rivals present. Males that guarded females bellowed more on days that females were in estrus, when a greater number of males surrounded them, and just prior to copulation. Bellowing rates were inversely related to the number of days of participation at the rut, but unaffected by female reproductive status. Males vocalized neither before nor after copulating when rivals were absent, but did so when rivals were present, which sug-

gests that bellows functioned as intrasexual displays, not as advertisements to females.

3. Bulls and spikes moved toward females with higher reproductive potential during the rut. Such cows had higher probabilities of calf production in the next season, probably because they were in better condition. Although the proximate mechanisms of mate selection were undetermined, the data suggest the occurrence of male mate choice in a nonhuman mammal.

4. Male reproductive success was estimated by the number of copulations with different females. Potential biases of this method were minimized by checking the possibility of differences in female reproductive behavior between day and night and by accounting for differences in monitoring efforts. About 10% of the males accounted for 50% of the copulations, but the skew in mating was due, in part, to differences in male age. Even when age was controlled, however, strong individual differences occurred; the most successful male accounted for twenty-eight offspring, and the least successful none. Male mating success was related to dominance, but only during the first half of the period that males participated at the rut. After that, a greater proportion of fights were lost. For prime males, mating success was not related to head size, body mass, rut tenure, or travel distance.

8.7 Statistical Notes

1. Comparison between (a) average September body weights of males aged 10 to 13 ($N = 39$) and 14 to 19 years ($N = 13$) and (b) variability in weights for the same 2 cohorts.
   (a) Mann-Whitney U Test: $z = 1.68$; NS,
   (b) F Maximum Test for Homogeneity of Variances: $F_{12,38} = 2.49$, $p < 0.05$

2. Comparison of effects of age class on the length of time that males spent at the rut. One-way Analysis of Variance: $F_{2,62} = 26.55$, $p < 0.001$ (all age categories differ significantly from one another; Student-Newman-Keuls Test)

3. Comparison of effects of (a) female presence, (b) age class, and (c) rut period (pre- or postmedian) on bulls' feeding rates in mixed groups of $100+$ and adult sex ratios of at least 0.2:1.0 during the 1987 breeding season. Three-way Analysis of Variance (data transformed by arc sine):

(a) $F_{1,23} = 18.46$, $p < 0.001$
(b) $F_{2,23} = 3.49$, $p < 0.05$
(c) $F_{1,23} = 0.03$, NS
Interaction: $F_{\text{female presence X age}} = 44.47$, $p < 0.001$ (all others NS)

4. Within- and between-category contrasts in the above analysis. Student-Newman-Keuls Test: For differences between feeding in the presence and absence of females for old and young bulls ($p < 0.05$), for prime bulls ($p < 0.01$), and for feeding in the presence of females, prime males differed from the other male categories ($p < 0.02$)

5. Comparison of effects of (a) age and (b) mating status on daily travel distances of bulls during the 1986 to 1988 breeding seasons. Two-way Analysis of Variance (data transformed by log):
   (a) $F_{2,42} = 7.20$, $p < 0.005$
   (b) $F_{1,42} = 3.05$, $0.05 < p < 0.10$
   Interaction: NS

6. Within- and between-category contrasts in the above analysis. Student-Newman-Keuls Test: Differences in travel significant ($p < 0.05$) for all contrasts between age categories, for mating status the only significant ($p < 0.05$) difference was between mated and unmated prime males.

7. Comparison of variation in daily travel distances between mated and unmated old bulls. F Maximum Test for Homogeneity of Variances:
   $F_{5,7} = 6.55$, $p < 0.025$

8. Comparison of effects of (a) year, (b) female presence, and (c) age on the proportion of encounters involving escalation using Three-way Analysis of Variance (data transformed by square root), and differences between old and prime males in the (d) absence and (e) presence of females.
   (a) $F_{1,92} = 2.48$, NS
   (b) $F_{1,92} = 12.84$, $p < 0.002$
   (c) $F_{2,92} = 5.99$, $p < 0.01$
   (d) $F_{11,17} = 1.53$, NS
   (e) $F_{11,17} = 6.27$, $p < 0.001$
   Interaction: all NS

9. Comparison of effects of (a) copulatory status, (b) attendant male group size, and (c) interval to mating on mean bellowing rate (data transformed by log):

(a) $F_{3,213} = 345.85$, $p < 0.0001$
(b) $F = 265.60$, $p < 0.001$
(c) $F = 12.34$, $p < 0.001$

10. The binomial probability that the 9 males who copulated with sequestered females would have the fewest bellows/period in the 0- 0.99 category of attendant males (from fig. 8.5) is 0.000038.

11. Comparison of bellowing rates of bulls when attendant males were present and during the 2-min period after potential rivals departed. Wilcoxon Matched Pairs Test:
    Ts = 10.5, n = 19, $p < 0.01$

12. Relationships between (a) bellowing rate and the number of social interactions per minute per male and (b) bellowing rate and duration (min) of precopulatory consortships. Spearman Rank Correlation:
    (a) $r_s = -.37$, df = 62, $p < 0.02$
    (b) $r_s = -.19$, df = 62, NS

13. Effect of interval to mating on bellowing when other variables are removed (from statistic 9). First Order Partial Correlation Coefficient:
    $r_{partial} = .20$, $p < 0.05$

14. Multiple regression of attendant number of males (X_1), days at the rut (X_2), and date (X_3) on precopulatory bellowing rate.
    $F = 44.62$, df = 93, $p < 0.0001$; $Y = .994 + .696X_1 - .019X_2 - .017X_3$.
    Partial correlation coefficients are .74, -.21, and -.31 ($p < .0001$, $p < 0.05$, and $p < 0.003$ respectively).

15. Comparison of effects of male group size and estrous state on bellowing rate. Two-way Analysis of Variance:
    $F_{group\ size} = 9.93$, df = 76, $p < 0.0001$;
    $F_{status} = 6.70$, $p < 0.025$

16. Comparison of body size between large and small 5-, 7-, and 9-year-old bulls. T Test:
    t = 4.99, df = 4, $p < 0.01$

17. Comparison of effects of body and group size on bellowing rates for the bulls of the above analysis with 2 and 4 replicates of each. Two-way Analysis of Variance.
    $F_{body\ size} = 5.60$; df = 2,35, $p < 0.03$; $F_{group\ size} = 3.68$; $p < 0.05$; Interaction: NS

18. Comparison of calf sex on fecundity of 81 cows in the next year. Chi Square Test:
    $X^2 = 0.67$, NS
19. Comparison of the distribution of males with respect to the cumulative weekly reproductive potential median in 1985. Chi Square Test:
    $X^2 = 91.18$, $p < 0.001$
20. Comparison of effects of female reproductive status (FRS) and quartile (Q) of the breeding season on the frequency of A-G investigations by males. Friedman Two-way Analysis of Variance:
    $X^2_{FRS} = 45.45$, $p < 0.001$; $X^2_Q = 42.42$, $p < 0.001$
21. Comparison of percentage of approaches (from fig. 8.9) by males 6 or more years of age and 3 to 5 years old to three categories of estrous females that were either unguarded or guarded. Female categories are Barren (B), Lactating (L), or Nulliparous (N). Multiple comparison of standard error in degrees using the q distribution (see Zar 1984). Older male approaches to (a) unguarded and (b) guarded females; younger male approaches to (c) unguarded and (d) guarded females. Q and p values are given for B vs L, L vs N, and B vs N.
    (a) 2.45, $p < 0.20$; 11.20, $p < 0.001$; 13.85, $p < 0.001$
    (b) 1.19, NS; 6.73, $p < 0.001$; 7.80, $p < 0.001$
    (c) 2.47, $p < 0.20$; 5.27; $p < 0.001$; 7.50 $p < 0.001$
    (d) 0.69, NS; 7.69, $p < 0.001$; 7.79 $p < 0.001$
22. Comparison of the change in mean proportion of recently copulated females during 12-h day and night periods on each of 10 days in 1986, 1987, and 1988. Mann-Whitney U Test:
    1986: U = 38, NS;
    1987: U = 36, NS
    1988: U = 41, NS
23. Comparison of observation hours until first mating and those of unmated 6- to 14-year-old males. T Test:
    1985: t = 1.46, df = 16, NS
    1986: t = 2.02, df = 26, $p < 0.05$
    1987: t = 0.97, df = 36, NS
    1988: t = 1.15, df = 40, NS
24. Comparison of male reproductive success and age per year for a 4-year period. (Data normalized by square root transforma-

tion). Analysis of Variance (Student-Newman-Keuls Test for intercohort contrasts):

$F_{6,194} = 5.13, p<0.001$

No differences exist between the following cohorts: 6 vs 13 to 14, 6 vs 15+, 13 to 14 vs 15, 7 to 8 vs 9 to 10, 7 to 8 vs 11 to 12, 9 to 10 vs 11 to 12 (all others significant at $p<0.05$)

25. Comparison of number of matings with different females by 7 prime-aged bulls (7 to 9 years old when the study began) from 1985 to 1988. Kruskal-Wallis Analysis of Variance (corrected for ties):

$H = 19.92, p<0.001$

26. Comparison of variance in RS between 7- to 12-year-old and 13+year-old males from 1985 to 1988. Test for Homogeneity of Variance:

$F_{77,47} = 1.79, p<0.02$

27. Comparison of number of matings with different females by 6 old bulls from 1985 to 1988. Kruskal-Wallis Analysis of Variance (corrected for ties):

$H = 8.71$, NS

28. Comparison of degree of concordance in mating success among (a) 7 prime-aged and (b) 6 old bulls from 1985 to 1988. Kendall's Coefficient of Concordance (corrected for ties):

(a) $X^2r_{4,7} = 12.95, p<0.002$

(b) $X^2r_{4,6} = 0.63$, NS

29. The binomial probability that prime males experienced decreased reproductive performances the year after copulating (a) 3+ or (b) 2 or fewer times. Binomial Test:

(a) $p<0.015, N = 18$

(b) $p = .145, N = 8$

PART THREE

Insularization: Individuals, Populations, Ecosystems

9. Mating Asymmetries and Their Consequences

Our common cock, whose pugnacious qualities are well known,
. . . is furnished for the combat with other males, the subject of dis-
pute being . . . the perpetuation of the stock in this line or that; as
if nature had intended that he who could best defend himself and
his, could be preferred to others for the continuance of the kind.

W. Harvey 1651

In this section we shift our attention away from bison behavior and reproductive success, focusing instead on evolutionary and conservation considerations of variation in breeding among individuals and between lineages. At least two principal reasons exist for wishing to understand possible consequences of asymmetries in mating success. First, they can shed light on processes related to sexual selection, thus providing a basis to examine potential genotypic changes in future generations. Second, when populations become disturbed, either directly by human manipulations or indirectly through effects of habitat fragmentation, long-term conservation must be based on knowledge of population structure. These seemingly disparate issues are actually closely related, principally because knowledge about the degree of reproductive variation that occurs within and between the sexes will be needed for prudent management.

For numerous taxa individual reproductive success is known for multiple year periods (Clutton-Brock 1988a). This is not the case for wild mammals, for which data are available for just a few species, including black-tailed prairie dogs (Hoogland 1982, 1992), lions (Packer et al. 1988), elephant seals (Le Boeuf and Reiter 1988), red deer (Clutton-Brock, Guinness, and Albon 1982), horses (Berger 1986; Feh 1990), and deer mice (Ribble 1992). In species maintained primarily in captivity, such as black-footed ferrets (Brussard and Gilpin 1989; Clark 1989), tigers (Ballou and Seidensticker 1987), or Pere David's deer (Foose and Foose 1983), simulations or actual information on the reproductive contributions of both sexes are also available. While these types of data are generally used by conservation biologists to project changes in heterozygosity through calculations of effective population size (N_e), evolutionary biologists have traditionally focused on unconfined populations to gain insights about how evolution works. But fragmented (and often captive) populations of large mammals may soon be all that are left.

In this chapter we discuss two issues. We first describe possible evolutionary consequences of polygyny in bison by evaluating the opportunity for selection and changes in N_e. Of course, problems exist in sorting out cause from effect because social behavior influences evolution and vice versa. Our second point deals with direct effects of variation in the reproductive abilities of males of different genetic lineages. Questions about the conservation of lineages and the extent to which humans should intervene have existed for at least 125 years (Shirley 1867), but few data on the persistence of lineages in natural populations have been available. In one of the male bison lines of our study animals, possible sex-linked traits are being lost through introgression. Of equal importance, however, is that our analysis of lineage losses is expanded to include natural populations from thirteen species of other mammals representing six orders. The loss of genetic lineages is apparently more widespread than has been previously known.

9.1 Estimates of Reproductive Variance

Uses and Caveats

Data on lifetime reproductive success (LRS) have been used to estimate the opportunity for selection, *"I"* (from Crow 1958), defined as "the variance in relative fitness associated with a particular component of the life history of an organism" (Wade 1987:198). The opportunity for selection is an important process because selection is capable of promoting observable changes in the means and variances of the phenotypic distribution of traits over a generation (Arnold and Wade 1984). Although reproductive success and fitness differ (Endler 1986; Grafen 1988), the former has been widely used as a marker for the latter, with estimates of variance in reproductive success being used to gauge *"I"* (see Clutton-Brock 1988b). Debate surrounds the appropriate definition of the term "selection." Some authors restrict its usage to those cases in which the heritability of traits are demonstrable (Endler 1986). Others employ it when phenotypes differ in LRS and assume a component of heritability exists (Clutton-Brock 1988b). Because information on the heritability of traits associated with bison reproduction is lacking and our analyses were confined to phenotypes within the same generation, we use the term "selection" in the latter sense.

"*I*" has been used as a way to distinguish the relative role of natural selection from that of sexual selection, the latter often being defined as variance in reproduction arising as a consequence of access to mates. For numerous species, both the distinction and the definition have been questioned because of practical problems in assessing mortality causes and other selective processes at different life stages (Koenig and Albano 1986). For bison the distinction is probably moot. Today's bison occur in reserves where their history and current conditions govern sex ratios, age structures, and genetic composition. The dilemma in distinguishing between sexual and natural selection is blurred because most bison females produce calves (i.e., there is relatively little variability; see below), and virtually all the calves survive (see chapter 5). Hence, the primary source of any reproductive variance will be among adult males and, possibly, in offspring quality (see fig. 8.11). The real issue seems to be sorting out what bison mating systems might have been like in the past and what the consequences might be for the future. Our Badlands data allow us to suggest something about the opportunity for selection; they cannot indicate much about selection pressures of the past. If the data are liberally stretched and we *assume* that the present measures are reflective of past conditions (a big if), it is possible to comment on probable evolutionary relationships between phenotypic traits and RS.

Three methodological issues remain concerning the uses and limitations of the data. First, LRS cannot be assessed in the absence of longitudinal studies. Our study spans five years. But bison are long lived, and data reflecting a portion of their lives do not equate to LRS. Second, where age-dependent reproduction and mortality occur and the variance in these parameters is high at any point in the life cycle, short-term studies may obscure effects of increasing age. Fortunately, neither concern is overwhelming. Our study was longitudinal, measuring the RS of the same individuals over multiple year periods. Individual bulls varied in their RS, and the probability that differences in LRS would be equilibrated was slight. (The greatest degree of reproductive variance occurred within the prime-aged class). Because individual differences in RS were not found in the other age classes, the only significant period in which variation in reproduction might affect LRS was during prime age. This contention would be untrue if age-dependent mortality occurred, but this was not the case at Badlands where adult mortality was exceedingly low (see chapter 5). In addition, the relatively minor reproductive variance detected for females suggests lifetime measures may in this case be unnecessary (Nishida 1989), although potential effects of study duration should not be dismissed swiftly. The possibility always exists that small or imperceptible differences in RS can lead to large differences when traits have high heritability and are carried over long enough periods. For instance, Fisher (1958) showed that an individual with a 1% advantage over conspecifics is likely to have that trait incorporated into a population within one hundred generations.

The final issue is demographic in nature. In nonstationary populations the number of females available to males will vary, and assessments of male RS may be seriously biased if males are compared during different portions of their lives or in different generations. While adjustments for the progeny count for each individual should be scaled to the population growth rate (Arnold and Wade 1984), we made no such adjustment because all intermale contrasts accounted for age and yearly variation in the number of females potentially available.

Females and Males

In any given year, RS for prime-aged animals was higher in males than in females. Means (and variances) for males and females, respectively, were: 1985 .88 (3.2), 0.72 (0.20); 1986 1.38 (6.1), 0.58 (0.24); 1987 1.36 (5.2), 0.70 (0.21); 1988 1.02 (4.0), 0.64 (0.23); 1989 (females only) .55 (.25). The discrepancy in mean RS between the sexes occurs because our sampling focused on a subset of the population (i.e., known individuals only). Not only were variances smaller than average for females, but their yearly variances ranged from only 0.20 to 0.25, whereas males varied from 4.0 to 6.1. However, measures based on a single season tend to inflate differences among individuals (Clutton-Brock, Guinness, and Albon 1982; Arnold and Wade 1984). Therefore we used cumulative RS data on the same prime individuals for continuous three- and four-year periods. Our measures are likely to yield conservative "I" values because any mortality that might have occurred at young ages would be omitted from the analyses. Inclusion of animals not surviving to different age classes merely results in heightened selection (Howard 1988). For males, means (and variances) from 1985 to 1987 were 5.70 (38.21), from 1986 to 1988 3.95 (19.47), and from 1985 to 1988 4.93 (33.52). Again, female values were considerably less during these periods: 1985 to 1987 1.91 (1.12), 1986 to 1988 2.06 (0.93), and 1985 to 1988 2.52 (1.90). By including a fifth year for females (1985 to 1989), the mean (2.91) increases less sharply than the variance (2.51).

The change in variance that occurs by including analyses based on multiple year periods is dramatic. For males, the most conservative disparity in reproductive variance (i.e., the lowest three variances relative to the highest annual variance) was 19.47/6.08, or more than a magnitude of 3. For the four-year period, the magnitude of difference was 5 1/2 times. Females, despite their lower overall variances, exhibited differences that were more impressive, reaching 1.91 over the 1985 to 1988 period, an increase of 8 times more than the annual RS variance observed in 1986.

Opportunity for Selection and Body Size

Using the above data, we calculated the opportunity for selection, "I," which is the RS variance divided by square of the mean. Based on annual measures, male RS is considerably higher than that of females, irrespective of whether the measures include all individuals (three years or older for females, five years or older for males) or only those in their prime (see table 9.1). But when calculated over different multiple year periods, "I" is lower for both sexes as is the relative intensity of selection on the two sexes—defined as the ratio of "I"$_{males}$/"I"$_{females}$ (Wade and Arnold 1980). Irrespective of the multiple year period, "I" for both males and females was always lower than that in any single year, although depending on the sequence of years the between-period variation for females might exceed that for males. Nevertheless, the variance per se was much larger for males than for females as reflected by "I"$_{males}$/"I"$_{females}$ ratios of 3.83 (1985 to 1987), 5.72 (1986 to 1988), and 4.61 (1985 to 1988) (see table 9.2). These results suggest that it may be imprudent to use single measures of data on variance ratios as representative measures of individual species without accounting for temporal or stochastic variation.

Comparative Effects of Body Size on RS in Horses and Bison.

In polygynous mammals, the opportunity for selection on body size is generally assumed to be stronger on males than on females because male RS is affected more by size than that of females (Clutton-Brock, Guinness, and Albon 1982). There is strong evidence for size-related reproductive advantages in many species including flies (Partridge, Hoffman, and Jones 1987), frogs (Howard 1988), and elephant seals (Le Boeuf and Reiter 1988), but not in others (Lott 1979). However, data on the comparative effects of size on mammalian RS have been gathered in very

TABLE 9.1

Intensity of selection measures based on different scenarios of annual reproductive success

	Prime individuals						All individuals			
	N	$"I"_{females}$	N	$"I"_{males}$	$"I"_m/"I"_f$	N	$"I"_{females}$	N	$"I"_{males}$	$"I"_m/"I"_f$
1985	28	.334	10	1.500	4.491	35	.386	25	4.176	10.80
1986	40	.324	20	2.686	8.290	59	.731	39	3.193	3.367
1987	51	.417	25	2.000	4.796	67	.425	50	2.827	6.652
1988	60	.429	34	3.850	8.974	69	.568	46	3.825	6.735
1989	41	.710	—	—	—	—	—	—	—	—

Prime males (7–12 yrs) and females (5–13 yrs) whereas all individuals include all females 3 years or older and all males 5 years and older

TABLE 9.2.
Intensity of selection measures based on different
scenarios for multiple-year periods

N	$"I"_{females}$	N	$"I"_{males}$	$"I"_m/"I"_f$	Time period (in years)
23	.307	10	1.176	3.83	3 (1985–87)
44	.218	20	1.248	5.72	3 (1986–88)
23	.299	10	1.379	4.61	4 (1985–88)
51	.197				3 (1987–89)
39	.171				4 (1986–89)
23	.296				5 (1985–89)

Females and males must be 5 and 7 yrs (respectively) when study began for inclusion here

few cases, and even if such data were widespread the putative relationship need not always be expected. In wild horses, which are polygynous but monomorphic, the $"I"_{males}/"I"_{females}$ ratio was about 4.5 (Berger 1986), a value well within the range reported for polygynous and dimorphic lions, elephant seals, and red deer (Clutton-Brock 1988b). Although the estimate for horses may be criticized on the grounds that it was based on maximal breeding performances of animals in their prime, it suggests not only that variance in male RS exceeds that for females but also that other factors may operate on RS.

Influences of estimated body mass were no more important in dimorphic bison than they were in monomorphic horses. In bison bulls, for example, there was no relationship between mass and RS (see table 8.2) even after correcting for a possible interaction between fighting success and mass [1; numbers in brackets correspond to statistical notes at end of chapter]. And two studies of horses found no association between male mass and RS (Berger 1986; Feh 1990). On the other hand, female horses and female bison accrued reproductive advantages with increasing mass. Heavier mares were more fecund than lighter ones once effects of age and home range quality were controlled (Berger 1986). However, such effects were not striking, and only a threshold value was detectable, above which size conferred no advantage. For bison cows the contrasts between mass and RS are more problematic because the currency in which reproductive advantages are gauged differs. For example, mass per se had no effect on female RS in cows, and only when a body mass/ condition interaction was considered did mass have a small effect on calf production. As in horses (Berger 1986), the effect occurs once a threshold is reached (see table 7.4). The evidence for mass-related effects on cow reproduction can be strengthened by considering the timing of estrus, which occurs one day earlier for every 10.7 kg of mass above a threshold (see section 7.3). Because earlier-born calves weigh more in their first fall (Green 1990) and weight and juvenile survivorship are related (Clutton-Brock, Guinness, and Albon 1982; Festa-Bianchet 1988b), heavier cows may derive reproductive benefits through offspring quality rather than the number of offspring. Why males and females do not become larger in each generation is unclear.

Problems in Measurements and Application of ''I'' Ratios.

The foregoing illustrates two points. First, it highlights practical problems in making meaningful interspecies contrasts. It may be that size has more important effects on RS in males than females or vice versa, but obtaining the appropriate data to demonstrate differences that may be very subtle will not be easy. Second, much of the variation that we report in size or fighting ability may have more to do with environmental (Clutton-Brock 1988b) or social sources of variation (e.g., development; Bekoff 1976; Byers 1986; Rothstein and Griswold 1991) than it does with heritability, which is the principal factor in quantitative models of sexual selection and dimorphism (Bradbury and Andersson 1987).

Other issues also warrant comment. Distinct sexual dimorphism is found among extant artiodactyls, whereas perissodactyls are essentially monomorphic. Thus, despite polygyny in a majority of the ungulates (Kleiman 1977; Owen-Smith 1977), different genetic histories preclude the expectation of any simple or straightforward influences of body size on RS in the two sexes. For instance, phylogenetic inertia may affect equids differently than it does other species (Berger 1988), and it may be premature to suggest that selective pressures today mirror those of the past. Although potential effects of phenotypic variation on reproduction can be examined, they indicate conditions only at a single point in time. With harsher environments, differing densities, or skewed sex ratios, some effects may be obscured or exacerbated.

9.2 Effective Population Size

The intensity of selection in captive populations must be relaxed relative to that in the wild. For numerous large mammals the difference certainly must wane because the space provided by small national parks approximates that found in the largest zoological reserves. Although we have expressed caution concerning the use of data on variance in RS for interpreting selection, similar types of data are used by conservation biologists to predict the loss of genetic diversity over time through estimates of effective population size (N_e) (Frankham et al. 1986). N_e is conceptually useful in this context because it is inversely related to the loss of heterozygosity in small populations (Wright 1931; Frankel and Soule 1981). When populations become very small, the amount of genetic diversity retained is often low and the opportunity for selection is reduced. The potential for genetic drift will then be high.

Although estimations of N_e have played increasingly prominent roles in the management of insularized populations (Foose and Foose 1983; Lande and Barrowclough 1987), most methods require information on the genotypes of individuals from one generation to the next (Wright 1931; Crow and Kimura 1970; Falconer 1981). This means that knowledge of survivorship and variance in RS during such time frames is critical. But such information has rarely been available, and measures of N_e have often been simplistic, based solely on estimates of adult sex ratios. These shortcomings have been explicitly recognized in the management of bison and other mammals (Brussard 1991). Shull and Tipton (1987:40) noted, "Due to a lack of age-specific data on reproductive rates of *male* bison, calculations for N_e for males were not possible" (our emphasis). This point has been further highlighted in the use of grizzly bears as a model for large polygynous mammals: "A critical component of estimating effective population size, for which data are lacking, is the distribution of reproductive contributions among males" (Harris and Allendorf 1989:182–83).

Assumptions and Methods

To estimate N_e, we first contrasted two methods employing formulas of Wright (1931) and Crow and Kimura (1970), respectively. The first, based on breeding sex ratio only, is

$$N_e = \frac{4N_m N_f}{N_m + N_f} \qquad \text{(Eq. 1)}$$

where N is the number of breeding males (m) and females (f) respectively.

The second

$$N_e = \frac{4N - 2}{V_k + 2} \qquad \text{(Eq. 2)}$$

accounts for the variance in progeny production (V_k) in each sex. The separate measures for males and females (Eq. 2) were then combined for an "ideal" population (i.e., assuming a binomial distribution) using Eq. 1 (after Koenig and Mumme 1987). The N_e incorporating variance in RS is designated $N_e V_k$. Generally, N_e should be lower than the census size (N) in polygynous populations because not all individuals will breed every year. If they did, N would equal $2N_e$, an unlikely situation in polygynously breeding mammals, in which some males will inevitably be more successful at leaving behind progeny than others. The resultant asymmetry in mating success would increase the mean relatedness of the population and lower the N_e (Crow and Kimura 1970). The ratio of N_e/ N is the proportional reduction in the genetic size of the population (Falconer 1981).

In estimating N_e, we did not adjust for the non-Poisson variance in LRS, although this was suggested by Reed, Doerr, and Walters (1986). The possible effects of non-normality on the shape of this distribution remain uncertain, and assumptions about the variance of RS in offspring have generally seemed unwarranted (Harris and Allendorf 1989). We thought it was more prudent to report N_e estimates derived from effects of sex ratios (Eq. 1) and reproductive variance (Eq. 2), although we were forced to rely, at least initially, on the simplistic notion of nonoverlapping generations. In comparing annual variation, however, we adjusted for fluctuating population size as recommended by Lacy and Clark (1989) and Crow and Kimura (1970) (see table 9.3).

Comparison of Estimates

Estimates of N_e based on breeding sex ratio and reproductive variance from 1985 to 1988 differed, which was not surprising, as the number of known animals (breeding and nonbreeding adults plus juveniles and offspring) in each of the four years changed. The number of known and breeding (in parentheses) animals in each year were: 1985 112 (30), 1986 139 (40), 1987 169 (53), and 1988 181 (58). The adjustments due to fluctuations in population size had negligible influences on N_e; nor did the method of calculation alter N_e greatly. However, a fundamental change that resulted from the method of calculation was that the ratio of N_e/N was lower in all years except 1985, and it was more consistent when a V_k value was employed (see table 9.3).

As with measures of the opportunity of selection, any values based on a single season are likely to be biased because they do not account for

TABLE 9.3.
Summary of annual N_e and N_e/N estimates

	Breeding adults only		Reproductive variance	
	N_e	N_e/N	N_e	N_e/N
1985				
(a)	16.00	.286	23.91	.427
(b)	14.89	.266	23.12	.413
1986				
(a)	33.71	.449	28.06	.374
(b)	33.33	.444	27.44	.366
1987				
(a)	44.37	.431	41.42	.402
(b)	44.42	.431	41.35	.401
1988				
(a)	44.51	.420	44.67	.421
(b)	44.57	.420	44.74	.422

Based on breeding adults only and variance in reproduction as described in the text, employing adjustments for fluctuating population size according to (a) Lacy and Clark 1989 and (b) Crow and Kimura 1970

the possibility that differences in reproduction may be equilibrated over multiple year periods. For instance, in acorn woodpeckers, differences in parental production of progeny varies considerably, depending on whether annual or lifetime measures are used (Koenig and Mumme 1987; Koenig 1988). Therefore, we recalculated N_e using data on only prime-aged animals from 1986 to 1988, the period with the greatest number of known males and females. The same procedures as in table 9.3 were used. Total population size (harmonic mean) over this period was 137, which included 68 adults. The N_e/N based on sex ratio using the Lacy and Clark (1989) and Crow and Kimura (1970) adjustments, is 0.61 and 0.68, respectively. It is 0.68 and 0.32, respectively, for V_k. The N_e/N for breeding adults and reproductive variance (from table 9.3) changes substantially when measures include multiple year periods. That is, given a population of 137 bison with 68 adults, the N_e ranges from 21 to 46 depending on which measure is used. The V_k reduction in N_e/N over this period was greatest, 25% (a mean of 0.40 divided by 0.32 minus 1.0) over that of annual breeding seasons; when LRS was taken into account, the reduction over annual breeding in acorn woodpeckers was approximately 60% (Koenig 1988).

Numerous aspects of a species' social organization decrease N_e; the most important include variance in access to mates, differences in parental production of progeny, individual differences in survivorship, decreased generation interval, and overlapping generations (Melnick, Pearl, and Richard 1984; Chepko-Sade and Shields et al. 1987). For bison, simulations by Shull and Tipton (1987) revealed that increased reproductive rates or variance in LRS had stronger influences on N_e than did generation interval and that N_e can range from 8.4% to 29.6% of the actual population size. In their simulation model, data on variance in male LRS were unavailable so Shull and Tipton (1987) assumed a stationary population with 50% males and ratios of effective (breeding) to actual males of 90% and 60%. Our data on males (see table 9.3), whether based on annual or multiple year values, are in agreement with Shull and Tipton's suspicions that their measures were conservative. Although they report lower N_e/N ratios than we estimated, the discrepancy may be more apparent than real. Their simulations were based on lifetime estimates, whereas our data represented multiple years within the lives of individuals. Evidence exists to support the idea that when data are expanded over longer periods of time the N_e/N ratio declines, as is the case with our Badlands data. Therefore the simulations of Shull and Tipton (1987) are within the range of our findings. Despite necessary simplifying assumptions, it is encouraging that results of their simulations and our empirical data are comparable.

9.3 Introgression of a Male Lineage

The preceding sections have dealt with reproductive variance in the context of selection and N_e, but we have yet to consider the degree to which socially restricted mating leads to the differential representation of genetic lineages at Badlands. Animals derived from two founding populations were the basis for the lineages at Badlands, designated here as CL and NL to delineate their Colorado and Nebraska ancestries (see chapter 3).

The National Park Service introduced the CL bison to genetically enhance the NL bison. At that time (1984) it was not known that the CL stemmed from only three founders (one male and two females), and the hope was that males and females from the two different lineages would mate freely. All animals were unrestricted in their movements and a high degree of sympatry existed (see appendix 4).

Although lineages have supplemented extant populations of different species many times (e.g., bighorn sheep, alpine ibex; Greig 1979), for most ungulates information on the subsequent breeding performances or survivorship of known individuals has been lacking. This omission has had serious consequences; ignorance about individual breeding performances has resulted in inadequate assessment of most management actions designed to enhance conservation genetics. Nevertheless, much interest has been expressed about the introgression of different genetic lines. About 125 years ago concern was expressed about the incorporation of inbred deer into existing lines on British estates (Shirley 1867). Similarly, the loss of endangered trout subspecies in California's Sierra Nevada Range as a result of genetic swamping by aggressive non-native trout (introduced for fisherman) has been the source of frustration (Cowan 1973). In bison the widescale hybridization of *B. b. athabascae* by the introduction of *B. b. bison* was opposed by different groups earlier in this century (see chapter 2), and concerns about the loss of alleles through introgression or drift in small populations (zoo or wild) have been regularly expressed (Thompson 1986; Stanley-Price 1989), although counterexamples are available as well (Lacy, Petric, and Warneke 1993).

Lineage Differences in Reproductive Competition

To determine whether males or females of either bison lineage at Badlands were more successful, three life history traits were examined—female fecundity, juvenile mortality, and variation in male reproductive success. Neither annual juvenile mortality nor calf production/yr varied between lineages [2]. Although females of both lineages produced young, all matings were with NL males.

The extent to which lineage affected male reproduction was further noted by matching 37 (32 NL and all 5 CL) males by age to compare the number of offspring sired over a four-year period (between-year contrasts were avoided because different numbers of females were available in each year). Of 131 matings that resulted in offspring, only 19 of the 37 males bred. All were from the NL and none from the CL (see fig. 9.1). Whether this lack of reproduction resulted from a sampling bias due to a low number of CL males or as a biological consequence of poor CL competitive ability, was considered by addressing three possibilities. First, we used a binomial coefficient to determine that the probability that the 5 CL males would be selected at random from the total sample of nonbreeding males was 0.011. Therefore, the lack of reproduction by CL males would not have been predicted solely by their frequency in the population. However, our failure to observe breeding of CL males might have been an artifact of less intensive sampling, but this was not the case.

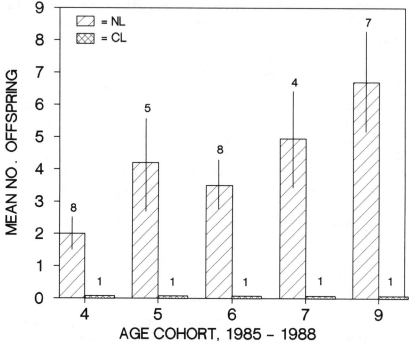

FIGURE 9.1. Distribution of estimated number of offspring produced by CL and NL males from 1985 to 1988. Only single CL males exist in each cohort; none reproduced. At the end of the study, individuals in each cohort are four years older (i.e., data for CL male and NL males in the age-four cohort reflect average contributions when individuals were from four through seven years old). Sample sizes and standard errors as indicated.

CL, Colorado line; *NL,* Nebraska line.

On average, CL males were observed 50% more than NL males ($\bar{X}$/CL male = 67.6 hrs vs 45.9 hrs for NL male) [3].

Second, the amount of time that males of each lineage spent defending females during the rut was compared. Defense time was calculated as the amount of time spent in consort with females divided by the total time spent in mixed groups. NL males spent nearly 2.8 times more in female defense [NL $\bar{X}$ = 18.49 ± 2.37, CL $\bar{X}$ = 6.58 ± 1.95%) (see fig. 9.2). In fact, CL males were nearly 1.75 times more likely than NL males to cease such defense when approached by possible competitors (58% vs 33%) [4]. Data of this type may be difficult to interpret because individuals of one lineage or the other may consistently attract larger (or smaller) opponents. Finally we considered interactions between CL and NL males of the same age when body sizes were within 1 standard deviation; CL males were displaced nearly 2.7 times more often [5], a strong indication of low social standing.

Implications of Mating Asymmetries

These results indicate that CL males were more timid, less aggressive, less able to defend females, and less competitive than NL males. In addition, the probability of CL males breeding is low, and the extinction of sex-linked traits from this lineage appears imminent as introgression between the NL males and CL females proceeds. Although the introduction of the CL was clearly intended to promote the breeding of CL females and males, only the former mated.

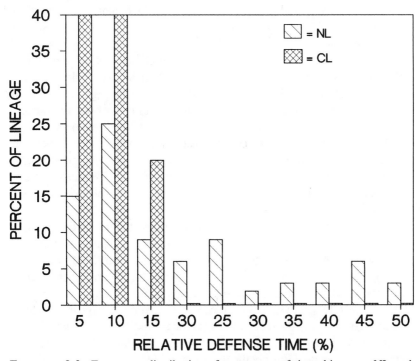

FIGURE 9.2. Frequency distribution of percentage of time thirty-two NL and five CL males defended females. Four of the five CL males were in the last quartile of respective age cohorts for the 1985 to 1988 period.
CL, Colorado line; NL, Nebraska line.

If the goals of national parks are to simulate natural conditions, then the loss of a line due to the noncompetitive nature of some individuals may not be so unfortunate, because selection continues in one form or another. On the other hand, although bison at Badlands roam the largest shortgrass prairie park in the world, conditions can hardly be considered natural. Perhaps the lesson to be learned from Badlands is that males were assimilated less readily as breeding members of the population than females, a situation exactly opposite to the practice of rotating domestic bulls in and out of livestock herds.

Darwin was well aware of the difficulties and consequences males faced as a result of reproductive competition: "This form of selection depends . . . on a struggle between the individuals of one sex, generally the males, for the possession of the other sex. The result is not death to the unsuccessful competitor, but few or no offspring" (Darwin 1859:98–99). Although many nuances of how selection operates are appreciated today, one of the challenges facing managers of the fragmented faunas of tomorrow will be how best to prevent the erosion of genetic diversity. Because most bison females mate and a substantial number of males apparently do not, the prudent way to infuse new animals into a gene pool will be to introduce females, not males. Clearly, when populations are large, the loss of a lineage through introgression may not be so serious, but the loss of alleles from small populations can be critical because of the enhanced possibility for drift (Frankel and Soule 1981). Because a high degree of variation is likely to exist between lineages that are inbred (Lasley 1978; Falconer 1981), one possibility is to preserve healthy inbred lines (e.g., Speke's gazelle; Templeton 1987), while promoting introgression in those lines where deleterious effects have been noted (Smith 1979).

To what extent does socially restricted mating prevent introgression of immigrant lines in the wild? The data are limited. Life-history studies of marked individuals are uncommon, and fortuitous circumstances must accompany observations of reproductive competition. Some information is available on interspecific relationships. Adult male olive baboons have immigrated into yellow baboon troops in the Amboseli Basin of Kenya where offspring may have been sired (Samuels and Altmann 1986, 1991). To the north, olive and Hamadryas baboons overlap. Male Hamadryas baboons may mate intraspecifically or with female olive baboons, but evidence that olive males have mated with Hamadryas females is lacking, the interspecific differences arising from differences in courtship patterns (Gabow 1975). For other species, witnessed interactions are nonexistent, even though interbreeding has been documented multiple times, for instance, between mule and white-tailed deer in the Rocky Mountains (Cowan 1962; Cronin, Vyse, and Cameron 1988) and between the native brush rabbit and the introduced eastern cottontail in Oregon (Verts and Carraway 1980).

9.4 Loss of Lineages in Other Mammals

How frequently are lineages lost from natural populations? Because the Badlands data were generated from a quasi-experimental introduction, they provide only indirect support for the idea that some lines may be lost, in this case as a result of lack of competitive ability. The question, however, is important. In the absence of knowledge about the extent of losses, it will be difficult to weigh arguments about the importance of human intervention in the conservation or recovery of populations. Because information on the retention of patrilines is generally lacking from wild populations, we focused on the persistence of matrilineages where data are available for six orders—ungulates, primates, carnivores, pinnipeds, rodents, and hyracoids. Patriline losses were also included for wild dogs because males are the philopatric sex (Frame et al. 1979). Our analyses are based on data gathered from the long-term field studies listed in figure 9.3.

Small-bodied species like viscachas, marmots, ground squirrels, and hyraxes kept only 13% to 46% of lineages over three to twenty-two years, but species the size of lions, black bears, yellow baboons, red deer, and elephant seals retained 63% to 97% of matrilines over twenty-year periods. Body size has an important influence on turnover rates (Clutton-Brock and Harvey 1983), especially in long-lived species studied for only a portion of their generation interval. Because generation intervals can best be approximated only by data from life tables when populations are stationary (Caughley 1977), information that does not exist for most species, a different measure was used to account for size. Following Western (1979), we expressed birth rate (BR = % annual recruitment) as a function of adult body weight (W) where BR = 3.09- 0.33 log W ($r^2 = 0.98$). This value is inversely related to the percentage of lineages retained, suggesting that species with higher birth rates experience more rapid turnover ($r^2 = .62$; see fig. 9.3).

Among the parameters that might affect this relationship, two stand out. First, because small species are typically studied over more generations than larger ones, the duration of individual studies must also be

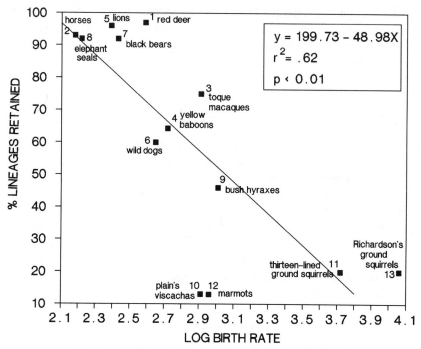

FIGURE 9.3. Relationship between percent of lineages retained and log birth rate. Data for respective studies as follows: (1) Clutton-Brock, Albon, and Guinness 1988; (2) Berger 1986; (3) Dittus 1986; (4) Altmann 1980, pers. comm. 1990; (5) Packer et al. 1988; (6) Frame et al. 1979; (7) Rogers 1987, pers. comm. 1990; (8) Le Boeuf and Reiter 1988; (9) Hoeck 1982; (10) Branch 1989; (11) McCarley 1970; (12) Armitage 1984; (13) Michener 1980. Additional life history data taken from Albon, Mitchell, and Staines 1983; Armitage 1981; Costa et al. 1986; Eisenberg 1981; and Gittleman 1986.

considered. We did this by dividing a species' study duration (in years) by its log BR. The percentage of lineages retained is still significant ($p<0.05$) although the amount of variance explained is reduced to 0.33. Nevertheless, the general finding that fewer lineages of small-bodied mammals persist over equivalent time frames seems to hold. Second, although six orders and thirteen species were included in the analyses, potential phylogenetic effects were omitted. When the analysis is restricted to members of the same family and average values are used for sciurid rodents (three species) and cercopithecid primates (two species), the sample is reduced to ten species. The simple regression of percent lineages retained plotted against log BR is still significant ($p<0.05$;

$r^2 = .43$), but with study duration included, only 1% of the variance in lineage retention is explained. What seems clear is that among-population differentiation may arise due to numerous processes (Wright 1931), one of which will be the frequent loss of matrilines in small-bodied species; the apparent lower rate of lineage loss in larger species may lead to less population subdivision in these taxa, at least over short time frames. Irrespective of the mechanisms affecting population structure, which range from stochastic environmental and genetic events to such behavioral phenomena as territoriality (Pope 1992) or poor intrasexual competitive abilities as in one of our reintroduced bison lines, these results make clear that lineages can be rapidly lost. Unless immigration occurs with successful breeding, genetic deterioration is likely to occur (Gilpin and Soule 1986; Stacey and Taper 1992).

9.5 Summary

1. The degree of variance in reproductive success was estimated for both sexes by attributing the number of offspring born to respective parents. In any given year variance among males exceeded that of females by a factor that ranged from 3 to 5.5 depending on the method of calculation. Similarly, the opportunity for selection, "I," was greater for males than females, varying from 3.83 to 5.72.

2. The comparative effects of body mass on reproduction were contrasted between bison, a dimorphic ungulate, and feral horses, a monomorphic species. For females of both species body mass influenced reproduction; for horses, the primary effect of additional weight was increased fecundity, for bison, it was an acceleration in estrus date. For males, additional weight conferred no reproductive advantage.

3. Effective population size (N_e) was estimated using measures based on the sex ratio of breeding adults and on variance in individual reproductive success ($N_e V_k$); the ratio of N_e/N was then calculated. Although variation in annual N_e was minimal over each of four years, when the more realistic $N_e V_k$ term was used, annual variance was greater. However, measures based on data gathered over multiple year periods resulted in dramatic N_e/N reductions. For our known population of 137 bison with 68 adults the N_e ranges from 21 to 46 depending on the measure used. These data are a little higher than those predicted by simulation.

4. At Badlands, one (CL) of two male bison lineages is being lost through introgression; that is, no reproduction is occurring by CL males although CL females are readily mating with males from the other line. CL males are more timid, less aggressive, less able to defend females, and less competitive than males from the other lineage. The intent of Park Service management was to increase genetic diversity by adding females and males from an additional lineage, but the reintroduction has been only partially successful.

5. The rate of lineage loss in natural populations was estimated for thirteen other mammals from six orders. From 3% to 87% of the lineages were lost in less than twenty-year periods.

9.6 Statistical Notes

1. Relationship between mean weight and RS after correcting for the effect of fighting success (during the first half of the rut) for 6 prime-aged males. Kendall Rank Order Correlation Coefficient:

   $tau = 0.33$; NS

2. Comparison between (a) juvenile mortality (1985 to 1989) and (b) calf production/year for equal-aged cohorts of NL and CL females. Chi Square Test:

   (a) $X^2 = 0.01$, $N = 236$, NS
   (b) $X^2 = 0.09$, $N = 161$, NS

3. Comparison between average number of hours of observations/ focal animals during the rut. T Test:

   $t = 2.15$, df $= 17$, $p < 0.05$

4. Comparison between frequency of departures by CL and NL males when approached by conspecific males. Chi Square Test:

   $X^2 = 18.47$, $N = 364$, $p < 0.001$

5. Comparison between the frequency that CL and NL males won interactions when encountering males of the same size, but of the opposite lineage. Chi Square Test:

   $X^2 = 5.54$, $N = 26$, $p < 0.02$

10. Bottlenecks and Lineage Mixing

Excerpts from Three Letters to W. T. Hornaday, President, American Bison Society

Concerning the number of herds of Bison which should be established . . . I should say the more the better. . . . Assuming for argument's sake that there are 500 Bison in this country, available for the purpose of perpetuating the race, it would not in my opinion be wise to divide this number into less than five herds, each to be maintained on a separate range. . . . Ten herds would be better than five if we could have the greater number.
Ernest Harold Baynes (18 January 1906; American Bison Society 1/1)

I think the greatest dangers at present to American bison are (1) Inbreeding. (2) Restriction to small ranges. (3) Protection by feeding, thus eliminating the element of self-protection.
Henry Fairfield Osborne (24 January 1906; American Bison Society 1/1)

It would certainly be well to have at least three herds situated in as many different localities, but my experience has gone to prove that under favorable conditions the infusion of new blood is unnecessary to the highest development of the species.
James Philip (9 February 1906; American Bison Society 1/1)

Reaching consensus on the best conservation tactics has never been an easy task. James (Scotty) Philip, whose herd prospered on the northern prairies in the late 1800s, believed the addition of new animals was unnecessary to enhance genetic diversity. Henry F. Osborne, of the American Museum of Natural History, thought the opposite—that inbreeding represented a danger. Harold Baynes, Secretary of the American Bison Society, did not address the question of inbreeding, but felt that population subdivision was the prudent way to minimize the possibility of catastrophic losses, particularly as a result of disease. More than eighty-five years later, there is still disagreement about how best to incorporate demographic and genetic principles when managing small populations.

Subdivision will contribute to higher overall genetic diversity among subpopulations (Wright 1978), but this would be an imprudent tactic for managers of single small populations. By lowering N_e the potential for inbreeding and drift increases within populations (Crow and Kimura 1970; Allendorf 1986), an unacceptable situation because extinction rates in inbred lines can be extremely high (Wright 1931; Dobzhansky 1970). Inbreeding in itself is not always harmful, and in unusual instances it may be promoted (Templeton 1987). It has occurred in European bison and is practiced in multiple breeds of cattle (Hall 1990). Although much evidence suggests extreme inbreeding has deleterious effects (Ralls, Brugger, and Ballou 1979; Ballou and Ralls 1982), the possibility also exists that the mating of genetically distant individuals can result in outbreeding depression (Shields 1982, 1993) or have little effect at all (Lacy, Petric, and Warneke).

This chapter considers how inbreeding and genetic variability are related to possible correlates of fitness. First, we summarize information on how genetic variation affects population performances and then speculate about potential genetic effects of demographic contractions in population size (referred to as bottlenecks). Second, given the different histories of the two lineages at Badlands, we examine the extent to which they differ phenotypically and genetically. Third, potential deleterious effects of inbreeding and outbreeding are explored. We conclude the chapter by identifying the possible roles of natural and sexual selection and how these affect the bison lineages at Badlands.

10.1 Historical Demography and Population Contractions

Bottlenecks and Genetic Diversity

When a population crashes precipitously, reduction in genetic diversity coupled with a loss of rare alleles may be expected (Allendorf 1986), the decline being dependent on N_e. If the population rebounds quickly, the overall loss of genetic variability is affected by the rate of population growth (Nei, Maruyama, and Chakraborty 1975). However, for populations that remain isolated, an inescapable consequence will be breeding with relatives. This may cause harmful effects because, in the absence of strong selection, deleterious alleles are more likely to be expressed in future generations. The assessment of past population sizes based primarily on narrative accounts, paleoecological reconstructions, or educated guesses may be referred to as historical demography, and it involves subsequent estimation of genetic changes and potential effects on fitness (Dinerstein and McCracken 1990; Packer et al. 1991).

Historical demography has been applied to Asian and African lions (Wildt et al. 1987), ferrets (Lacy and Clark 1989), ibex (Stuwe and Nievergelt 1991), and greater one-horned rhinos (Dinerstein and McCracken 1990). In species like elephant seals and fallow deer, both experiencing past bottlenecks, genetic variation has not been detected (Bonnell and Selander 1974; Pemberton and Smith 1985), and current survival is not jeopardized. It is also commonly pointed out that highly inbred species like European bison or Pere David's deer do not show harmful effects of inbreeding (O'Brien et al. 1985; Hall 1990). Nevertheless, much evidence points to negative effects of close matings between relatives (summarized for wild and domestic ungulates in table 10.1). While most of the information on this topic is limited to captive populations where pedigrees are available, inferences drawn from genetic surveys in wild populations strengthen the findings. Of particular interest is a drop in reproductive performance associated with decreasing heterozygosity in lions of the Ngorongoro Crater (Packer et al. 1991) and a high incidence of speculative reports of dental anomalies in wild populations of tule elk, bison, waterbuck, and feral goats (see table 10.1). Dental malformations have also been noted in bison populations from the northern prairies ten thousand years ago (Frison 1978), but the causes remain unclear. Deleterious effects of a small number of founders are well known. In addition to the effects noted in table 10.1, an inverse relationship between birth weight and inbreeding coefficients exists in a population of Speke's gazelles founded by just three animals (Templeton and Read 1983); for every 10% increase in inbreeding, birth weight dropped by 0.19 kg (see fig. 10.1).

Based on the literature for domestic animals, Frankel and Soule (1981) suggested that, as a rule of thumb, the per generation rate of inbreeding should not exceed 1%, although even this amount might not allow for long-term adaptation to changing environments (Franklin 1980). The rate of loss of selectively neutral heterozygosity (F) is estimated as $F = 1/2N_e$. Hence, a population can retain 99% of its heterozygosity each generation under ideal conditions if the minimum population size is kept at fifty breeding animals. Nevertheless, ideal conditions do not usually exist, and the 1% rule is only a short-term measure. Polygynous mammals maintained at a population size of fifty will soon lose genetic variation because of variance in reproductive success and overlapping generations. And exceptions occur. Although low genetic variability characterizes chamois

TABLE 10.1.
Summary of reported inbreeding effects in wild and domestic ungulates

Species	Environment	Effect	Reference
Indian elephant	Zoo	Increased juvenile mortality*	Ballou and Ralls (1982); Ralls and Ballou (1983)
Plain's zebra	Zoo	Increased juvenile mortality	Ballou and Ralls (1982); Ralls and Ballou (1983)
Pygmy hippo	Zoo	Increased juvenile mortality*	Ballou and Ralls (1982); Ralls and Ballou (1983)
Muntjac	Zoo	Increased juvenile mortality	Ballou and Ralls (1982); Ralls and Ballou (1983)
Eld's deer	Zoo	Increased juvenile mortality*	Ballou and Ralls (1982); Ralls and Ballou (1983)
Pere David's deer	Zoo	Increased juvenile mortality	Ballou and Ralls (1982); Ralls and Ballou (1983)
Giraffe	Zoo	Increased juvenile mortality	Ballou and Ralls (1982); Ralls and Ballou (1983)
Kudu	Zoo	No effect	Ballou and Ralls (1982); Ralls and Ballou (1983)
Sitatunga	Zoo	Increased juvenile mortality*	Ballou and Ralls (1982); Ralls and Ballou (1983)
Sable antelope	Zoo	Increased juvenile mortality*	Ballou and Ralls (1982); Ralls and Ballou (1983)
Scimitar-horned oryx	Zoo	Increased juvenile mortality*	Ballou and Ralls (1982); Ralls and Ballou (1983)
Wildebeest	Zoo	Increased juvenile mortality	Ballou and Ralls (1982); Ralls and Ballou (1983)
Dik dik	Zoo	Increased juvenile mortality	Ballou and Ralls (1982); Ralls and Ballou (1983)
Dorcas gazelle	Zoo	Delayed puberty; increased juvenile mortality*	Ralls, Brugger, and Glick 1980
Serow	Zoo	Increased juvenile mortality*	Ralls and Ballou 1983
Eland	Zoo	Increased skeletal deformities	Treus and Labanov 1971
Przewalskii horse	Zoo	Decreased lifespan	Bouman 1977

TABLE 10.1. *(Continued)*

Species	Environment	Effect	Reference
		and increased juvenile mortality	
Okapi	Zoo	Increased juvenile mortality	De Bois, Dhondt, and Van Prijenbroeck 1990
Gaur	Zoo	Increased juvenile mortality and more males born	Hintz and Foose 1982
Arabian oryx	Reserve	Increased juvenile mortality	Stanley-Price 1989
Wisent	Reserve	Decreased lifespan*; increased juvenile mortality*; decreased skull size	Olech 1987 Kobrynczuk 1985
Domestic sheep	Farm	Reduced fertility*	Lamberson and Thomas 1984
Domestic cattle	Farm	Reduced fertility*	Brink and Knapp 1975
Domestic horses	Farm	Mixed evidence	Cothran et al. 1984
Feral goats	Island	Malpositioned teeth?	Van Vuren and Coblentz 1988
Tule elk	Wild	Cleft palate?	Gogan and Jessup 1985
Waterbuck	Wild	Abnormal tooth wear?	Foley and Atkinson 1984
White-tailed deer	Wild	Decreased fetal weight	Cothran et al. 1983
Reindeer	Island	Reduced skull and body size?	Kistchinski 1971
Red deer	Island	Reduced mortality in female heterozygotes*, but increased mortality in male homozygotes	Pemberton et al. 1988
Bison	Wild	Supernumerary teeth?	Van Vuren 1984
	Park	Reduced growth*; late puberty*; origin of effects unclear	This study

*Significant at $p<0.05$; ?—admittedly speculative by the authors

(Pemberton et al. 1989), ibex (Stuwe and Nievergelt 1991), black-footed ferrets (Ballou 1989), and elephant seals (Bonnell and Selander 1974)—all having experienced bottlenecks—other species retain high levels of heterozygosity. Despite being reduced to an N_e of twenty-one to twenty-eight, greater one-horned rhinos in Nepal have more genetic variation than expected (Dinerstein and McCracken 1990). High levels of heterozygosity may result from the recent nature of the bottleneck, long generation times, or large N_e's prior to the bottleneck (Dinerstein and McCracken

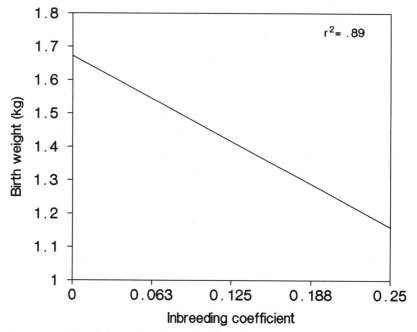

FIGURE 10.1. Relationship between inbreeding coefficient and birth weight in twenty-one captive, live-born Speke's gazelle fawns Y (weight) = 1.638 − 1.888X (inbreeding coefficient). Redrawn from Templeton and Read 1983.

1990), but whether other species had higher levels *before* the demographic contractions is unknown (Pimm et al. 1989).

Population Changes and N_e in Bison

Numbers of plains bison were estimated at 30 to 60 million prior to their decimation last century (Roe 1970; McHugh 1972). Although actual numbers will never be known, clearly bison were reduced to about 1,000 animals at their low point (Hornaday 1889; Roe 1970), and most populations today are descended from far fewer animals. What are the genetic implications of such demographic bottlenecks, and to what extent do bison lineages at Badlands differ from each other?

A reduction in heterozygosity because of a population bottleneck may be associated with a loss in fitness. Whether this supposition applies to bison is uncertain, but three scenarios are possible. Fitness may be unrelated; it may increase linearly; or it may have an asymptotic relationship with heterozygosity. Whatever the form of the actual relationship, heterozygosity should have been reduced both at the species level and to a greater extent in the CL than the NL at Badlands since the former is based on three founders (see below and fig. 10.2).

If genetic diversity is associated positively with traits capable of promoting increased fitness, evidence should be detectable in the NL animals. Although this line was founded in 1907 with six animals (two males and four females), some uncertainty exists about the source of the original animals. In the 1890s J. W. Gilbert of Friend, Nebraska, had

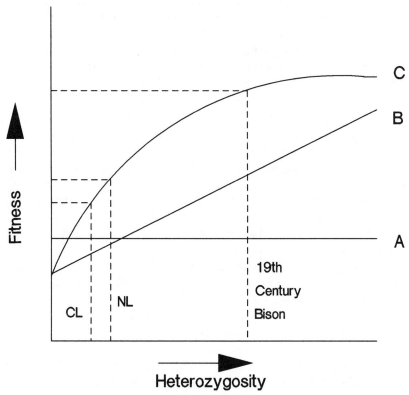

FIGURE 10.2. Hypothetical relationship between fitness and heterozygosity (based on Frankel and Soule 1981) for nineteenth-century bison and CL and NL populations. A, no effect; B, lineage effect on fitness; C, asymptotic effect (overall) with lineage effect on fitness.
CL, Colorado line; NL, Nebraska line.

about "forty head of elk, deer, and buffaloes." In a letter of 6 August 1965, Librarian R. Doner of the Gilbert Public Library wrote, "In my search I finally found one man who said he remembered Mr. Gilbert got the first buffaloes out of a wild herd in northcentral Nebraska, and the others came from Valentine" (USFWS n.d.). The NL was later supplemented with eleven males (two two-year olds from Yellowstone in 1913; four males from Custer in 1935, descended from James Philip's herd in South Dakota; and five males from the National Bison Range in 1952 that, in turn, were descended from three different herds; Malcolm 1983). Whether any of these males mated is unknown. However, the NL experienced at least three major bottlenecks; the first was in 1907 when the population was formed, another when animals were transplanted to Theodore Roosevelt National Memorial Park in the 1950s, and a third when twenty-five founders were transplanted to the Badlands in 1964 (see fig. 10.3). Although population sizes fluctuated from just a few to hundreds, three major demographic contractions occurred within sixty years.

In contrast, the CL line was totally isolated from other bison. In 1902 the governor of Colorado, James Ornran, declared, "The only buffalo in captivity in the state consists of six bison in the City Park in Denver" (American Bison Society 1/1), and in 1907 John Land, the Superintendent of City Park, wrote Hornaday to indicate that six males and ten females were in the city's possession (American Bison Society 4/8). In 1925 three animals (two females and a male) from this herd were transplanted to Colorado National Monument in the western part of the state, where they and their descendants remained until 1984 when reintroduced into Badlands. Thus although both lineages are inbred, the CL had no immigrants and began with fewer founders.

To assess potential losses in heterozygosity from the inception of the two lineages prior to their sympatry in Badlands in 1984, it was necessary to estimate N_e over multiple, unstudied generations. Because demographic data except population sizes were lacking over most of these periods, we made several simplifying assumptions: (1) the generation interval is 6.75 years, (the mean of the eight populations simulated by Shull and Tipton 1987); (2) a 50:50 birth sex ratio; (3) 100% neonate survivorship; (4) removal of twice as many adult males as females (given the sex ratio of reintroduced CL adults was 1:2); and (5) between 28% to 40% of adult males and 68% to 80% of adult females reproduce annually (see chapter 9). Breeding ages for females and males began at three and five years respectively. The means and variances in male and female reproduction were taken from our actual Badlands data. Assuming that

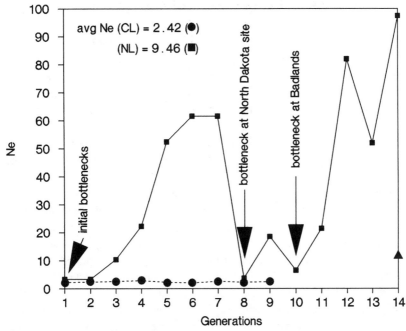

FIGURE 10.3. Changes in estimated N_e for fluctuating NL and stable CL bison populations prior to sympatry in 1984. For thirteenth and fourteenth generations N_e was combined for both lineages. Average N_e values and that for the fourteenth generation (triangle at 10.10) were calculated using Eq. 2 from the text.
CL, Colorado line; *NL*, Nebraska line.

the skew in mating asymmetries we report is representative for bison as a whole (undoubtedly it is not since variation among sites will occur for many reasons), the N_e for prior generations of bison descended from the CL and NL can now be estimated retrospectively. In addition, since information on population size was not available for every past generation, we used data from the year closest to that which would have represented the next generation. This was done be devaluing a lineage's population size by the exponential rate of increase (16.7% for the Badlands population during the field study) for years when demographic estimates were unavailable.

Following Lande and Barrowclough (1987), average N_e was calculated by $N_e = 1/2[1 - \{ \prod_{i=1}^{t} [1 - 1/2 \, N_e(i)] \}^{1/t}$ where ^{t} is the number of generations.

This equation, which uses the geometric mean, takes into account the disproportionate influence that the smallest N_e in prior generations will have on the long-term N_e (Lande and Barrowclough 1987).

During the nine generations spanning 1925 to 1981, the CL population fluctuated very little in size, numbering most often between 30 and 40 animals (Wasser 1977). Using the above formula N_e never exceeded 3 (see fig. 10.3). Assuming the best-case scenario to retain the greatest amount of heterozygosity (i.e., parity in reproduction), the N_e can be increased to 9.1; hence, over the nine generations since the CL has been in existence, N_e could have ranged from the more realistic 2.5 to 3 to the less conservative value of 9.

For the NL animals, fluctuations in population size and N_e per generation were much greater, being as high as 82 in the twelfth generation (see fig. 10.3). Calculations for subsequent generations combined the CL and NL animals. When based solely on animals in the population during the fourteenth generation, N_e approaches 100. Nevertheless, because populations may increase substantially over even a few generations and the overall N_e will be strongly affected by the number of animals during the first bottleneck, it is desirable to account for the number of generations (Lande and Barrowclough 1987). Therefore, we have highlighted our overall long-term value of N_e, accounting for generations not only for the CL (2.42) and NL (9.46) separately (that is, prior to their sympatry in 1984) but also in a combined value (10.10; the triangle in fig. 10.3) for the fourteenth generation.

Given the dramatic reductions in N_e, what is the per generation loss in heterozygosity of neutral alleles? Using the values from figure 10.3, we calculated the per generation rate of loss of heterozygosity for CL and NL animals. Based on the assumption that a 1% loss of heterozygosity in small populations may be tolerable in the short term (Frankel and Soule 1981), the CL losses are from 17 to 23 times higher than is desirable; the NL per generation losses exceed the recommended level by up to 15 times. Although the loss of heterozygosity may have been less in the NL because immigration occurred through the addition of males, the expected reduction in heterozygosity is well in excess of the recommended loss (see table 10.2).

One way to express the magnitude of per generation loss in heterozygosity is by comparing actual lineage data with the theoretical number of breeding males and females that would be needed to prevent losses greater than 1% and 0.5% per generation. In eight of thirteen generations, the NL did not have the number of breeding adults needed to minimize

TABLE 10.2.
*Deterministic simulation of per generation
loss-rate of heterozygosity (F) for bison
derived from Colorado and Nebraskan
lineages based on N_e estimates from figure
10.4 assuming no immigration*

| Generation | Lineages | |
	Colorado	Nebraska
1	.217	.145
2	.214	.146
3	.178	.048
4	.172	.022
5	.217	.009
6	.230	.008
7	.178	.008
8	.214	.135
9	.200	.027
10		.076
11		.023
12		.006
13		.010
14		.005 *
Avg./generation	.202	.051
$\overline{H}$	12.46	49.33

*Designates heterozygosity predicted to be lost per generation if
population size remains at the 1990 level
The assumption is violated for the NL population because 1 male
and 2 females from the Fort Niobrara population in 1963 and 2
to 3 males from Yellowstone in 1965 were added: for the CL no
immigrants occurred. $\overline{H}$ is the expected heterozygosity remaining
after T generations.

potential losses of greater than 0.5%, and during *every* generation the CL
animals fell well below the critical values to meet Frankel and Soule's
1% rule (see fig. 10.4).

These results make clear that populations numbering in the hundreds
have not dramatically increased N_e at Badlands, and they raise three
issues concerning relationships among historical demography, levels of
explanation, and conservation genetics:

1. In extant large-bodied polygynous mammals that have experienced bottlenecks, a high proportion of heterozygosity may already have been lost. For bison, this scenario seems to be the

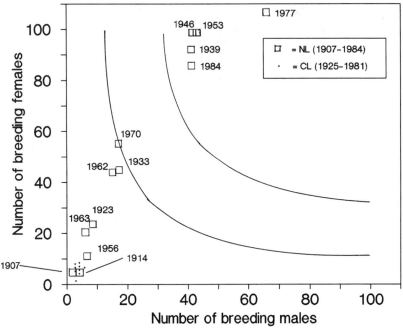

FIGURE 10.4. Relationship between number of breeding males and females needed to account for less than 1% ($N_e = 50$; lower continuous line) and 0.5% ($N_e = 100$; upper continuous line) loss of heterozygosity per generation. Points represent each generation for NL and CL bison by year (designated for NL; omitted for CL). Number of breeding males and females based on expectations using Badlands data (see text).

CL, Colorado line; *NL,* Nebraska line.

most probable, given the reduction in population size, but it remains speculative since the level of genetic diversity prior to the human-induced bottlenecks is unknown. If bison are similar to other large mammals of northern temperate regions, then they may have already been characterized by low heterozygosity (Sage and Wolff 1986). In addition, bison travel over large areas. If discrete populations were lacking, there may have been little genic differentiation. Even the allopatric bison populations noted from the 1850s to 1880s may have been separated from others for short time periods due to recent human disturbance and hunting pressures (see chapter 2).

2. A different reason for expecting low levels of diversity concerns

effects of male reproduction on N_e. There is some evidence that bison lived shorter lives during paleoecological periods (Frison 1978; Speth 1983) than they do today, and the degree of variance in reproduction during historic periods may have been closer to parity, a scenario that would reduce effects of a small founding population.

3. Several shortcomings are inherent in demographic reconstructions. Assumptions about population growth, sex ratios, and survivorship schedules may or may not be correct. And because our data were treated as if discrete generations occurred, the equations we used do not strictly apply. However, when the approximate generation time and number of adults are known, potential changes in gene frequencies in the population can be treated as if generations are distinct (Nei and Tajima 1981).

Despite these caveats, the results are important because they highlight expected losses based on current theory and indicate that in a large mammal such as bison genetic problems may arise; these can include dental anomalies, reduced life span or survivorship (see table 10.1), and the morphological deformities we report at the end of this chapter.

10.2 Differentiation of Lineages

Phenotypic Markers: Morphology and Coat Color

In chapter 3 we indicated that the two lineages at Badlands differed. The traits that were obvious to us were head configuration and pelage. Among domestic bovids, traits appearing early in life often serve as markers for specific breeds (Hall 1990), but whether such traits also characterize lines of native bovids is unclear. Each year when we first taught our coworkers how to identify individuals we regularly described the faces of CL males as shorter and stouter—almost piglike—compared to NL males. And although our impression was that these traits were good diagnostic characters, our identification based on head shape alone appeared to be influenced by pelage coloration since we noticed that the CL was darker.

We evaluated body color through use of the Munsell System, which provides color scores for hue (range of true color), value (relative darkness) and chroma (relative value of strength, that is, deviation from a neutral value of the same lightness) (Munsell soil color chart 1954). Cape and underhair from animals immobilized or captured at roundups were contrasted by lineage when both dry and wet. The cape fur was "brown-to-dark-brown'' for the CL animals and ''dark reddish-to-brown'' for the NL, differences that were statistically significant [1; numbers in brackets correspond to statistical notes at end of the chapter]. Although the underhair did not differ statistically, color values were not identical; the CL was ''brown-to-dark-brown'' while the NL was ''dusky red.'' Precipitation had no effect on pelage color [1].

These results confirmed our suspicions that the CL animals were darker and that pelage coloration, at least at the Badlands, was a valid marker. Because of small samples, head size could not be evaluated independently of color. Why the lineage differences occur is unknown, but they did not persist, because the hybrid offspring (of the NL male x CL female crosses) did not differ qualitatively from their fathers.

Genetic Markers: Allozymes and DNA

Although we considered lineage effects on reproductive competition (see section 9.3) and expected losses of heterozygosity (see section 10.1), selection cannot operate in the absence of genetic variation. Given the different histories experienced by the two lineages, it is important to know not only whether they differ genetically but also the amount of variation present. Most prior work on bison genetics has involved the use of blood groups (Stormont 1982); however, where the goal is to study genetic variability, these may be inappropriate genetic markers because assumptions of selective neutrality are violated (Knudsen and Allendorf 1987) and selection on blood groups may be intense (Yamazaki and Maruyama 1974). Therefore allozymes with starch gel electrophoresis were used to examine variation at twenty-four presumptive loci in adults from both lineages at Badlands (McClenaghan, Berger, and Truesdale 1990).

Neither line had unique alleles and only one locus (MDH-1) was polymorphic. Allele frequencies in MDH-1 did not differ between lineages, but within the NL the observed genotypic frequencies differed from those expected on the basis of Hardy-Weinberg equilibrium [2], suggesting a deficiency in heterozygotes, although the reasons for this are unclear. For the CL line genotypic frequencies did not differ from that expected [2]. Because only one locus was polymorphic, genic variability in the population appeared low. The proportion of polymorphic loci in the individual lineages and in the pooled samples was 0.042; for the total population, the observed heterozygosity was just 0.012 (see table 10.3).

TABLE 10.3.
Alleles and genotype frequencies at the Malate Dehydrogenase-1
(MDH-1) locus, proportions of polymorphic loci (P), observed (H$_o$)
and expected (H$_e$) heterozygosities

	NL sample[1]	CL sample[2]	Pooled sample[3]
MDH-1^{95}	0.448	0.400	0.446
MDH-1^{100}	0.552	0.600	0.554
95/95	0.417 (0.305)	0.400 (0.360)	0.416 (0.307)
95/100	0.271 (0.495)	0.400 (0.480)	0.277 (0.494)
100/100	0.313 (0.201)	0.200 (0.160)	0.307 (0.199)
P	0.042	0.042	0.042
H$_o$	0.011	0.017	0.012
H$_e$	0.021	0.020	0.021

[1] N = 96
[2] N = 5
[3] N = 101
Genotype frequencies expected from the Hardy-Weinberg equilibrium in parentheses; expected and
observed frequencies for the NL and pooled samples were significantly different ($p<0.01$).
From McClenaghan et al. 1990.

Compared to the only other population studied with allozymes, variability at Badlands is low. At the National Bison Range, Baccus et al. (1983) sampled seven animals and found the proportion of polymorphic loci to be 0.053 and an observed mean heterozygosity of 0.023, and Knudsen and Allendorf (1987) reported values of 0.150 and 0.047, respectively, from their sample of twenty-five animals. The greater variability at the National Bison population may arise from a greater number of founders and subsequent immigrants (Malcolm 1983), or the differences may only be apparent, stemming from laboratory differences in the levels of skill (Pemberton et al. 1989). Whatever the reason(s), Badlands bison have low amounts of genetic variability and the lineages do not differ from one another. Both were polymorphic at the same locus (MDH-1) suggesting that drift had not led to between-lineage differentiation. On the other hand, variation among populations does occur since animals from the National Bison Range were polymorphic at the GOT-1, not the MDH-1, locus (Baccus et al. 1983).

The range of genetic variation reported in the above studies was large, and it is difficult to say how bison compare to other large mammals. Several temperate ungulates, including some cervids (roe deer, elk, reindeer, mule and white-tailed deer; Smith et al. 1990), are characterized by higher levels of heterozygosity than reported in bison except for the Knudsen and Allendorf (1987) study. However, at least one large polygynous ungulate of northern climes, musk ox, has similar levels to that found in Badlands bison. Fleischman (1986) found average heterozygosity in a population founded by thirty-four animals reintroduced into Alaska to be 0.011, and it was lower (0.006) in native Greenlandic musk ox. Bison, rather than showing consistently low levels of heterozygosity, may have a considerable range depending upon a population's past.

Because the histories of lineages at Badlands differed, we were perplexed that differences were not noticeable in allozyme loci. This was probably naive since the detection of variation resulting from a bottleneck using allozymes is difficult unless the bottleneck is severe (we believe it was) and a large number of loci are studied (twenty-four were probably too few) (Nei, Maruyama, and Chakraborty 1975). Alternatively, mitochondrial DNA (mtDNA) has proved useful at resolving differences between subgroups or populations. Because it is maternally inherited without recombination and restriction fragment length polymorphisms have been used to identify female parentage (Avise 1986), mtDNA may indicate the number of maternal lineages of individuals within an area. Our interest in using mtDNA has been in assessing the number of maternal lines within the CL and NL bison at Badlands.

Prior use of mtDNA with respect to bison has involved estimation of divergence between subspecies and populations where mtDNA fragment sizes were contrasted with size standards generated by cutting with four or six base restriction endonucleases (Cronin 1986). Samples of plains bison from Yellowstone, the Henry Mountains, the Nielson Herd (Alberta, Canada), wood bison from Elk Island National Park, and presumed hybrids between plains and wood bison from the Northwest Territories showed no interpopulation variation in restriction fragment patterns (see table 10.4). The lack of differentiation between bison subspecies and in discrete herds spread over broad geographical regions is disappointing since mule deer in Montana show distinct mitochondrial genomes over spatially small areas (Cronin, Vyse, and Cameron 1988). In fact, estimates of base substitutions per nucleotide for mtDNA between wood and plains bison using six restriction enzymes revealed *no* divergence (Cronin 1986). Given the relatively brief periods of existence of the CL and NL bison (nine to thirteen generations) differences may not exist, a possibility we hope to report on in the future. Other species, such as harvest mice (Ashley 1989) and black rhinos (Ashley, Melnick, and Western 1990), also show a lack of mtDNA polymorphisms.

TABLE 10.4.

Restriction enzymes and fragment patterns (expressed as size of fragments [kilobases] generated by enzyme digestion), and number of animals sampled from EINP, NWT, YNP, HM, and NH populations

Enzyme	EINP	NWT	YNP	HM	NB	Restriction fragment pattern
EcoRI	1	1	3	4		7.3, 4.6, 4.2
BamHI	1	1	3	1		5.9, 5.2, 3.7
HindIII	1	2	2	1	1	15.0, 1.67
XbaI	1			1	1	6.5, 3.7, 3.0, 2.6
BgIII		1				9.8, 6.6
PvuII	1	2			1	14.0, 2.7
ClaI	1	1		1		7.2, 6.4, 1.6
BcII		2				12.0, 4.0
SacI	1	2			1	11.0, 2.8, 2.3
HaeIII		2				2.0, 1.5, 1.3, 1.1, 0.8
Sau96I		2				5.6, 3.5, 1.6

EINP—Elk Island National Park
NWT—Northwest Territories
YNP—Yellowstone National Park
HM—Henry Mountains
NH—Nielson Herd
From Cronin 1986

10.3 Inbreeding or Outbreeding? Expectations, Evidence, and Reality

Because detectable genetic variation is lacking, does it follow that deleterious effects of inbreeding do not occur? At least one argument favors the idea. Both bison and wisent passed through successive bottlenecks, and because current reproduction is robust, harmful alleles may have been purged (Slatis 1960; Hall 1990). A different issue, however, is whether it would be prudent to neglect the absence of variation in populations that have obviously become inbred over many generations, especially since potentially negative effects of consanguineous matings have been reported in species with little electrophoretically noticeable variation. In Pere David's deer, bred in captivity for perhaps three thousand years and with a captive population derived from fewer than about eighteen founders, inbred juvenile animals may experience higher mortality despite little genetic variability (Foose and Foose 1983; Ballou 1989). Similarly, cheetahs are well known for being monomorphic, but inbred animals may also incur higher mortality than noninbred ones (O'Brien et al. 1985). Further, demographic analyses of mink on ranches in Sweden revealed that, although historically inbred, the more inbred lines experienced greater mortality (Johannson 1961). Thus despite the commonly cited expectation that deleterious recessive alleles have been lost from populations with a long history of inbreeding, negative effects may occur. On the other hand, black-tailed prairie dogs exposed to high levels of inbreeding seem not to suffer, as evidenced by little change in five reproductive parameters (Hoogland 1992).

Do bison lineages at Badlands differ with respect to traits possibly correlated with fitness? We examine this question using some of the information already presented and with new data. Because the analyses focus on juveniles of the F_1 generation, it is important to recall that no CL males mated (see section 9.3); therefore the F_1 juveniles are products of either NL male x NL female (i.e., inbred or purebred; also designated linebred by breeders of domestic livestock) or NL male $\times$ CL female (i.e., hybrid or, in our case, outbred) matings. Maternal lines were either NL or CL, but because of the lack of mating by one lineage the paternal lines were always NL.

Detection of Direct and Indirect Correlates of Fitness

The differential survivorship of phenotypes with heritable variation is among the most dramatic demonstration of fitness (Endler 1986), and, indeed, among wild red deer, juvenile heterozygote females had reduced mortality and male juvenile heterozygotes died more (Pemberton et al. 1988). In juvenile bison, survival is so high (in excess of 97% annually; chapter 5) that to show statistical disparities between lineages would be nearly impossible, even if they existed; a sample of one hundred births annually would preclude detection of differences unless extreme (Ballou 1989). And in favorable environments or under conditions of resource abundance, any putative negative effects of inbreeding might not be evident. Therefore it was not unexpected that neither juvenile mortality nor calf production varied between the bison lineages (for analyses see section 9.3).

However, less direct but still important effects are possible. These include modification of growth rates, ages at puberty, developmental stability, and disease resistance, all of which have genetic bases (Allendorf and Leary 1986). For instance, heterozygous oldfield mice from the southeastern United States were better buffered against weight losses when food was scarce than were more homozygous conspecifics (Teska, Smith, and Novak 1990). In addition, an association exists between fetal growth rate and heterozygous protein loci in white-tailed deer (Cothran et al. 1983), although this is complicated by the possibility that faster growing fetuses may have compensated for late conceptions (as may be the case for bison; see chapter 6). Nevertheless, influences of reduced heterozygosity or inbreeding are not always apparent; an effect of consanguineous matings on fetal growth and development in humans was not evident in Tamil Nadu State, India, (Rao and Inbaraj 1980), and for deliberately inbred and outbred deer mice, reproductive differences were traceable to a population's history (Ribble and Millar 1992).

At least three difficulties confront study of possible relationships between genetic lineages and fitness correlates of juvenile organisms not held in the laboratory. First, where populations differ genetically but occur in varied locations, such as salmon in different streams (Beachum and Murray 1987), environmental rather than genetic variation may account for differing performances. Second, even at the same site, maternal influences on juvenile growth or survivorship may be great if mothers vary widely in body size or dominance (Silk 1983; Derrickson 1988; Trombulak 1991). Third, environmental stochasticity, including climatic variation or predation, may exert effects on juveniles that are independent of the mothers.

To show genetic effects in wild populations will always be problematic because it is nearly impossible to control for the effects of all potentially relevant environmental sources of variation—food, age, social status, degree of genetic differentiation, population history, weather, predation, parental effects, and undoubtedly other variables. Nonetheless, some information on associations between fitness correlates and changes in genetic history among wild populations are available (Packer et al. 1991). Because both genetic and environmental factors underlie reproduction, it seemed reasonable to expect differing performances of the two Badlands bison lineages given their differing histories and effective population sizes.

Growth Rates and Puberty.

Our data allowed examination of lineage effects on growth rates and ages at puberty, both factors ultimately related to reproduction. Fortunately, many of the difficulties raised above could to a large extent be avoided at Badlands. Both bison lineages occurred at the same site, had similar home ranges (see appendix 4), and were unaffected by predation (see chapters 4 and 5). Unlike several other ungulates (Berger 1986; Gosling 1986), bison do not use discrete home ranges or practice resource defense, making it unlikely that any growth-related variation among juveniles would be a consequence of differences in home range quality. And possible influences of maternal size, condition, and age, all of which are known to affect juvenile growth in other species (Clutton-Brock, Guinness, and Albon 1982; Trites 1991), could be controlled statistically because detailed life-history information was available (see below).

To calculate juvenile growth rates we used the photogrammetric device described in chapter 3 in which known head sizes were scaled to actual body weights explaining 84% to 87% of the variance in body mass (see chapter 6). To assess the extent to which the neonate's mass (the dependent variable) was affected by its age, its mother's mass, and its year of birth, we used multiple regression. Only calf age produced a significant effect [3]. Growth trajectories were then contrasted between the sexes within a lineage and then between lineages.

Irrespective of lineage, calves of either sex did not differ in their growth trajectories. F_1 males of both outbred (CL females × NL males)

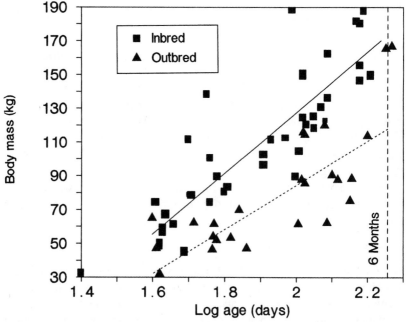

FIGURE 10.5. Comparison of calf growth rates of F_1 inbred (squares: NL x NL) and outbred (triangles: NL x CL) matings. Regression lines are both significant at $p < 0.001$ and differ from one another (see text).
CL, Colorado line; NL, Nebraska line.

PHOTO 10.1. Two ten-week-old male calves of different size.

and inbred (NL females x NL males) descent were a little heavier than respective females (6.6% and 6.9%), but because neither slopes nor elevations differed [4], data from the sexes were pooled. In contrast, between-lineage variation in calf growth was dramatic (see fig. 10.5 and photo 10.1). Simple linear regressions of calf mass (Y) on log age (X) were, $Y_{CL} = 132.95$ log X- 179.12 ($r^2 = 0.66$, $p<0.001$) and $Y_{NL} = 176.33$ log X- 225.68 ($r^2 = 0.75$, $p<0.001$). At 180 days of age, inbred juveniles weighed 172 kg, whereas outbred juveniles weighed 121 kg, or only 70% the mass of their inbred counterparts; these differences were highly significant [5].

In addition to growth, the ages at which young females of outbred (CL x NL) and inbred (NL x NL) descent produced their first calves were contrasted. For F_1 outbred females it was later ($\bar{X} = 3.9 \pm 0.2$ years) than for F_1 inbred primiparous cows ($\bar{X} = 3.2 \pm 0.1$) [6], an unsurprising find given the slower growth rates of outbred juveniles (see fig. 10.5). What was unanticipated was that outbred young females were more than 30 kg lighter ($\bar{X} = 385.1 \pm 9.8$ kg for outbred; $\bar{X} = 416.2 \pm 12.3$ for inbred) when they first reproduced, despite being older than those of pure NL descent [6].

With respect to direct and indirect correlates of fitness, the results can be summarized as follows. Lineage differences in juvenile survivorship or mortality were absent. Hybrid juvenile males and females (i.e., those of maternal CL descent) grew slower; age of first calf production was later and body mass was less for outbred females than for young purebred (= inbred) females. Two not necessarily exclusive consequences of these lineage differences in growth may be expected. First, because additional body mass buffers against mortality when environmental conditions are extreme (Murie and Boag 1984; Calambokidis and Gentry 1985; Iason 1989), descendants of the outbred line might experience strong negative selection during cold winters. Second, and more importantly, is that differences in the age at puberty usually result from tradeoffs between growth and later reproduction. If, by maturing later, females of CL (outbred) descent were larger and produced more lifetime offspring, then few costs of delayed reproduction would exist. Northern elephant seal cows that gave birth as three-year olds experienced greater mortality and were less likely to achieve high reproductive success than those that pupped later (Reiter and Le Boeuf 1991). But the opposite appears to be true for bison, at least based on data from Wind Cave National Park. Over a seven- to nine-year period, female bison that matured early had more offspring; somatic growth was sacrificed for reproduction and age at first reproduction explained 33% of the variance in offspring production (Green and Rothstein 1991a). The differences in lifetime reproduction likely to accrue with early offspring production, at least in bison, is well in excess of the 1% advantage that Fisher (1958) maintained would be incorporated in one hundred generations if the population was large. Hence the differences in growth trajectories and correlated age at first reproduction between F_1 inbred and outbred juveniles would be likely to result in long-term selection against the animals of outbred descent. These mixed results from other studies may arise due to true interspecies differences, or they may stem from variation in the relative abundance of food resources. Wind Cave animals are maintained on a high nutritional plane by biannual roundups.

Evidence for Inbreeding or Outbreeding?

Although our analyses demonstrate retarded growth in both calves and young females in the lineage (CL) with fewer founders and no immigrants, the data were for the F_1 generation only. Whether the effect arose as a consequence of inbreeding or outbreeding is difficult to say. If the former, then the CL x CL and NL x NL matings (scenarios [A] and [D] from table 10.5) should have produced purebred offspring that were slower growing than the hybrids. Alternatively, if outbreeding depression occurred, hybrid (outbred) offspring of NL x CL matings ([B] and [C] from table 10.5) should be slower growing than those of the purebred lines. Unfortunately, the absence of breeding by CL males prevents discrimination between the conflicting predictions. Nevertheless, because data on growth in the F_1 purebreds (i.e., inbred juveniles) exceeded that of the F_1 hybrids (i.e., outbred juveniles), the idea of outbreeding depression cannot be rejected. To support the contention that relatively greater depressive effects of inbreeding (instead of outbreeding) occur requires the demonstration that the growth rates of F_1 hybrids exceed those of the inbred juveniles in the absence of competing sources of environmental variation; the actual data show the converse to be true. Irrespective of the cause(s) of differences in growth and sexual maturation, our results suggest that when future programs are designed to bolster genetic diversity in previously inbred populations, it will be prudent to consider the possibility of outbreeding effects (see table 10.5).

Possible Effects of Other Variables.

As is true of virtually any field study, the available data do not allow a clean separation of environmental effects from genetic ones. Of the many potential sources of variation, four stand out.

1. Although maternal size had no effect on calf growth trajectories, if the CL and NL mothers differed consistently in body condi-

TABLE 10.5.

Summary of possible and actual mating relationships of male and female bison of CL and NL lineages at Badlands National Park and effects of mating relationships on four life-history traits for F_1 generation

Male	Female	F_1	Comment or Parameter
A) CL ×	CL	Pure (inbred); none produced	CL males did not mate
B) CL ×	NL	Hybrid (outbred); none produced	CL males did not mate
C) NL ×	CL	Hybrid (outbred)	Growth slower*; puberty later*; fecundity[NS]; juvenile mortality[NS]
D) NL ×	NL	Pure (inbred)	Growth faster*; puberty earlier*; fecundity[NS]; juvenile mortality[NS]

CL = Colorado lineage
NL = Nebraska lineage
*Differences between F_1 outbred (CL × NL) and inbred (NL × NL) progeny are significant at $p < 0.05$.

tion rather than mass per se, offspring growth could have been compromised. This was not the case, as lineage effects on body condition were not detectable [7].

2. The CL animals may have become locally adapted to desertlike conditions in western Colorado before their reintroduction into Badlands. This seems improbable because the CL and NL animals shared the same home ranges (see appendix 4). However, because CL mothers were exposed to different foods during their ontogeny in Colorado, the possibility exists that they may have learned to eat different grasses than did NL mothers when at Badlands. If so, neonatal growth trajectories would have been a consequence of the indirect effects of milk provisioning by mothers during their calves' first six months. Although this scenario cannot be dismissed, it too seems unlikely because both wild and domestic herbivores tend to select the most nutritious forage (Hudson and White 1985), and, in cattle, stronger inbreeding effects are usually most apparent before, rather than after, weaning (Dinkel et al. 1968).

3. Although nonlinear equations are often employed in analyses of growth (Zullinger et al. 1984), where the aim is to assess short-term changes, linear models seem appropriate and have been used regularly (Falconer 1984; Smith et al. 1987; Altmann and Alberts 1987; Foltz, Hoogland, and Koscielny 1988).

4. Either noninherited or genetically based maternal effects might account for lineage differences in calf growth and correlated ages at puberty. For instance, maternal nutrition affects neonate body mass (a nongenetic influence), and it is possible that individuals who display effects of a particular gene may not even possess that gene (Riska 1991). Although we examined for effects of the former through assessments of maternal condition [7], in bison it is not possible to assess the latter. Our data do permit us to assess whether mothers of the two lineages consistently differed in dominance. We restricted analyses to five- to thirteen-year olds, the cohort in which reproductive variation was undetectable (see chapter 7). Matrices of interactions were constructed and dominance ranked ordinally by the outcomes of winners and losers on a per year basis (see appendix 5). Individuals were assigned to the highest dominant rank when they had the greatest disparity in wins versus losses; for ties, individuals were given a higher status when an additional win would give

them a higher percentage (as for bison # NL-1 in appendix 5).
Because the calves of outbred descent grew slower (see fig.
10.5), we expected CL mothers to be subordinate to NL cows.

Lineage dominance was gauged in two ways. First, using the total
number of interactions irrespective of the lineage of the dyadic partner,
we asked whether an association between rank and lineage existed. None
did over the four-year period 1985 to 1988 [8] (see appendix 5). Second,
we checked for the predicted relationship using data only when interactions were with dyad members of the opposite lineage; that is, the between-lineage winners and losers of interactions were assessed with
within-lineage interactions being excluded. Nevertheless, in only one of
four years did the dominance rankings of mothers of one lineage approach
statistical significance [8]. These were CL, not NL, mothers, the opposite
of what we predicted, had maternal social dominance contributed to the
enhanced neonatal growth rates of calves of inbred descent. Thus, although not all variables were controlled, the available data suggest that
the hypothesis that outbreeding may have contributed to diminished
growth of F_1 calves of CL origin cannot be rejected.

Comparisons with Wild and Domestic Mammals

Studies of effects of genetic diversity or inbreeding on growth both
contradict and support our findings. In prairie dogs, for instance, neither
maternal nor offspring heterozygosity influenced juvenile growth rates
(Foltz, Hoogland, and Koscielny 1988), and in domestic sheep, lamb
weight at birth and at thirty days was unaffected by inbreeding (Dassat
and Sartore 1960). However, in captive rhesus macaques, birth weight
was lower for inbred animals, but subsequent effects on growth were not
found (Smith 1986). Mice of lineages under intense selection varied with
respect to age and weight at puberty (Falconer 1984). The most extensive
data for ungulates come from studies of domestic cattle (Barlow 1978),
and myriad effects have been reported. Among the most common are
inverse relationships between inbreeding and survivorship, growth, and
fertility (Burgess, Landblom, and Stonaker 1954; Dinkel et al. 1968;
Urick et al. 1968; MacNeil et al. 1989). The findings for cattle in
particular, although based on huge sample sizes relative to ours for bison,
confirm that even when inbreeding is deliberately practiced it can be a
problem and lead to a diminution in fitness-related traits.

Deformities of Unknown Origin at Badlands

From 1985 to 1990 we discovered twelve morphological anomalies in bison. Nine involved NL animals, of which eight had malformed feet or limbs. Three were already present when the study began; a yearling female with a deformed left rear hoof, a male yearling with rear legs badly bowed and recurved hooves that prevented rapid locomotion, and a spike missing part of his rear leg (see photos 10.2, 10.3, 10.4, and 10.5). The leg injuries might have stemmed from barbed wire that remains on the ground in a few locations where homesteaders cordoned off areas for their cattle during the early part of the century. This seems an unlikely explanation, given our discovery in subsequent years of five additional

PHOTO 10.2. Comparison of malformed left rear and normal right hoof in a yearling female.

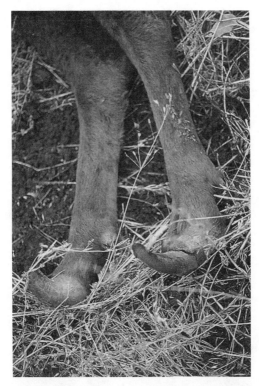

PHOTO 10.3. Abnormal hooves of a two-year-old male

PHOTO 10.4. The male from photo 10.3 as a four-year-old, rolling in an aggressive display

PHOTO 10.5. Diminutive four-year-old male missing a portion of his right rear foot, which does not reach the ground

PHOTO 10.6. Calf missing a portion of his right front leg

leg malformations, all in calves, including two less than a week old and one on its first day of life. The deformities included two individuals with parts of their front legs missing at the metacarpus, another lacking a hoof on the front leg, and two missing hooves from rear legs (see photo 10.6). In cattle these types of conditions are referred to as "amputated" and "arthrogryposis" (bowed or twisted limbs) and are presumed to be genetically based (Lasley 1978). An additional anomaly was the occurrence of an umbilical hernia in a female calf. The final three malformations, all in CL male bison, were cases of kinked tails, a condition known as "screwtail" in cattle (Kanpp, Emmel, and Ward 1937).

The origins of these morphological deformities are unclear. They may have resulted from the maternal ingestion of plants high in alkaloid levels during pregnancy, a recurring problem for livestock operators on public lands (Keeler et al. 1977). If so, it seems odd that similar deformities are not found in other bison populations, some of which have been extensively studied and occur in prairie habitats not dissimilar to Badlands. On the other hand, if such problems arose as a result of extensive inbreeding, then enhanced genetic management will be needed at Badlands.

10.4 Overview of Natural Selection, Sexual Selection, and Bison Conservation Genetics

In free-roaming undisturbed vertebrates, breeding with individuals from widely separated areas is not likely to be a serious concern of conservation geneticists. It is of theoretical importance because of its implications for understanding evolutionary events. But the specter of inbreeding and outbreeding effects in fragmented populations, or those reintroduced into former habitats, is real. For the "islandlike" bison of the Badlands, the effects of lineage were evaluated at multiple levels and suggest underlying processes that we had not considered when our study began.

Sexual selection, operating through effects of male-male competition, caused social restrictions on mating whereby adult males of an entire lineage were denied access to estrous females (see figs. 9.1 and 9.2); their failure to breed can result in a loss of sex-linked traits through introgressive hybridization. Other effects of lineage were expressed. However, rather than implicating sexual selection, the source can be traced to natural selection; F_1 juveniles of outbred descent experienced slower growth and gains in body mass (see fig. 10.5). With other factors equal, delayed puberty will result in fewer lifetime offspring and, therefore, have serious fitness consequences because the lineage of juveniles (in this case, outbreds) characterized by slow growth would be selected against. Given enough time, selection could be witnessed at two levels at Badlands: first, through intrasexual effects on male reproduction, and second, by natural selection operating on a female's ability to produce fast-growing calves that mature early and live to reproduce.

Regrettably, the lack of mating by one lineage of males prevents the best possible separation of inbreeding effects versus those of outbreeding. With the exception of African lions (Packer et al. 1991) and possibly Arabian oryx (Stanley-Price 1989), the detection of such effects has proved enormously challenging in natural or reintroduced populations of large mammals, principally because detailed data on individuals have been lacking. For bison, any putative demonstration of bottleneck effects has further suffered from widespread claims that a long history of inbreeding has purged potentially deleterious alleles. However, by controlling for sources of environmental variation, maintaining detailed life-history profiles, and having a fortuitous research design in which descendants of two small founding groups were known, it has been possible to identify potentially negative effects, perhaps of a genetic origin, on two correlated fitness traits, growth and puberty.

Despite an apparent absence of allozyme differentiation between the two inbred lines, the F_1 juveniles that experienced more retarded growth also had fewer founders and no immigrants during their recent history. The possibility of outbreeding depression was assessed, but only indirectly; an absence of comparable F_1 juveniles in the Badlands sample was prevented because of a lack of mating by CL males. Such is the nature of fieldwork.

It is worthwhile to remember that our results do not stem from truly wild populations, as the bison of Badlands' lineages experienced multiple, human-caused bottlenecks. Therefore the extent to which our findings may be generalized to wild situations remains speculative. On the other hand, many of the world's reintroductions may involve groups of different origins—some probably subjected to different levels of inbreeding—and it will be useful to anticipate the biological outcome(s) of lineage mixing in advance.

Data for wisent (Olech 1987) and now for reintroduced wild plains bison demonstrate limitations of phenotypic traits derived from small founding events a minimum of sixty-five years ago. Although bison enjoy a distinguished history of conservation achievements that include reintroduction into multiple areas and sometimes spacious reserves, as a species bison may be in need of serious genetic management because

N_e's have generally fallen well below recommendations for long-term conservation. Even in the Badlands population, which is larger and less manipulated than many populations in the United States (see table 2.2), it is not possible to conclude that growth, puberty, or morphological anomalies are not attributable to small founder size or lineage. Any future reintroductions will have to proceed with caution, noting the sexes, ages, sources, and histories of the new migrants.

10.5 Summary

1. The historic size of founding groups for the lineages at Badlands was determined, and the expected per generation rate of loss of genetic diversity was then calculated. During nine generations the CL fluctuated little in population size, but the average N_e varied from the more realistic 2.5 or 3 to the less conservative 9. For NL animals fluctuations in annual N_e were as high as 82 in the twelfth generation, but when the number of animals during initial bottlenecks was taken into account, the overall (average) N_e was less than 10. Based on current models, the number of breeding males and females at Badlands appears to be insufficient to prevent losses of 1% heterozygosity per generation.

2. The two lineages at Badlands differed phenotypically. Males of the CL line were darker, but analyses of allozymes revealed no differentiation. The proportion of polymorphic loci (pooled sample) and the observed heterozygosity at Badlands was 0.042 and 0.012, respectively. Bison from a Montana population showed greater variation, perhaps due to a greater number of founders or more immigrants. Based on the literature, mtDNA did not vary among other populations of bison.

3. Because the two Badlands lineages were both inbred but one was founded with more individuals, the possibility that one would perform better than the other was examined. Of the four traits examined, no lineage differences were found in fecundity or juvenile mortality. However, growth rates were lower and puberty later for F_1 hybrids of the CL female x NL male crosses than they were for the F_1 purebreds of the NL female x NL male crosses. The absence of reproduction in CL males prevented analyses of additional mating combinations. Possible consequences of the differing performances of the F_1 hybrids versus those of the F_1 purebreds include higher winter mortality of juve-

niles of the slower growing line and decreased lifetime production of young.

4. The observed reduction in traits potentially related to fitness of the F_1 hybrids relative to those of the inbred F_1 purebreds is not inconsistent with an outbreeding depression hypothesis, an idea that cannot be tested with rigor except in laboratory experiments.

5. Twelve morphological anomalies were detected during the five-year study. Eight involved leg deformities of unknown origin, all in NL animals.

6. Potential effects of sexual and natural selection were apparent. The former operated principally through intrasexual competition in which adult males from one lineage never mated. Evidence for the latter was suggested by the differing growth and maturation processes between inbred and outbred F_1 juveniles. Although the National Park Service intended to enhance genetic variability in the initial Badlands population by reintroduction of a new line, sexual and natural selection may prevent this from happening; males from the new line have been unable to reproduce, and the F_1 hybrid (outbred) neonates from it grew slower and reached sexual maturity later than young from the F_1 (inbred) young.

10.6 Statistical Notes

1. Comparison of effects of (a) lineages and (b) fur condition (wet or dry) on pelage coloration (cape and underhair). Analysis of Variance with Student-Newman-Keuls (SNK) Test:
    (a) $F_{1,31} = 15.64$, $p < 0.001$ (for cape $p < 0.001$, for underhair NS, SNK)
    (b) $F_{1,31} = 3.30$, NS

2. Comparison of observed and expected genotypic frequencies for MDH-1 on the basis of Hardy-Weinberg equilibrium in (a) 96 NL and (b) 5 CL bison. Chi Square Test:
    (a) $X^2 = 19.64$, $p < 0.01$
    (b) $X^2 = 0.32$, NS

3. Comparison of (a) amount of variance and (b) second order partial correlation coefficients for the multiple regression of maternal mass of 5- to 13-year-old cows (r_1), calf age (r_2), and year of birth (r_3) on F_1 juvenile mass (Y).

NL (inbred) males: $F_{3,17} = 71.25$, $p<0.001$ (a) 0.91; (b)
$r_1 = 0.59$, $r_2 = 0.96$, $r_3 = 0.14$
NL (inbred) females: $F_{3,24} = 20.59$, $p<0.001$ (a) 0.71; (b)
$r_1 = 0.31$, $r_2 = 0.76$, $r_3 - = 0.04$
CL (outbred) males: $F_{3,7} = 6.33$, $p<0.05$ (a) 0.76; (b)
$r_1 - = 0.48$, $r_2 = 0.93$, $r_3 = 0.83$
CL (outbred) females: $F_{3,9} = 11.33$, $p<0.005$ (a) 0.78; (b)
$r_1 = 0.23$, $r_2 = 0.90$, $r_3 = 0.41$

4. Comparison between partial correlation coefficients for differences in (a) slopes and (b) elevations in the above comparisons (statistic 3) for CL (outbred) males versus CL (outbred) females and NL (inbred) males versus NL (inbred) females.

   (a) $t_{males} = 1.38$, df $= 23$, NS; $t_{females} = 1.78$, df $= 40$, NS
   (b) $t_{males} = .96$, NS; $t_{females} = 1.31$, NS

5. Comparison of partial correlation coefficients (from statistic 3) of differences in growth of calves of CL (outbred) and NL (inbred) descent.

   $t = 3.88$, df $= 63$, $p<0.001$

6. Comparison of (a) ages and (b) weights (estimated from a photogrammetric device) at which NL and CL females produced their first calf. T Test:

   (a) $t = 2.10$, df $= 28$, $p<0.05$
   (b) $t = 1.72$, df $= 25$, $p<0.10$

7. Comparison between body condition (as described in chapter 3) of parous NL and CL females. G Test:

   $G = 0.38$, $N = 65$, NS

8. Comparison of annual differences (1985 to 1988) in dominance status (win-loss ratios assessed ordinally) between CL and NL cows that were 5 to 13 years old with respect to (a) cumulative frequency of interactions irrespective of lineage of the dyadic member and (b) only members of the opposite lineage. N is the number of different cows; the cumulative number of interactions for all cows included in the analysis is in parentheses. Median Test (as recommended by Siegel and Castellan 1988):

   1985 N $= 17$ (610)   1987 N $= 19$ (731)
   (a) $p = 0.58$ (a) $p = 0.21$
   (b) $p = 0.58$ (b) $p = 0.61$
   1986 N $= 19$ (546)   1988 N $= 18$ (571)
   (a) $p = 0.40$ (a) $p = 0.32$
   (b) $p = 0.55$ (b) $p = 0.08$

11. Landscapes and the Conservation of Charismatic Mammals

The preservation of animal and plant life, and of the general beauty of Nature, is one of the foremost duties of the men and women of today. It is an imperative duty, because it must be performed at once, for otherwise it will be too late. Every possible means of preservation—sentimental, education, and legislative—must be employed.

H. F. Osborne 1912

In recent decades conservation tactics have included the preservation of small remnant habitats, restoration of communities, captive breeding, and the awakening of public interest in environmental affairs. We now find village-based sanctuaries for red howler monkeys in Belize (Horwich 1990), the reintroduction of zoo-reared California condors and black-footed ferrets, and the proliferation of large and small environmental nongovernment organizations. All signify support for conservation at various levels, as do multiple features on wildlife desecration adorning the covers of *Newsweek, Time,* and *U.S. News and World Report.* Nevertheless, the sad reality is that chances for setting aside large tracts of habitat for protection in most areas of the world are now remote. The United States' newest national park, less than 80,000 acres in the sparsely populated Great Basin Desert, is testimony to this lamentable fact. No longer is it tenable to claim that national parks are enough for effective conservation. New methods, shaped by changes in attitudes, are necessary. The magnitude of the problem was already evident when John Vincent (1970:7) wrote of the Umfolozi Game Reserve in Natal "although on the surface appearing as a vignette of a natural environment such as was encountered by our early hunters and travelers, [the reserve] is far from being so. There have been far too many upsets in the natural order, such as the interruption of traditional migration routes by artificial boundaries, the virtual elimination of predators, and the resulting drastic changes in the habitat."

Virtually all of the world's medium-size parks, and many of the larger ones, face similar dilemmas. Disturbance is the rule. The issue is not whether a park or ecosystem is pristine; it is the degree to which species can persist and processes continue in the absence of additional human perturbations. The prospects are not good. Food production for humans continues its per capita decline in Africa as the population increases at more than 3% annually (Sinclair and Wells 1989). Less than 5% of the earth's terrestrial surface area is likely to be protected. In just over one hundred years, grizzly bears, wolves, black-footed ferrets, bison, elk, and swift foxes were lost from prairies in both Canada and the United States.

In this chapter we contrast dilemmas facing managers of bison at Badlands and coincident problems at the ecosystem level with those of other isolated reserves. Among the subtle but significant issues is how best to assure space for bison while still maintaining enough habitat for prairie dogs to support viable populations of black-footed ferrets and other carnivores. We also consider costs of conservation research and conclude by offering guidelines for managers of bison and suggestions for how behavioral ecologists can contribute to broader issues.

11.1 Insular Reserves

Badlands National Park typifies many of the world's reserves. At 98,463 ha, it is larger than about 70% of the 320 federal reserves of the United States (Schonewald-Cox 1983). And because the 9 largest are situated in Alaska, relatively speaking Badlands would fall closer to the seventy-fifth percentile. Nonetheless, Badlands is not large enough to be a self-contained ecological unit, and even with the adjacent Buffalo Gap National Grasslands, many mammals will require some degree of management if they are to persist (see photo 3.2). Bison there are truly insularized as are bighorn sheep that also cannot move the 100 km that separate them from adjacent populations; plowed fields and fences effectively sever any successful migration. Species from Badlands or areas to the east have disappeared in the last twenty years. Black-footed ferrets became extinct in South Dakota in the 1970s; we saw one beaver in 1985 but none since; and the last puma known at Badlands occurred in the early 1980s. Yet swift fox were reintroduced in 1987 and plans to reestablish ferrets in the park are underway, despite impending legislation by the state of South Dakota to prevent this.

In many ways the problems confronting managers of Badlands' 1,000 km^2 differ little from those of other isolated reserves, although both the temporal and spatial scales vary with specific conditions. The Hluhluwe-

Umfolozi Reserve is an area (920 km^2) in Natal, South Africa, similar in size to Badlands, for which we have extracted information (Brooks and Macdonald; 1983; Vincent 1970; and Walker et al. 1987). The area was set aside as a game conservation area in 1897 and research was first implemented in 1953. Elephants were exterminated in the late nineteenth century; white rhinos were driven to near extinction; and a rinderpest epidemic in 1896–97 nearly depleted African buffalo. Lions, brown hyenas, cheetahs, and wild dogs were gone by 1920, when the only remaining large predators were leopards and spotted hyenas. To eradicate tsetse flies, several ungulates, including zebras and wildebeest, were removed. Some ungulates migrated back into the area naturally, and lions and cheetahs were reintroduced. By 1967 a boundary fence was completed. As a result, existing and reintroduced ungulate populations experienced dramatic increases and culling was necessary to slow soil erosion and minimize permanent damage to vegetation. The biomass of five grazers (white rhino, wildebeest, zebra, buffalo, and impala) was reduced by 45% between 1976 and 1983, an action that included a significant number of removals from 1978 to 1981: 1,136 wildebeest, 1,524 warthogs, 36 waterbucks, 7,468 nyalas, 9,810 impalas, about 50 rhinos, and 973 buffalo. Ecosystem damage has been reduced, and compared to adjacent reserves with less active management programs, starvation-induced mortality has been prevented. Although extensive intervention remains an emotional issue, active management has been the rule for this park.

At Chitwan National Park—slightly smaller than Badlands—the problems differ radically. Established in 1973 as Nepal's first park and expanded in 1978 to 894 km^2, Chitwan is surrounded by 320 villages comprising more than 250,000 people. The density of domestic cattle adjacent to the park may be nearly as high as 28,000 kg/km^2 (Mishra 1984). Two endangered species, greater one-horned rhinos and tigers, reside in the park, and problems confront humans and wildlife. Several stand out. People have been killed by tigers and rhinos both within and outside of park boundaries; as a result, animals have been killed. In addition, villagers rely on grasses in the park for materials for their homes and are permitted to gather it on an annual basis (Sunquist and Sunquist 1988). If wildlife is to persist despite insularization, it will have to coexist with humans.

Some of the primary biological effects of geographical isolation include problems associated with small population sizes—short-term persistence, demographic jeopardy, and subsequent genetic concerns—most of them caused by human expansion and poverty. Agriculture is largely responsible for insularization of mountain gorilla and numerous species of lemurs, as well as islandlike populations of tigers, plains zebras, wildebeest, bison, and possibly pampas deer. The loss of migration corridors has resulted in the fragmentation of populations of alpine bovids, and the compression of elephants and other big mammals into small parks has not only created problems stemming from overabundance but also spawned controversial arguments about control methods. Not even reserves the size of Yellowstone park (9,000 km^2) or the Greater Yellowstone Ecosystem (57,000 km^2) are immune (Berger 1991b). Grizzly bears, which roam in and out of the park, kill and are killed by people; bison and elk carrying brucellosis leave the park and are shot; and elk are so numerous that damage to vegetation is commonplace. The establishment of a natural carnivore community, facilitated by the reintroduction of wolves, is likely to be the issue of the 1990s (see table 11.1).

11.2 A Clash Between Single-Species and Ecosystem Conservation

Biodiversity is the provenance of conservation, but how best to assure it is the subject of heated dispute. The restoration of ecosystems is an appropriate goal, but effective restoration practices are in their infancy (Hudson 1991), and even reintroduced populations may be in need of help. Our focus has been solely on bison, but to champion a landscape perspective at Badlands or beyond means tackling complex sociopolitical and ecological issues. Inevitably these will include how best to manage biodiversity. And at Badlands this will require, at a minimum, understanding the indirect effects of bison on other species.

The Cornerstone of the Ecosystem: Prairie Dogs

One consequence that arises when species are confined is that interactions with community members may be exacerbated. Black-tailed prairie dogs are an excellent example. They occur not only at Badlands but also at other prairie parks, where they create highly conspicuous, modified sections of the prairie (see photos 11.1, 11.2). Early naturalists described the colonial "towns" as "one of the curiosities of the Far West" (Irving 1859:189–90), noting that owls and rattlesnakes used their burrows. Catlin (1841:72) observed that prairie dogs "dig their hole[s] . . . to a depth of eight or ten feet, [their] villages are sometimes several miles in

TABLE 11.1.

Summary of recognized and suggested effects of insularization in three mammalian taxa

Species	Location	Type of isolation and presumed effect	Reference
Primates			
Mangabey	Tana River, Kenya	Habitat loss; hunting-related decline (?)	Oates 1986
Tana River red colobus	Tana River, Kenya	Habitat loss; hunting-related decline (?)	Oates 1986
Mountain gorilla	Virunga NP, Rwanda	Agriculture; loss of heterozygosity	Harcourt and Fossey 1981
Syke's monkey	Kibale Forest, Uganda	Habitat loss; declining population	Skorupa 1986
Red colobus	Kibale Forest, Uganda	Habitat loss; declining population	Skorupa 1986
Lemurs (many species)	Madagascar	Agriculture; declining populations	Jolly 1986
Mentawai monkeys	Mentawai Islands, Indonesia	Deforestation; small populations	MacKinnon 1986
Golden lion tamarins	Poço das Antas Reserve, Brazil	Deforestation; population reintroduced	Kleiman 1989
Carnivores			
Tiger	Java/Bali, Indonesia	Agriculture; small populations	Seidensticker 1987a
Tiger	Sundarbans, Bangladesh	Human pressure; change in land use	Seidensticker 1987b
Tiger	Chitwan NP, Nepal	Agriculture; small population	Sunquist 1981; Mishra, Wemmer, and Smith 1987
Asian lion	Gir Forest, India	Deforestation; prey on domestic species	Saharia 1984
African lion	Central Kalahari Reserve, Botswana	Cropped when outside reserve	Owens and Owens 1984
African lion	Ngorongoro, Tanzania	Habitat loss; sperm abnormalities	Wildt et al. 1987; Packer et al. 1991
Grizzly bear	Yellowstone NP, U.S.	Conflicts with humans; small population	Craighead 1979
Gray wolf	Isle Royal NP, U.S.	Small island; population fluctuations	Peterson 1988
Giant panda	Wolong Reserve, China	Deforestation; small population	Schaller et al. 1985
Cheetah	Throughout Africa	Prior bottleneck (?); loss of heterozygosity	O'Brien et al. 1986

Ungulates			
White-lipped peccary	Guanacaste NP, Costa Rica	Area effect; poaching (?)	Janzen 1986a
Collared peccary	Santa Rosa NP, Costa Rica	Increased seed dispersal due to restricted movements	Janzen 1986b
Plains zebra	Tarangire NP, Tanzania	Agriculture; loss of migration	Borner 1985
Wildebeest	Tarangire NP, Tanzania	Agriculture; loss of migration	Borner 1985
North American bison	Yellowstone and Teton NP's, U.S.	Agriculture; loss of migration	Berger 1991
Elk	Teton NP and Elk Refuge, U.S.	Habitat loss; artificial feeding	Boyce 1989
Greater one-horned rhino	Chitwan NP, Nepal	Agriculture; conflicts with local people	Mishra 1984
Asian elephant	Anamalais–Palani Hills, India	Hydroelectric projects; loss of heterozygosity	Sukumar 1986
African buffalo	Kruger NP, South Africa	Restricted reserve; overabundance	Hanks 1981
African elephant	Hwange NP, Zimbabwe	Habitat loss; overabundance	Cumming 1981
Hartebeest	Kasunga NP, Malawi	Agriculture; increased elephants affect other species	Bell 1981
Pampas deer	Emas NP, Brazil	Agriculture and ranches; population isolated (?)	Redford 1985, 1987
Arabian oryx	Jiddat-al-Harasis, Oman	Reintroduced population; genetic concerns	Stanley-Price 1989
Spanish ibex	Valle de Ordesa, Spain	Habitat loss; isolation	Alados 1985b
Bighorn sheep	Southwestern deserts, U.S.	Habitat loss; rapid extinctions	Berger 1990
Markhor	Pakistan	Habitat loss; small populations	Schaller 1977
Bharal	Pakistan and India	Habitat loss; small populations	Schaller 1977
Alpine ibex	Switzerland	Fragmentation; low heterozygosity	Stuwe and Scribner 1989
White-lipped deer	Qinghai Province, China	Habitat loss (?) due to grazing; small population size	Miura et al 1989

NP = national park

PHOTO 11.1. A prairie dog town with bison, a coyote, and prairie dog family. Sage Creek drainage is in background.

PHOTO 11.2. A pronghorn male and three females cross a prairie dog town. Note ear tag in left ear of female bison in left portion of photo.

extent, [and] these curious little animals belong to almost every latitude in the vast plains of prairies in North America." Recent studies demonstrate that prairie dog colonies may support increased avian diversity. For mammals, colonies may enhance abundance but not increase the number of species (Agnew et al. 1986). Prairie dogs also facilitate energy flow and nutrients to ungulates by creating vegetation patches with higher nitrogen content and digestibility than surrounding areas (Coppock et al. 1983; Krueger 1986; Whicker and Detling 1988).

During the past sixty years, prairie dog colonies have shrunk from approximately 40,000,000 ha to 600,000 ha (Miller, Wemmer, and Biggins 1990). Despite the prairie dog's critical role in maintaining biodiversity and promoting high-quality vegetation, from 1980 to 1984 alone, more than $6.2 million was spent on poisoning prairie dogs on the Pine Ridge Reservation just south of Badlands. And prairie dog hunting is apparently an exciting "sport" on the Buffalo Gap National Grasslands (Sharps 1988). Prairie dogs are unwanted denizens of the ecosystem because of their alleged negative impacts on cattle because food habits overlap (Koford 1958; Uresk 1985; Uresk and Bjugstad 1983; Uresk and Paulson 1989). One result of prairie dog eradication has been the unintentional extinction of wild black-footed ferrets (Clark 1989). These somewhat disparate facts have immediate consequences for ecosystem restoration because the U.S. Fish and Wildlife Service has listed Badlands as one of the primary sites for the reintroduction of ferrets.

Ameliorating human concerns and ecological processes will be difficult. Healthy prairie dog populations exist within the park, and dispersing individuals colonize areas beyond the park boundaries. As a result, ranchers and other users of adjacent lands (both public and private) request that the Park Service control populations within the park. Compromises have been reached, and the Park Service uses control measures along its boundaries. But for ferrets to have a high probability of persistence, multiple large populations need to be established (Harris, Clark, and Shaffer 1989). Sustaining populations of fifty or more ferrets will require interagency cooperation because Badlands is too small to support viable populations of ferrets. And the help of ranchers will be essential. Prairie dog expansion will benefit ferrets because additional prairie dog habitat means more ferret habitat.

Among the most critical factors governing the expansion of prairie dog colonies is the height of vegetation at the colony's edge because prairie dogs rely on vision to detect predators (Hoogland 1981), and vegetation height will be governed by the interaction of prairie dog density and the intensity of ungulate grazing (Cincotta, Uresk, and Hansen 1987). Where prairie dog densities are higher, the amount of available habitat for cattle is reduced (Uresk and Paulson 1989). This suggests that, at places like Badlands, the unlimited expansion of prairie dogs although good for ferrets would ultimately set limits on the size of the bison population. But the interaction is not as straightforward as it might seem. Carrying capacity depends on both food quantity and quality, and plant productivity on prairie dog towns changes with age. Older colonies are dominated more by forbs than by grasses (Whicker and Detling 1988). Any relevant discussion of ferret reintroduction will have to consider not only the dynamic nature of prairie dog colonies and bison population size, but also the management of public lands beyond park boundaries.

Although black-footed ferrets are one of the most endangered mammals on earth and rightfully deserve assistance, other mammalian carnivores are also present at Badlands and need to be considered within the context of ecosystem restoration. The Park Service reintroduced swift foxes during our bison study, but the extent to which they are affected by coyotes and badgers is unclear because so little is known of Badlands' carnivores. In other areas, coyotes kill kit foxes regularly (Ralls, pers. comm. 1988) and limit the spatial distribution of red foxes (Sargeant, Allen, and Hastings 1987). It seems reasonable to expect that responses of swift foxes to predators at Badlands would be strongly affected by the height of the canopy, visibility, and the availability of burrows. If so, then the degree to which bison and prairie dogs alter their environment will influence the success of swift foxes. This admittedly simplistic construct of community-level interactions ignores, of course, both the direct and indirect effects of insect herbivory, which can be substantial in prairie environments (Reichman 1987).

Dilemmas When Two Protected Species May Compete

In nonprairie ecosystems the conflicts that arise due to differing mandates are equally as dramatic. In the eastern Mojave Desert in Arizona, California, and Nevada, desert tortoises and feral burros are federally protected species, but how potential conflicts will be mitigated if (or when) burros consume food destined for tortoises remains undecided. Among rare species of native cattle, both gaur and banteng occur in fragmented populations, the former from India through Southeast Asia (Schaller 1967; Conry 1989). Banteng are endangered in Bali but not in Java's Ujung Kulon National Park. However, the endangered Javan rhino also occurs in this park. Because interspecific relationships are unknown, active management has not been encouraged. But if research demonstrates that banteng reduce the carrying capacity of rhinos, then translocations of banteng to other reserves will be necessary (Ashby and Santiapillai 1988).

These examples illustrate the frailty of conservation biology as a new discipline. Without a firm theoretical base to deal with immediate conservation dilemmas, problems in one area may have to be resolved with solutions entirely different from those applied in another area (Caro 1986). Mitigation tactics for tortoises and burros, or banteng and rhinos, are not necessarily applicable to ferrets, prairie dogs, and bison.

11.3 Research, Funding, and Conservation

How much does it cost to gather conservation-related data, and what will it cost to do the study? These are recurring questions in scientific research. The former is not easily addressed; simple answers are nonexistent and opinions vary with respect to what constitutes conservation-related data. The latter question is less problematic because expenditures can be summed. Funding for applied and basic research on rare vertebrates is anything but trivial. Millions of dollars are spent annually on rhinos, elephants, grizzly bears, spotted owls, and California condors. The cost to produce one surviving golden lion tamarin reintroduced to its native Atlantic coastal rain forest is approximately $22,000 (Kleiman et al. 1991); to secure fifty survivors requires more than $1 million. The more critical issue concerns the utility and efficacy of the data once a study has been completed.

There are both advantages and disadvantages to studies like ours. In chapter 1 we pointed out why we suspected that bison were a good model species, concluding, in part, that they offered splendid opportunities to evaluate questions about mating systems and the behavior and reproductive contributions of individuals. In addition, because the bison we studied had traceable histories, possible effects of lineage, individuals, and traits on potential correlates of fitness could be examined. Despite restricting some sampling events to the F_1 progeny, we believe that our data set is relatively unusual among studies of large, polygynous mammals. But the study was not inexpensive. The funding in actual dollars was about $310,000, and when the value of volunteers and Park Service support (coworkers, horses, vehicles, gasoline, etc.) are included, the cost exceeded $400,000 (see table 11.2).

TABLE 11.2.
Approximate expenditures for components of the bison study

	1984	1985	1986	1987	1988	1989	1990	Total
Actual								
Vehicle and gas	3,300	1,200	1,200	12,000	1,200	1,200		$20,100
Travel	3,000	2,700	500	700	500	700		8,100
Salary[1]		40,000	40,000	40,000	40,000	40,000	50,000	250,000
Field assistants			3,000	3,000	3,000	3,000		12,000
Veterinary and genetic subcontracts			2,500	3,000				5,500
Photographic files		1,700	1,200	1,200	1,200	1,200		6,500
Supplies/miscellaneous	1,300	2,200	1,500	1,500	1,500	1,500		9,500
								311,700
Donated or Volunteer								
Salary[2]	20,000							20,000
Roundup help[3]		1,600	1,600	1,600	1,600	1,600		8,000
Vehicle			300	300	300			900
NPS rangers		1,000	1,000	1,000	1,000	1,000		5,000
Trailer		500						500
Vehicles for field assistants		2,000	2,000	2,000	2,000	2,000		10,000
Field assistants		12,000	12,000	12,000	12,000	6,000		54,000
								98,400
Total								$410,100

[1] Includes project-related salaries for the principal investigators
[2] Estimated salary had PI's received one
[3] Includes deferred costs of National Park Service employees to assist for the 1 to 3-day capture and processing of bison
Actual costs are real dollar amounts; donated or volunteer support are estimates

Bearing these figures in mind, what can realistically be achieved by studying large mammals? If conservation-oriented research is to be judged solely by contributions to evolutionary issues or questions about genetics in organisms with long generation times, then large mammals will make poor paradigms. As evident in our data, information on N_e or the opportunity for selection will necessarily employ numerous assumptions and not be easily gathered. The time frame (i.e., number of generations) covered by field studies will always be comparatively short and open to the criticism that events noted in one study generation may be reversed in the next. Even though statistical means are available to attenuate this problem, it is fruitless to argue that large (or even small) mammals will regularly be good investments for research dollars where the primary aim is to develop or refine evolutionary theory. Fortunately, conservation-oriented studies are rarely directed toward evolutionary theory. Study of mammals, especially those of the flagship variety, continue to serve as rallying points for the development of political and social support as well as for understanding components of ecosystems. Although there should be no substitute for rigorous data collection or concept-based science, the lessons to be learned from studies of organisms that differ in life histories will inevitably prove to be important in conserving biodiversity.

Decade-long studies are not an option available to most management agencies, nor are they feasible as a mechanism for saving most of the earth's endangered species. Relatively inexpensive ways to generate data include modeling and simulation. Both are critical in planning and in science, but neither should be used if empirically derived tests are possible. Although neither government nor nongovernment organizations have the fiscal reserves or the time for long-term studies, education and planning for future changes are one way to avoid crisis management.

Funding for the maintenance and understanding of biodiversity will have to be increased if conservationists are not destined to fail. Startling asymmetries exist. During the Reagan and Bush administrations, the federal government spent approximately $58 million annually on public lands for "range improvements," although only 2% of the total U.S. beef is produced there. An additional $10 million was committed each year to the management of feral horses and burros. About $27 million was spent annually on endangered species (Berger 1991c). Given that more than four hundred species are listed by the U.S. government as threatened or endangered, for every federal dollar allocated for exotic mammals on public lands, less than 0.1 cent was directed toward each threatened and endangered species (Berger 1991c). If we are not to witness the unconscionable loss of thousands (perhaps millions) of species in the coming decades, more will have to be done.

11.4 Applications of Research

General Guidelines for Bison

For bison, two major issues of the future are the retention of genetic diversity and the unavoidable flurry of difficulties that arise because of increasing (yet confined) populations in predator-free environments. Badlands' bison, with the unusual string of morphological anomalies in the Nebraskan lineage (see chapter 10) and the lack of mating by males of the Colorado lineage (see chapter 9), highlight the problem of retaining genetic diversity. The possible spread of diseases such as brucellosis and tuberculosis and the potential damage to fences, humans, and agriculture outside parks, and the damage to vegetation within them illustrate the second problem. Because no unifying theory has yet been developed to encompass such issues once populations have been confined in small reserves or ecosystems have been fragmented, we outline major issues and how to deal with them. Although we distinguish between ecosystem and population management, it is a rather arbitrary distinction.

Actions at the Level of Ecosystems.

1. Reserves designed for more than a single species (e.g., bison farms) should be guided by a scientific advisory committee composed of animal and plant ecologists, a resource manager, a population geneticist, and a behavioral ecologist.
2. Where areas are sufficiently large, bison migration should be encouraged, much as a rest-rotation system is employed to minimize damage by cattle on vegetation.
3. Where reserves are small, bison need to be intensively managed so that plant communities are not irreparably harmed. However, what constitutes harm is a matter of debate and often dependent on one's background (Houston 1982; Coughenour and Singer 1991; Brussard 1992). Clearly, intensive monitoring systems of plant communities are needed.
4. The possibility of a vast federal reserve, a "buffalo commons," in the northern prairies has been suggested (Popper and Popper 1987).The human population (400,000) in an area nearly

350,000 km² is declining, and it may cost American taxpayers more to subsidize farms there than to restore the area ecologically and then attract tourists (Mathews 1992). Although intriguing, the plan needs to be scrutinized by various people from economists, local landowners, ecologists, and sociologists to local, state, and federal politicians and policymakers.

Actions at the Level of Populations.

Continentwide, bison are no longer in demographic jeopardy, and attention should now turn toward ensuring the maximum genetic diversity so that opportunities for further adaptation are available. This involves many steps:

1. When populations become too large, "excess" animals that are not killed should be used to subsidize other herds or begin new ones.
2. Rules for monitoring and detailed record keeping should be developed so that bison in different reserves can be managed as a metapopulation. Either the U.S. National Park Service or the U.S. Fish and Wildlife Service should take the lead.
3. The extent of genetic diversity in different populations must be determined and efforts to conserve rare alleles formalized.
4. Migration between herds must be induced through artificial means. To some extent this is already being done, but formal guidelines are not in place. Because females have a better chance of reproducing than males, females should be relocated.
5. Migrants should always be identified and their reproductive fates noted and compared to those of resident individuals.
6. A common argument is that populations should be as large as possible and stabilized at carrying capacity (Foose and Foose 1983), but it may be impossible to reconcile this goal with those of ecosystem managers (see below).
7. Culling strategies should not be random, but based on increased attention to demographic and genetic consequences (Shull and Tipton 1987).

Among the most contentious of these recommendations will be the maintenance of the largest populations possible. Where migration is prevented in mobile species, damage to the ecosystem is unavoidable because heavy grazing impedes plant growth and reproduction (Walker et al. 1987; Sinclair and Wells 1989). Although early travelers to the prairies reported large, even huge, bison herds, they also noted that days or weeks could pass with only an occasional sign of bison (Catlin 1841; Allen 1875a; Hornaday 1889; Grinnell 1892), an indication that herd movements allowed the vegetation a respite from incessant grazing. To-day's confinement of large herds within small reserves is not the best way to approximate past conditions although it may result in large effective population sizes. An alternative to the maintenance of large N_e's is the artificial migration of females every few generations.

Some Guidelines for Behavioral Ecologists

How can behavioral ecologists enhance conservation efforts? We see two primary avenues, one research-related, the other dealing with broader issues. From a research perspective, valuable study can be achieved in numerous areas (see table 11.3). These include:

1. Dispersal, which is critical to understanding the spatial dispersion of individuals as well as the potential for inbreeding and other aspects of population structure;
2. Social structure and reproductive success, which bear directly

TABLE 11.3.

Selected examples of themes in mammalian behavioral ecology that have been applied to conservation

Theme	Application	Species	References
Dispersal	Inbreeding/population structure	Horses, prairie dogs, baboons	1–4
Social structure and re-productive success	Population structure	Primates and numerous other taxa	5–8
Sexual selection and mate choice	Population structure	Bison	This study
Social demography	Population dynamics	Baboons, red deer	9–11
Foraging-predation trade-offs	Reintroduction and as-sessment of human dis-turbance	Tamarins, ferrets, pronghorn	12–14
Spatial distribution	Reserve size/corridors	Tigers	15–16
Communication	Reintroduction/dispersal	Hyraxes, ground squirrels	17

1—Berger and Cunningham 1987; 2—Hoogland 1982; 3—Packer 1979; 4—Ralls, Harvey, and Lyles 1986; 5—Chepko-Sade and Halpin 1987; 6—Melnick and Pearl 1987; 7—Pope 1992; 8—Clutton-Brock (1988a); 9—Dunbar 1985; 10—Altmann 1980; 11—Clutton-Brock et al. 1982; 12—Berger et al. 1983; 13—Kleiman et al. 1986; 14—Miller et al. 1990; 15—Sunquist 1981; 16—Smith and McDougal 1991; 17—Smith and Peacock 1990

on assessments of the genetic organization of species or populations;

3. Sexual selection and mate choice, which are related to the above issues and have fundamental links to quantitative genetics and population structure, particularly where the research goal is to identify variance in reproduction;

4. Social demography, especially after factors that affect recruitment and mortality are identified and might be manipulated;

5. Optimality theory, which can enhance ways to reintroduce species by identifying when trade-offs between avoiding predation and gathering food may be critical to a project's success;

6. Communication, which is relevant to identifying which cues (i.e., olfactory, visual, auditory) direct the movements of nonrandom dispersing individuals;

7. Spatial distributions of individuals differing in age, sex, and status, which will be important when considering issues in reserve design since patterns of land use may result in the eviction of certain types of individuals.

Behavioral ecologists can also help in other ways, such as collaborating with government agencies, offering short courses and workshops, and guiding students. Specialized behavioral ecology journals are usually unavailable to nonacademicians. Why not place interesting demographic data or other information in more accessible publications? Although some academicians still refuse to publish in applied journals, the tide is turning. Articles should be published where they will do the most good; journals in the host countries and those for specialists, such as *Pachyderm* or *Desert Bighorn Council Transactions,* should be more frequent outlets. Popular articles are another way to contribute to conservation efforts. They can be an effective means of educating and instructing the public. If behavioral ecologists wish to play an active role in conservation, they must be prepared to do more than simply conduct scientific studies.

11.5 Concluding Remarks

We opened this book by posing questions about lessons learned from the past, the extent to which polygyny in isolated populations reduces N_e, and strategies for the future. History should have taught us that ecosystem processes are as important as the preservation of single species. Consequences of polygyny vary among species with different histories; for bison at Badlands, one of the surprising finds has been that F_1 (outbred) hybrids may have lower fitness than individuals of an inbred lineage. And strategies for the future will have to be flexible, both broad and specific— tailored for species and the vagaries of ecosystems, geography, and sociopolitical environments.

The only successful formula is environmental education, increased awareness of earth's fragile and complex ecosystems, and a true commitment to conservation. Researchers may capture some glory, but it is the hard-working practitioners in government offices, educators in classrooms, devoted people of nongovernment organizations, and the interested populace who will, in the long run, make conservation work. When eye-catching big species cannot be saved through sound research, campaigns designed to arouse public awareness, and environmental programs in schools, what hope remains for the smaller, less conspicuous species? If the decisive issue is not one of "bigness" or "smallness," but how to mobilize support for all forms of life in a continuously shrinking world, then to be sanguine about the loss of species of noneconomic value is to discard the essence of living.

11.6 Summary

1. Badlands seems typical of many of the world's temperate zone parks; it is less than 100,000 ha and dispersal of some of its large mammals to adjacent populations is effectively severed. As with other medium-size reserves, management of its big mammals is necessary to prevent ecosystem damage.
2. The management objectives for single species and ecosystems often clash. Theory dictates that the loss of genetic diversity can be minimized by maintaining large stable populations. This would be unrealistic for bison because other components of the ecosystem would be adversely affected. However, intensive grazing facilitates the expansion of prairie dogs. Because the park is designated as one of the sites likely for the reintroduction of black-footed ferrets and ferret survival is dependent on prairie dogs, ecosystems must be managed for more than a single species. In other areas of the world, conflicts arise between management objectives for different species. Because theory is insufficiently developed, solutions to such problems must be considered on a site-by-site basis.
3. Field research is expensive, and empirically derived results can-

not easily be circumvented by simulation and modelling. The real dollar expenditures of the bison study were more than $300,000; when the time committed by volunteers, donated equipment, and other help was assessed, costs exceeded $400,000.

4. Large mammals like bison offer opportunities to evaluate ideas about reproduction and factors that affect individuals. These data can be applied to questions about population structure. Smaller organisms, because of their more rapid generation times, are better suited for examining issues about evolutionary and conservation genetics. The study of large species, however, more readily stimulates public awareness and education.

APPENDIX 1
Common and Scientific Names of Mammals Mentioned in Text

ORDER MARSUPIALIA
Red kangaroo	*Macropus rufus*

ORDER PRIMATA
Gorilla	*Gorilla gorilla*
Orangutan	*Pongo pygmaeus*
Siamang gibbon	*Hylobates syndactylus*
Yellow baboon	*Papio cynocephalus*
Olive baboon	*Papio anubis*
Hamadryas baboon	*Papio hamadryas*
Black-and-white colobus	*Colobus guereza*
Red colobus	*Colobus badius*
Toque macaque	*Macaca sinica*
Rhesus monkey	*Macaca mulatta*
Red howler	*Alouatta seniculus*
Mangabey	*Cercocebus* spp.
Sykes monkey	*Cercopithecus mitis*
Vervet monkey	*Cercopithecus aethiops*
Squirrel monkey	*Ateles* spp.
Golden lion tamarin	*Leontopithecus rosalia*

ORDER LAGOMORPHA
White-tailed jackrabbit	*Lepus townsendii*
Black-tailed jackrabbit	*Lepus californicus*
Desert cottontail	*Sylvilagus audubonii*
Eastern cottontail	*Sylvilagus floridanus*
Brush rabbit	*Sylvilagus bachmani*

ORDER INSECTIVORA
Solenodon	*Solenodon paradoxus*

ORDER RODENTIA
Spotted ground squirrel	*Spermophilus spilosoma*
Richardson's ground squirrel	*Spermophilus richardsonii*
Thirteen-lined ground squirrel	*Spermophilus tridecemlineatus*
Columbian ground squirrel	*Spermophilus columbianus*
Yellow-bellied marmot	*Marmota flaviventris*
Harvest mouse	*Reithrodontymys megalotis*
Deer Mouse	*Peromyscus californicus*
Northern grasshopper mouse	*Onychomys leucogaster*
Black-tailed prairie dog	*Cynomys ludovicianus*
Ord's kangaroo rat	*Dipodomys ordii*
Beaver	*Castor canadensis*

North American porcupine   *Erethizon dorsatum*
Prairie vole   *Microtus ochrogaster*
Meadow vole   *Microtus pennsylvanicus*
Plain's viscacha   *Lagostomus maximus*

ORDER CARNIVORA
African lion   *Panthera leo*
Tiger   *Panthera tigris*
Cheetah   *Acinonyx jubatus*
Puma   *Felis concolor*
Wolf   *Canis lupus*
Coyote   *Canis latrans*
Wild dog   *Lycaon pictus*
Swift fox   *Vulpes velox*
Kit fox   *Vulpes macrotis*
Red fox   *Vulpes Vulpes*
Giant panda   *Ailurpoda melanoleuca*
Grizzly bear   *Ursus arctos*
Black bear   *Ursus americana*
Black-footed ferret   *Mustela nigripes*
Long-tailed weasel   *Mustela frenata*
Striped skunk   *Mephitis mephitis*
Badger   *Taxidea taxus*

ORDER HYRACOIDEA
Rock hydrax   *Procavia johnstoni*

ORDER PROBOSCIDEA
African elephant   *Loxodonta africana*
Asian elephant   *Elephas maximus*

ORDER PERISSODACTYLA
Przewalskii's horse   *Equus przewalskii*
Feral horse   *Equus caballus*
Feral burro   *Equus asinus*
Plain's zebra   *Equus burchelli*
Malay tapir   *Tapirus inducus*
Greater one-horned rhino   *Rhinocerus unicornis*
Javan rhino   *Rhinocerus sondaicus*
Black rhino   *Diceros bicornis*

ORDER ARTIODACTYLA
River hippo   *Hippopotamus amphibius*
Pygmy hippo   *Choeropsis liberiensis*
Warthog   *Phacochoerus aethiopicus*
Okapi   *Okapia jonhstoni*
Giraffe   *Giraffa camelopardis*
Muntjac   *Muntiacus spp.*
White-lipped deer   *Cervus albirostris*

Pere's David Deer	*Elaphurus davidianus*
Elk	*Cervus elaphuss*
Red deer	*Cervus elaphus*
Mule deer	*Odocoileus hemionus*
White-tailed deer	*Odocoileus virginianus*
Axis deer	*Axis axis*
Fallow deer	*Dama dama*
Roe deer	*Capreolus caprelus*
Eld's deer	*Cervus eldi*
Moose	*Alces alces*
Caribou	*Rangifer tarandus*
Reindeer	*Rangifer tarandus*
Plains Bison	*Bison bison bison*
Wood Bison	*Bison bison athabascae*
Wisent	*Bison bonasus*
Cattle	*Bos taurus*
Gaur	*Bos gaurus*
Banteng	*Bos banteng*
Kouprey	*Bos sauveli*
Anoa	*Anoa depressicornis*
Tamarou	*Anoa mindorensis*
Yak	*Bos grunniens*
Water Buffalo	*Bubalus bubalis*
African buffalo	*Syncerus caffer*
Ibex	*Capra ibex*
Bharal	*Pseudois nayaur*
Tahr	*Hemitragus* spp.
Markhor	*Capra falconeri*
Chiru	*Pantholops hodgsoni*
Serow	*Capricornis sumatraensis*
Saiga antelope	*Saiga tartarica*
Domestic goat	*Capra hircus*
Chamois	*Rupicapra rupicapra*
Bighorn sheep	*Ovis canadensis*
Dall sheep	*Ovis dalli*
Domestic sheep	*Ovis aires*
Dromedary camel	*Camelus dromedarius*
White-eared kob	*Kobus kob*
Dik dik	*Madoqua kirki*
Wildebeest	*Connochaaetes taurinus*
Hartebeest	*Alcelaphus buselaphus*
Sable antelope	*Hippotragus niger*
Arabian oryx	*Oryx leucoryx*
Gemsbok	*Oryx gazella*
Scimitar-horned oryx	*Oryx dammah*
Sprinbok	*Antidorcas marsupialis*
Dorcas gazelle	*Gazella dorcas*

Dama gazelle	*Gazella dama*
Speke's gazelle	*Gazella spekei*
Nyala	*Tragelaphus angasi*
Kudu	*Tragelaphus strepsiceros*
Sitatunga	*Tragelaphus spekei*
Eland	*Tragelaphus eland*

ORDER PINNIPEDA

Northern elephant seal	*Mirounga anugustirostris*

APPENDIX 2
Overview of Early Captive Populations of Prairie Bison

Herds established by the U.S. Government from 1888 to 1919, and their founding population sizes. Asterisks identify reserves no longer in existence.

1888: National Zoological Park, Washington, D.C.. One male and one female

1907: Wichita National Forest and Game Preserve, southwestern Oklahoma. Six males and nine females

1908: Montana National Bison Range, southwestern Montana. Fourteen males and twenty-six females

1913: Niobrara Reservation, near Valentine Nebraska. Three males, five females

1913: Wind Cave National Park, near Hot Springs, South Dakota. Seven males and seven females

1918: *Sully's Hill National Park, near Fort Totten, North Dakota. Exhibition herd, two males and four females

1919: *Pisgah National Forest and Game Preserve, Mt. Pisgah, North Carolina. Exhibition herd, three males and three females

1919: *Platt National Park, Sulphur, Oklahoma. Exhibition herd, one male and one female

APPENDIX 3
Variation in Vigilance in Badlands Ungulates

Summary of differences between centrally and peripherally located Badlands ungulates in mean vigilance rates, A, and variability per 180-s observation bouts, B.

Group Size	Pronghorn	Bighorn	Mule Deer	Bison
A				
2–5	*(34,16)	NS (41,27)	***(29,38)	NS (19,17)
6–10	*(23,14)	**(38,21)	***(37,30)	NS (40,27)
11 +	*(13,24)	***(37,19)	NS (44,24)	NS (46,15)
B				
2–5	**	NS	**	NS
6–10	NS	NS	**	NS
11 +	***	**	***	NS

Statistical comparisons by Mann Whitney U Test (A) and F Test for Homogeneity of Two Independent Samples (B).
NOTE: Sample size (in parentheses) for central and peripheral animals, respectively, are the same for A and B: *$p<0.05$; **$p<0.01$; ***$p<0.001$; NS = not significant.

APPENDIX 4
Home Range Locations of Females of Two Lineages

Our analyses of home ranges illustrate patterns of land use at two levels: (1) home range size during our most common sampling period and (2) degree of spatial overlap among individuals and between lineages. The data set is derived from four adult females of each lineage during ninety-seven field days from 9 May to 17 September 1988. The NL females were selected at random; the CL cows were those that were resighted most often. We designated an animal's home range as the area it used 90% of the time (shown below as frequency-use polygons) and used the first sighting per day to plot locations on maps gridded into 270-acre quadrats. Known buttes, trees, ravines, and creeks served as reference points.

Home Range Size

The figure below is scaled to the schematic shown in fig. 3.2 of the 250-km^2 Sage Creek WA. The estimated home range sizes (km^2) and number of resightings (in parentheses) for cows (A ... D) of the NL and CL lineages are: CL-A 64.8 (32), CL-B 131.8 (38), CL-C 113.4 (36), CL-D 130.7 (36), NL-A 142.6 (65), NL-B 122 (65), NL-C 88 (37), and NL-D 96.1 (37). However, the estimates are not strictly comparable because of inequalities in sampling effort. On average the NL females were resighted 51 and the CL cows 35.5 times. The difference is noteworthy because the home range size (Y) of the eight cows was positively associated with the number of resightings (X), a relationship best described by 55.99 log X-97.68 (r = 0.59) and not improved on by log transformation.

Spatial Overlap

We examined spatial overlap by females within and between lineages in two ways. First, percent overlap was expressed as the area in common divided by the sums of exclusively used regions plus the area in common; no adjustment was made for sampling intensity. Spatial overlap for the two lineages was 76%, a value derived by pooling the home ranges of cows of each lineage separately and then comparing the distributions between the lineages. We also constructed matrices for each lineage so that mean spatial overlap between each pair of cows could be determined as illustrated below.

	NL-A	NL-B	NL-C	NL-D		CL-A	CL-B	CL-C	CL-D
NL-A-		69.5	66.9	74.6	CL-A-		66.9	73.5	57.3
NL-B-		-	47.6	82.2	CL-B-		-	65.7	41.2
NL-C-		-	-	70.4	CL-C-		-	-	40.0

By incorporating the pairwise contrasts, mean (within-lineage) overlap for NL and CL cows was reduced (68.5% [SE ± 4.7] and 57.8 [± 5.5] respectively)) (t = 1.19, NS), although given the small sample, a significant difference between lineages would be difficult to detect. However, without accounting for variation in sampling intensities it would be impossible to reach any conclusion.

Second, we adjusted for the total number of sightings and then used simulation to estimate home range size and overlap. A random number generator selected for thirty-two dates that each female was seen (the minimum number for CL-A, the cow seen least) so that home range locations could then be produced and compared for the eight cows. This procedure was repeated fifty times. Although home ranges were reduced in size (NL-26.8%, CL-14.7%) in both lineages, sampling intensities were equilibrated and mean spatial (within-lineage) overlaps were then determined. For the two lineages spatial overlap was 63%, a value we derived in the same manner as above (i.e., by pooling the home ranges of cows of each lineage separately and then comparing the distributions between the lineages). With the simulations, mean (within-lineage) percent overlap for the NL and CL cows was 50.1 (± 0.7) and 49.3 (± 0.7) (t = 0.62; df = 299; NS). In other words, based on the simulations, the NL and CL cows used the same areas half the time and neither lineage was characterized by females whose ranges were more disparate than the other.

Analyses of these sorts pose several problems (White and Garrott 1990). A lack of independence can result if the location of any animal is not independent of its previous location (time-based), or if its membership in a herd is affected by others (socially based), or both. Circumventing the latter is difficult in herd-dwelling species; the former might be prevented by maximizing the length between sampling intervals. In addition, we were unable to sample all areas with the same rigor. For instance, Tyree Basin (see fig. 3.2) was used more regularly in late spring than our data suggest. But because the animals were not used to seeing people

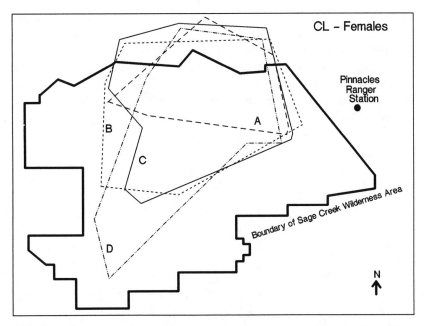

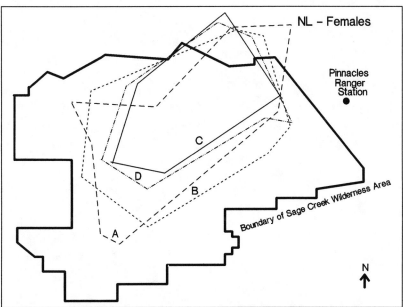

Appendix 4. Home ranges (90% frequency polygons) of 4 cows each from the Colorado (CL) and Nebraska (NL) lineages from May to September 1988. Sample sizes as follows: NL- A (65), B (65), C (37), D (37) and CL - A (32), B (38), C (36), D (36).

there, they ran, and it was often impossible to identify individuals. Although the possibility clearly exists that spatial overlap may be more (or less) there than elsewhere, we assume that the patterns we report from the northern end of the wilderness area represent those in other regions of the Sage Creek WA.

APPENDIX 5
Example of Dominance Matrix for Adult Females

Dominance matrix for 5- to 13-year-old females (in 1985) of NL and CL descent

ID	CL-1	CL-2	CL-3	CL-4	CL-5	CL-6	CL-7	NL-1	NL-2	NL-3	NL-4	NL-5	NL-6	NL-7	NL-8	NL-9	NL-10
CL-1	-	2	4	8	0	1	1	3	0	0	0	2	4	1	5	1	9
CL-2	2	-	5	1	3	0	0	1	7	2	0	3	1	4	0	1	3
CL-3	0	1	-	5	0	1	3	2	4	1	0	0	0	1	4	0	3
CL-4	1	2	8	-	7	1	6	2	7	1	0	4	0	1	3	1	4
CL-5	4	2	0	7	-	1	3	0	0	1	0	0	3	7	1	2	0
CL-6	5	0	1	1	3	-	4	2	5	0	5	0	4	1	1	3	0
CL-7	8	0	1	0	1	2	-	0	1	4	2	3	6	4	3	1	5
NL-1	4	5	1	3	4	6	0	-	0	0	0	1	5	0	1	2	2
NL-2	2	1	3	0	0	0	0	1	-	3	5	1	4	1	6	0	0
NL-3	6	0	3	3	7	1	0	0	0	-	1	7	4	5	0	1	4
NL-4	0	2	0	2	1	0	0	2	8	3	-	3	5	0	3	2	5
NL-5	1	9	7	3	0	0	0	0	0	7	3	-	0	4	1	4	6
NL-6	4	5	0	5	0	3	0	1	4	0	5	6	-	5	2	3	8
NL-7	4	0	0	4	0	0	3	6	0	4	2	1	5	-	1	4	0
NL-8	1	2	3	0	3	3	3	4	3	3	2	1	2	0	-	2	0
NL-9	7	1	2	0	3	1	4	0	1	9	4	2	3	0	0	-	3
NL-10	4	1	0	0	6	3	0	0	1	2	3	0	8	0	2	0	-

Summary

ID	Within-lineage interactions		Between-lineage interactions		Cumulative total		
	W	L	W	L	W	L	Rank
CL-1	16	20	25	33	41	53	14
CL-2	11	7	22	26	33	33	10
CL-3	10	19	15	20	25	39	16
CL-4	25	22	19	20	44	42	9
CL-5	17	14	21	21	38	35	8
CL-6	14	6	21	14	35	20	1

CL-7	12	17	29	10	41	27	2
NL-1	13	14	23	10	36	24	3
NL-2	21	17	6	24	27	41	15
NL-3	16	31	17	12	33	43	13
NL-4	35	25	7	7	42	32	5
NL-5	21	22	12	12	33	34	11
NL-6	33	27	19	18	52	45	7
NL-7	23	10	15	19	38	29	6
NL-8	16	16	13	17	29	33	12
NL-9	19	18	20	9	39	27	4
NL-10	12	29	12	24	24	53	17
Totals	314	314	296	296	610	610	

NOTE: Wins (W) are recorded horizontally and losses (L) vertically.
NL = Nebraska lineage; CL = Colorado lineage.

References

Numbers in brackets at the end of each citation refer to chapters in which the work is cited.

Agnew, W., Uresk, D. W., and Hansen, R. M. 1986. Flora and fauna associated with prairie dog colonies and adjacent ungrazed mixed-grass prairie in western South Dakota. *J. Range Manage.* 39: 135–39. [11]

Ahren, T. G. 1926. Condensed report of the progress of the international society for the preservation of the wisent. *Sond. Ber. Int. Gesell. Erhal. Wisents.* 3: 85–91. [2]

Alados, C. L. 1985a. Distribution and status of the Spanish ibex (*Capra pyrenaica* Schinz*). In S. Lovari, ed., *The Biology and Management of Mountain Ungulates,* pp. 204–11. London: Croom Helm. [2,11]

———. 1985b. An analysis of vigilance in the Spanish ibex (*Capra pyrenaica*). *Z. Tierpsychol.* 68: 58–64. [4]

Alados, C. L. and Escos, J. M. 1992. The determinants of social status and the effects of female rank on reproductive success in Dama and Cuvier's gazelles. *Ethol. Ecol. Evol.* 4: 151–64. [7]

Albon, S. D., Clutton-Brock, T. H., and Guinness, F. E. 1987. Early development and population dynamics in red deer. II. Density-independent effects and cohort variation. *J. Anim. Ecol.* 56: 69–81. [8]

Albon, S. D., Mitchell, B., Huey, B. J., and Brown, D. 1986. Fertility in female red deer (*Cervus elaphus*): The effects of body composition, age, and reproductive status. *J. Zool., Lond.* 209: 447–60. [7]

Albon, S. D., Mitchell, B., and Staines, B. W. 1983. Fertility and body weight in female red deer: A density-dependent relationship. *J. Anim. Ecol.* 52: 969–80. [5]

Alexander, R. D., Hoogland, J. L., Howard, R. D., Noonan, K. N., and Sherman, P. W. 1979. Sexual dimorphism and breeding systems in pinnipeds, ungulates, primates, and humans. In N. A. Chagnon and W. Irons, eds., *Evolutionary Biology and Social Behavior,* pp. 402–35. No. Scituate: Duxbury Press. [1]

Allee, W. C. 1938. *The Social Life of Animals.* Boston: Beacon Press. [5]

Allen, J. A. 1875a. The American bisons: Living and extinct. *U.S. Geol. Surv. Ann. Rep.* 9: 443–587. [2,4,11]

———. 1875b. *History of American Bison.* Washington, D.C.: U.S. Government Printing Office. [2]

Allendorf, F. W. 1986. Genetic drift and the loss of alleles versus heterozygosity. *Zoo Biol.* 5: 181–90. [1, 10]

Allendorf, F. W. and Leary, R. F. 1986. Heterozygosity and fitness in natural populations of animals. In M. E. Soule, ed., *Conservation Biology: The Science of Scarcity and Diversity,* pp. 57–76. Sunderland, Mass.: Sinauer. [1,10]

Altmann, J. 1974. Observational study of behaviour: Sampling methods. *Behaviour* 49: 227–67. [3]

———. 1980. *Baboon Mothers and Infants*. Cambridge: Harvard University Press. [3,8,9,11]

Altmann, J. and Alberts, S. 1987. Body mass and growth rates in a wild primate population. *Oecologia* 72: 15–20. [6,10]

Amann, R. P. 1981. A critical review of methods for evaluation of spermatogenesis from seminal characteristics. *J. Androl.* 2: 37–58. [8]

American Bison Society. 1908–30. Archives of the New York Zoological Society. Bronx, New York. [2,10]

Anderson, C. M. 1986. Female age: Male preference and reproductive success in primates. *Int. J. Primatol.* 7: 305–326. [8]

Apollonio, M., Festa-Bianchet, M. and Mari, F. 1989. Correlates of copulatory success in a fallow deer lek. *Beh. Ecol. Sociobiol.* 25: 89–97. [8]

Armitage, K. B. 1981. Sociality as a life-history tactic of ground squirrels. *Oecologia* 48: 36–49. [9]

———. 1984. Recruitment in yellow-bellied marmot populations: Kinship, philopatry, and individual variability. In J. O. Murie and G. R. Michener, eds., *The Biology of Ground-dwelling Squirrels*, pp. 377–403, Lincoln: University of Nebraska Press. [8,9]

Arnold, S. J. and Wade, M. J. 1984. On the measurement of natural and sexual selection: Applications. *Evolution* 38: 720–34. [8,9]

Arthur, G. W. 1975. An introduction to the ecology of early historic communal bison hunting among the northern plain's Indians. *Archael. Survey Canada, Mercury Ser.* 37: 1–136. [2]

Ashby, K. R. and Santiapillai, C. 1988. The status of the banteng (*Bos javanicus*) in Java and Bali. *Tiger Paper* (October–December): 6–26. [11]

Ashley, M. V. 1989. Absence of differentiation in mitochondrial DNA of island and mainland harvest mice, *Reithrodontomys megalotis*. *J. Mamm.* 70: 383–86. [10]

Ashley, M. V., Melnick, D. J., and Western, D. 1990. Conservation genetics of the black rhinoceros (*Diceros bicornis*), I: Evidence from the mitochondrial DNA of three populations. *Cons. Biol.* 4: 71–77. [10]

Avise, J. C. 1986. Mitochondrial DNA and the evolutionary genetics of higher animals. *Philos. Trans. R. Soc. London B*. 312: 325–42. [10]

Ayala, F. J., Powell, J. R., Tracey, M. I., Mourao, C. A., and Perez-Salas, S. 1972. Enzyme variability in the *Drosophila willistoni* group. IV. Genic variation in natural populations of *Drosophila willistoni*. *Genetics* 70: 113–39. [3]

Baccus, R., Ryman, N., Smith, M. H., Reuterwall, C., and Cameron, D. 1983. Genetic variability and differentiation of large grazing mammals. *J. Mamm.* 64: 109–20. [10]

Ballou, J. 1989. Inbreeding and outbreeding depression in the captive propagation of black-footed ferrets. In U. S. Seal, E. T. Thorne, M. A. Bogan, and S. H. Anderson, eds., *Conservation Biology and the Black-footed Ferret*, pp. 55–68. New Haven: Yale University Press. [10]

Ballou, J. and Ralls, K. 1982. Inbreeding and juvenile mortality in small populations of ungulates: A detailed analysis. *Biol. Cons.* 24: 239–72. [10]

Ballou, J. D. and Seidensticker, J. 1987. The genetic and demographic characteristics of the 1983 captive population of Sumatran tigers. In R. L. Tilson and U. S. Seal, eds., *Tigers of the World*, pp. 329–47. Park Ridge, N.J.: Noyse. [9]

Bamforth, D. B. 1987. Historical documents and bison ecology on the great plains. *Plains Anthrop.* 32: 1–16. [4]

Barlow, R. 1978. Biological ramifications of selection for preweaning growth in cattle: A review. *Anim. Breed. Abst.* 46: 469–94. [10]

Barrette, C. 1987. Mating behaviour and mate choice by wild Axis deer in Sri Lanka. *J. Bombay Nat. Hist. Soc.* 84: 361–371. [7]

Barrette, C. and Vandal, D. 1985. Social rank, dominance, antler size, and access to food in snow-bound wild woodland caribou. *Behaviour* 97: 118–46. [7]

Barrowclough, G. F. and Rockwell, R. F. 1993. Variance of lifetime reproductive success: Estimates based on demographic data. *Amer. Nat.* 141: 281–95. [1]

Barsness, L. 1977. *The Bison in Art*. Flagstaff, Ariz.: Northland Press. [2]

Bateson, P. 1983. *Mate Choice*. Cambridge: Cambridge University Press. [7]

Baynes, E. H. 1906. Letter to W. T. Hornaday. Archives of the American Bison Society, New York Zoological Society. [2,10]

Beachum, T. D. and Murray, C. B. 1987. Adaptive variation in body size, age, morphology, egg size, and developmental biology of chum salmon (*Oncorhynchus keta*) in British Columbia. *Can. J. Fish. Aquat. Sci.* 44: 244–61. [10]

Beasom, S. L., Wiggers, E. P., and Giardino, J. R. 1983. A technique for assessing land surface ruggedness. *J. Wildl. Manage.* 47: 1163–66. [4]

Beck, B. and Wemmer, C. 1983. *The Biology and Management of an Extinct Species, Pere David's Deer*. Park Ridge, N.J.: Noyes. [2]

Bekoff, M. 1976. Animal play: Problems and perspectives. *Pers. Ethol.* 2: 165–88. [9]

———. 1977. Mammalian dispersal and the ontogeny of individual behavioral phenotypes. *Amer. Nat.* 111: 715–32. [8]

Bell, R. H. V. 1981. An outline of a management plan for Kasungu National Park, Malawi. In P. A. Jewell, S. Holt, and D. Hart, eds., *Problems in Management of Locally Abundant Wild Mammals*, pp. 69–90. New York: Academic Press. [11]

Belovsky, G. 1981. Optimal activity times and habitat choice of moose. *Oecologia* 48: 22–30. [4]

———. 1987. Extinction models and mammalian persistence. In M. E. Soule, ed., *Viable Populations for Conservation*, pp. 35–37. New York: Cambridge University Press. [1]

Belovsky, G. E. and Slade, J. B. 1986. Time budgets of grassland herbivores: Body size similarities. *Oecologia* 70: 53–62. [4]

Bercovitch, F. B. 1983. Time budgets and consortships in olive baboons (*Papio anubis*). *Folia Primatol.* 41: 180–90. [8]

———. 1989. Body size, sperm competition, and determination of reproductive success in male savanna baboons. *Evolution* 43: 1507–21. [8]

Berger, J. 1978. Group size, foraging, and antipredator ploys: An analysis of bighorn sheep decisions. *Beh. Ecol. Sociobiol.* 4: 91–100. [4]

———. 1979. Social ontogeny and behavioural diversity: Consequences for bighorn sheep inhabiting desert and mountain environments. *J. Zool., Lond.* 188: 251–66. [4]

———. 1980. The ecology, structure, and functions of social play in bighorn sheep. *J. Zool., Lond.* 192: 531–42. [4]

———. 1986. *Wild Horses of the Great Basin: Social Competition and Population Size.* Chicago: University of Chicago Press. [1,5,6,7,8,9,10]

———. 1987. Reproductive fates of dispersers in a harem-dwelling ungulate: The wild horse. In D. B. Chepko-Sade and Z. T. Halpin, eds., *Mammalian Dispersal Patterns: The Effects of Social Structure on Population Genetics*, pp. 41–54. Chicago: University of Chicago Press. [1]

———. 1988. Social systems, resources, and phylogenetic inertia: An experimental test and its limitations. In C. Slobochikoff, ed., *Ecology of Social Behavior*, pp. 159–86. New York: Academic Press. [9]

———. 1989. Female reproductive potential and its apparent evaluation by male mammals. *J. Mamm.* 70: 347–58. [1,3,4,6,7,8]

———. 1990. Persistence of different-sized populations: An empirical assessment of rapid extinctions in bighorn sheep. *Cons. Biol.* 4: 91–98. [1]

———. 1991a. Pregnancy, predation constraints, and habitat shifts: Experimental and field evidence from wild bighorn sheep. *Anim. Beh.* 41: 61–77. [1,4]

———. 1991b. Greater Yellowstone's native ungulates: Myths and realities. *Cons. Biol.* 5: 353–63. [1,2,11]

———. 1991c. Funding asymmetries for endangered species, feral animals, and livestock. *Bioscience* 41: 105–6. [11]

———. 1992. Facilitation of reproductive synchrony by gestation adjustment in gregarious mammals: A new hypothesis. *Ecology* 73: 323–29. [6]

Berger, J. and Cunningham, C. 1987. Influence of familiarity on frequency of inbreeding in wild horses. *Evolution* 41: 229–31. [11]

———. 1988. Size-related effects on search times of North American grassland female ungulates. *Ecology* 69: 177–83. [2,4]

———. 1991. Bellows, copulations, and sexual selection in bison. *Beh. Ecol.* 2: 1–6. [3,8]

Berger, J., Daneke, D., Johnson, J., and Berwick, S. H. 1983. Pronghorn foraging economy and predator avoidance in a desert ecosystem: Implications for the conservation of large mammalian herbivores. *Biol. Cons.* 25: 193–208. [4,11]

Berger, J. and Kock, M. D. 1988. Overwinter survival of carfentanil-immobilized male bison. *J. Wildl. Dis.* 24: 555–56. [3]

———. 1989. Type I and type II errors in the real world. *J. Wildl. Dis.* 25: 451–54. [3]

Berger, J. and Peacock, M. 1988. Variability in size-weight relationships of *Bison bison. J. Mamm.* 69: 618–24. [3,6]

Bertram, B. C. R. 1975. Social factors limiting reproduction in wild lions. *J. Zool., Lond.* 177: 463–82. [6]

Bewick, T. 1790. *A General History of the Quadrupeds.* Trowbridge, Eng.: Redwood Burn. Reprint. Trowbridge, Eng.: Winward. 1980. [4]

Bierzychudek, P. and Eckhart, V. 1988. Spatial segregation of the sexes of dioecious plants. *Amer. Nat.* 132: 34–43. [4]

Blaustein, A. R. 1981. Sexual selection and mammalian olfaction. *Amer. Nat.* 117: 1006–10. [8]

Boinski, S. 1987. Birth synchrony in squirrel monkeys *(Saimiri oerstedi):* A strategy to reduce neonatal predation. *Beh. Ecol. Sociobiol.* 21: 393–400. [6]

Boldenkov, S. V. 1977. Reintroduction of the European bison, *Bos bonasus,* in the Ukraine. *Congress Game Biol.* 13: 508–11. [2]

Bonnell, M. L. and Selander, R. K. 1974. Elephant seals: Genetic variation and near extinction. *Science* 184: 908–9. [10]

Borgerhoff Mulder, M. 1990. Kipsigis women's preferences for wealthy men: Evidence for female choice in mammals? *Beh. Ecol. Sociobiol.* 27: 255–64. [8]

Bork, A., Strobeck, C. M., Yeh, F. C., Hudson, R. J., and Salmon, R. K. 1991. Genetic relationship of wood and plains bison based on restriction fragment length polymorphisms. *Can. J. Zool.* 69: 43–48. [2]

Borman, E. G. 1971. *Homesteading in the South Dakota Badlands, 1912.* Stickney, S.D.: Borman. [3]

Borner, M. 1985. The increasing isolation of Tarangire National Park. *Oryx* 19: 91–96. [11]

Bouman, J. 1977. The future of Przewalski horses *Equus przewalskii* in captivity. *Int. Zoo Yrbk.* 17: 62–76. [10]

Bowyer, R. T. 1984. Sexual segregation in southern mule deer. *J. Mamm.* 65: 410–17. [1,2,4]

———. 1991. Timing of birth and lactation in southern mule deer. *J. Mamm.* 72: 138–45. [6]

Bowyer, R. T. and Kitchen, D. W. 1987. Sex and age-class differences in vocalizations of Roosevelt elk during rut. *Amer. Midl. Nat.* 118: 225–35. [8]

Boyce, M. S. 1989. *The Jackson Elk Herd: Intensive Wildlife Management in North America.* Cambridge: Cambridge University Press. [2,5]

Bradbury, J. W. and Andersson, M. B. 1987. *Sexual Selection: Testing the Alternatives.* Chichester: Wiley. [9]

Branch, L. 1989. Demography and social organization of the plain's viscacha. Ph.D. diss., University of California, Berkeley. [9]

Brink, J. S. and Knapp, B. W. 1975. Effects of inbreeding on performance traits of beef cattle in the western region. *Tech. Bull. Colorado Ag. Exp. Sta. 123.* [10]

Bronson, F. H. 1989. *Mammalian Reproductive Biology.* Chicago: University of Chicago Press. [6]

Brooks, P. M. and MacDonald, I. A. W. 1983. The Hluhluwe-Umfolozi Reserve: An ecological case history. In R. N. Owen-Smith, ed., *Management of Large Mammals in African Conservation Areas,* pp. 51–78. Pretoria: Haum. [11]

Brown, J. H. 1971. Mammals on mountaintops: Nonequilibrium insular biogeography. *Amer. Nat.* 105: 467–78. [1]

Brussard, P. F. 1991. The role of ecology in biological conservation. *Ecol. Appl.* 1: 6–12. [1,9]

———. 1992. The future of Yellowstone. *Science* 255: 1148–49. [11]

Brussard, P. F. and Gilpin, M. E. 1989. Demographic and genetic problems of small populations. In U. S. Seal, E. T. Thorne, M. A. Bogan, and S. H. Anderson, eds., *Conservation Biology and the Black-footed Ferret*, pp. 37–48. New Haven: Yale University Press. [9]

Bunnell, F. L. and Gillingham, M. P. 1985. Foraging behavior: Dynamics of eating out. In R. J. Hudson and R. White, eds., *Bioenergetics of Wild Herbivores*, pp. 53–80. Boca Raton, Fla.: CRC Press. [4]

Burgess, J. B., Landblom, N. L., and Stonaker, H. H. 1954. Weaning weights of Hereford calves as affected by inbreeding, sex, and age. *J. Anim. Sci.* 13: 843–51. [10]

Burley, N. 1981. Mate selection by multiple criteria in a monogamous species. *Amer. Nat.* 117: 515–28. [8]

Byers, J. A. 1980. Play partner preferences in Siberian ibex, *Capra ibex siberica*. *Z. Tierpsychol.* 53: 23–40. [8]

———. 1986. Natural variation in early experience in pronghorn fawns: Sources and consequences. In L. Passera and J. P. LeChaud, eds., *The Individual and Society*, pp. 81–92. Toulouse, France: Privat, I.E.C. [6,8,9]

Byers, J. A. and Kitchen, D. W. 1988. Mating system shift in a pronghorn population. *Beh. Ecol. Sociobiol.* 22: 355–60. [8]

Calambokidis, J. and Gentry, R. L. 1985. Mortality of northern fur seal pups in relation to growth and birth weights. *J. Wildl. Dis.* 21: 327–30. [6,10]

Calef, G. W. 1984. Population growth in an introduced herd of wood bison (*Bison bison athabascae*) In R. Olson, F. Geddes, and R. Hastings, eds., *Northern Ecology and Resource Management*, pp. 183–200. Edmonton: University of Alberta Press. [2,5,6]

Caraco, T. 1979. Time budgeting and group size: A test of a theory. *Ecology* 60: 618–27. [4]

Carbyn, L. N., Oosenbrug, S. M., and Anions, D. W. 1993. *Wolves, Bison, and the Dynamics Related to the Peace-Athabasca Delta in Canada's Wood Buffalo National Park*. Edmonton: Canadian Circumpolar Institute. [2,4,5]

Carbyn, L. N. and Trottier, T. 1987. Responses of bison on their calving grounds to predation by wolves in Wood Buffalo National Park. *Can. J. Zool.* 65: 2072–78. [4,6]

———. 1988. Descriptions of wolf attacks on bison calves in Wood Buffalo National Park. *Arctic* 41: 297–302. [4,6]

Caro, T. M. 1986. The many paths to wildlife conservation in Africa. *Oryx* 24: 221–29. [11]

Caro, T. M. and Sellen, D. W. 1989. The reproductive advantages of fat in women. *Ethol. Sociobiol.* 11: 51–66. [7]

Cates, J. 1986. *Home on the Range: The Story of the National Bison Range*. Helena, Mont.: Falcon Press. [2,3]

Catlin, G. 1841. Letters and notes on the manners, customs, and condition of the

North American Indians. Reprint. Minneapolis: Roos and Haines, 1965. [2,11]

Caughley, G. C. 1977. *Analysis of Vertebrate Populations.* London: Wiley. [5,9]

Chadwick, D. H. 1988. Protecting Soviet wildlife. *Defenders* 63: 24–29. [2]

Chase, A. 1986. *Playing God in Yellowstone.* Boston: Atlantic Press. [1,2]

Cheney, D. L., Seyfarth, R. M., Andelman, S. J., and Lee, P. C. 1988. Reproductive success in vervet monkeys. In T. H. Clutton-Brock, ed., *Reproductive Success: Studies of Individual Variation in Contrasting Breeding Systems,* pp. 384–402. Chicago: University of Chicago Press. [7]

Chepko-Sade, D. B. and Halpin, Z. T. 1987. *Mammalian Dispersal Patterns: The Effects of Social Structure on Population Genetics.* Chicago: University of Chicago Press. [11]

Chepko-Sade, D. B. and Shields, W. M., with Berger, J., Halpin, Z. T., Jones, W. T., Rogers, L., Rood, J. P., and Smith, A. T. 1987. The effects of dispersal and social structure on effective population size. In D. B. Chepko-Sade and Z. T. Halpin, eds., *Mammalian Dispersal Patterns: The Effects of Social Structure on Population Genetics,* pp. 287–312. Chicago: University of Chicago Press. [1,9]

Child, G. and Le Riche, J. D. 1969. Recent springbok treks (mass movements) in southwestern Botswana. *Mammalia* 33: 499–504. [1]

Cincotta, R. F., Uresk, D. W., and Hansen, R. M. 1987. A statistical model of expansion in a colony of black-tailed prairie dogs. In D. W. Uresk, G. L. Schenbeck, and R. Cefkin, eds., *Eight Great Plains Wildlife Damage Control Workshop Proceedings,* pp. 30–33. Rapid City, S.D.: U.S. Department of Agriculture, Forest Service Tech. Rep. RM-154. [11]

Clark, C. 1974. *The Badlands.* New York: Time-Life Books. [3]

Clark, T. W. 1989. Conservation biology of the black-footed ferret. *Wildlife Preservation Trust Spec. Sci. Rep.* 3: 1–175. [1,9,11]

Clutton-Brock, T. H., ed. 1988a. *Reproductive Success: Studies of Individual Variation in Contrasting Breeding Systems.* Chicago: University of Chicago Press. [9]

———. 1988b. Reproductive success. In T. H. Clutton-Brock, ed., *Reproductive Success: Studies of Individual Variation in Contrasting Breeding Systems,* pp. 472–86. Chicago: University of Chicago Press. [1,9]

Clutton-Brock, T. H. and Albon, S. D. 1979. The roaring of red deer and the evolution of honest advertisement. *Behaviour* 69: 145–70. [8]

———. 1982. Parental investment in male and female offspring in mammals. In King's College Sociobiology Group, ed., *Current Problems in Sociobiology,* pp. 223–47. Cambridge: Cambridge University Press. [1]

Clutton-Brock, T. H., Albon, S. D., and Guinness, F. E. 1988. Reproductive success in male and female red deer. In T. H. Clutton-Brock, ed., *Reproductive Success: Studies of Individual Variation in Contrasting Breeding Systems,* pp. 325–43. Chicago: University of Chicago Press. [7,10]

Clutton-Brock, T. H., Albon, S. D., and Harvey, P. H. 1980. Antlers, body size, and breeding group size in the Cervidae. *Nature* 285: 565–67. [1]

Clutton-Brock, T. H., Guinness, F. E., and Albon, S. D. 1982. *Red Deer: Ecology and Behavior of Two Sexes.* Chicago: University of Chicago Press. [1,4,5,6,7,8,9,10,11]

————. 1983. The costs of reproduction to red deer hinds. *J. Anim. Ecol.* 52: 367–83. [6,7]

Clutton-Brock, T. H. and Harvey, P. H. 1983. The functional significance of variation in body size among mammals. In J. F. Eisenberg and D. G. Kleiman, eds., *Advances in the Study of Mammalian Behavior*, pp. 632–63. Lawrence, Kans.: Allen Press. [9]

Clutton-Brock, T. H. and Iason, G. R. 1986. Sex ratio variation in mammals. *Q. Rev. Biol.* 61: 339–74. [1]

Clutton-Brock, T. H., Iason, G. R., and Guinness, F. E. 1987. Sexual segregation and density-related changes in habitat use in male and female red deer (*Cervus elaphus*). *J. Zool., Lond.* 211: 275–89. [4]

Coblentz, B. E. 1976. Functions of scent-urination in ungulates with special reference to feral goats (*Capra hircus* L.). *Amer. Nat.* 110: 549–57. [8]

Cole, G. F. 1972. An ecological rationale for the natural or artificial regulation of native ungulates in parks. *Trans. No. Amer. Wildl. Nat. Res. Conf.* 36: 417–25. [2]

Conaway, C. H. and Koford, C. B. 1965. Estrous cycles and mating behavior in a free-ranging band of rhesus monkeys. *J. Mamm.* 45: 577–88. [8]

Conry, P. J. 1989. Gaur *Bos gaurus* and development in Malaysia. *Biol. Cons.* 49: 47–65. [11]

Cooke, R. L. and Hart, R. V. 1979. Ages assigned to known-age Texas white-tailed deer: Tooth wear versus cementum analysis. *Proc. Ann. Conf. Southeast. Assoc. Fish Wildl. Agencies.* 33: 195–201. [3]

Coppock, D. L., Ellis, J. E., Detling, J. K., and Dyer, M. I. 1983. Plant-herbivore interactions in a North American mixed-grass prairie. II. Responses of bison to modification of vegetation by prairie dogs. *Oecologia* 56: 10–15. [4,11]

Costa, D. P., Le Boeuf, B. J., Huntley, A. C., and Ortiz, C. L. 1986. The energetics of lactation in the northern elephant seal, *Mirounga angustirostris. J. Zool., Lond.* 209: 21–33. [9]

Cothran, E. G., Chesser, R. K., Smith, M. H., and Johns, P. E. 1983. Influences of genetic variability and maternal factors on fetal growth in white-tailed deer. *Evolution* 37: 282–91. [10]

Cothran, E. G., MacCluer, J. W., Weitkamp, L. R., Pfennig, D. W., and Boyce, A. J. 1984. Inbreeding and reproductive performance in Standardbred horses. *J. Heredity* 75: 220–24. [10]

Coughenour, M. B. and Singer, F. J. 1991. The concept of overgrazing and its application to Yellowstone's northern range. In R. Keiter and M. S. Boyce, eds., *The Greater Yellowstone Ecosystem*, pp 209–30. New Haven: Yale University Press. [11]

Cowan, I. M. 1962. Hybridization between the black-tailed deer and the white-tailed deer. *J. Mamm.* 43: 539–41. [9]

————. 1973. Vanishing species: Habitat changes and reconciling conflict. IUCN *Pubs.* n.s. 28: 321–33. [9]

Cox, C. L. and Le Boeuf, B. J. 1977. Female incitation of male competition: A mechanism in sexual selection. *Amer. Nat.* 111: 317–35. [7]

Craighead, F. C., Jr. 1979. *Track of the Grizzly.* San Francisco: Sierra Club Books. [1,11]

Crockett, C. M. and Eisenberg, J. F. 1987. Howlers: Variation in group size and demography. In B. B. Smuts, D. L. Cheney, R. M. Seyfarth, R. W. Wrangham, and T. T. Struhsaker, eds., *Primate Societies*, pp. 54–68. Chicago: University of Chicago Press. [1]

Cronin, M. A. 1986. Genetic relationships between white-tailed deer, mule deer, and other large mammals inferred from mitochondrial DNA analysis. Thesis, Montana State University, Bozeman. [2,10]

Cronin, M. A., Vyse, E. R., and Cameron, D. G. 1988. Genetic relationships between mule deer and white-tailed deer in Montana. *J. Wildl. Manage.* 52: 320–28. [9,10]

Crow, J. F. 1958. Some possibilities for measuring selection intensities in man. *Human Biol.* 30: 1–13. [9]

Crow, J. F. and Kimura, M. 1970. *An Introduction to Population Genetics Theory.* New York: Harper and Row. [1,3,9,10]

Cumming, D. H. M. 1981. The management of elephants and other large mammals in Zimbabwe. In P. A. Jewell, S. Holt, and D. Hart, eds., *Problems in Management of Locally Abundant Wild Mammals*, pp. 91–118. New York: Academic Press. [11]

Custer, G. A. 1860. *My Life on the Plains.* Chicago: Quaife. [4]

Dalrymple, B. 1919. *The Gray Wolf of South Dakota.* Altoona, Penn.: Altoona Tribune. [3,4]

Darling, F. F. 1938. *Bird Flocks and the Breeding Cycle.* Cambridge: University of Cambridge Press. [6]

Darwin, C. 1859. *On the Origin of Species by Means of Natural Selection.* London: Murray. [1,9]

———. 1871. *The Descent of Man and Selection in Relation to Sex.* London: Murray. Reprint. New York: Hurst, 1874. [1,7,8]

———. 1872. *The Expression of the Emotions in Man and Animals.* New York: D. Appleton. Reprint. Chicago: University of Chicago Press, 1965. [7,8]

Dary, D. D. 1974. *The Buffalo Book.* Chicago: Swallow Press. [2]

Dassat, P. and Sartore, G. 1960. A note on the effect of inbreeding on lamb weights of Sardinian sheep. *Anim. Prod.* 2: 79–80. [10]

Davis, L. B. and Wilson, M., eds. 1978. Bison procurement and utilization: A symposium. *Plains Anthrop. Mem.* 14: 1–361. [2]

De Bois, H., Dhondt, A. A., and Van Puijenbroeck, G. 1990. Effects of inbreeding on juvenile survival of the okapi *Okapi johnstoni* in captivity. *Biol. Cons.* 54: 147–55. [10]

DeFries, J. C., Touchberry, R. W., and Hays, R. L. 1959. Heritability of the length of gestation period in cattle. *J. Dairy Sci.* 42: 598–606. [6]

de Girardin, E. n.d. A trip to the Badlands in 1849. *So. Dakota Historical Review* 1: 62

Derrickson, E. M. 1988. Patterns of postnatal growth in a laboratory colony of *Peromyscus leucopus*. *J. Mamm.* 69: 57–66. [10]

Despain, D., Houston, D., Meagher, M., and Schullery, P. 1986. *Wildlife in Transition: Man and Nature on Yellowstone's Northern Range.* Boulder, Col.: Rineharts. [2]

Dewsbury, D. A. 1982. Ejaculate cost and male choice. *Amer. Nat.* 119: 601–10. [8]

DeYoung, C. A. 1989. Aging live white-tailed deer on southern ranges. *J. Wildl. Manage.* 53: 519–23. [3]

Diamond, J. 1980. Patchy distribution of tropical birds. In M. E. Soule and B. A. Wilcox, eds., *Conservation Biology: An Eco-evolutionary Approach,* pp. 57–74. Sunderland, Mass.: Sinauer. [1]

———. 1984. Normal extinctions of isolated populations. In M. H. Nitecki, ed., *Extinctions,* pp. 191–246. Chicago: University of Chicago Press. [1]

———. 1985. How many unknown species are yet to be discovered? *Nature* 315: 538–39. [1]

Dinerstein, E. and McCracken, G. F. 1990. Endangered greater one-horned rhinoceros carry high levels of genetic variation. *Cons. Biol.* 4: 417–22. [1,10]

Dinkel, C. A., Busch, D. A., Minyard, J. A., and Trevillyan, W. R. 1968. Effects of inbreeding on growth and conformation of beef cattle. *J. Anim. Sci.* 27: 313–22. [10]

Dittus, W. P. J. 1977. The social regulation of population density and age-sex distribution in the Toque monkey. *Behaviour* 63: 281–322. [7]

———. 1979. The evolution of behaviours regulating density and age-specific sex ratios in a primate population. *Behaviour* 69: 265–302. [7]

———. 1986. Sex differences in fitness following a group takeover among Toque macaques: Testing models of social evolution. *Beh. Ecol. Sociobiol.* 19: 257–66. [9]

Dobson, F. S. 1982. Competition for mates and predominant juvenile male dispersal in mammals. *Anim. Beh.* 30: 1183–92. [1]

Dobzhansky, T. 1970. *Genetics of the Evolutionary Process.* New York: Columbia University Press. [10]

Downes, C. M., Theberge, J. B., and Smith, S. M. 1986. The influence of insects on the distribution, microhabitat choice, and behavior of the Burwash caribou herd. *Can. J. Zool.* 64: 622–29. [4]

Dubois, S. D. 1987. History of bison in Alaska and the Delta bison herd. In *North American Bison Workshop,* p. 21. Missoula, Mont.: U.S. Fish and Wildlife Service, Spec. Pub. [2]

Dunbar, R. 1985. *Reproductive Decisions.* Princeton: Princeton University Press. [11]

Duncan, P. 1980. Time budgets of Camargue horses: 2. Time budgets of adult horses and weaned subadults. *Behaviour* 72: 26–49. [4]

Duncan, P., and Vigne, N. 1979. The effect of group size in horses on the rates of attacks by blood-sucking flies. *Anim. Beh.* 27: 623–25. [4]

Durant, S. M., Caro, T. M., Collins, D. A., Alawi, R. M., and Fitzgibbon, C. D. 1988. Migration patterns of Thomson's gazelles and cheetah on the Serengeti Plains. *Afr. J. Ecol.* 26: 257–68. [1]

Dyrmundsson, O. R. 1978. Studies on the breeding season of Icelandic ewes and ewe lambs. *J. Agricul. Sci.* 90: 275–81. [6]

East, R. 1981. Area requirements and conservation status of large African mammals. *Nyala* 7: 3–20. [1]

———. 1983. Application of species area curves to African savannah reserves. *Afr. J. Ecol.* 21: 123–28. [1]

Eccles, T. R. and Shackleton, D. M. 1986. Correlates and consequences of social status in female bighorn sheep. *Anim. Beh.* 34: 1392–1401. [7]

Edwards, J. 1983. Diet shifts in moose due to predator avoidance. *Oecologia* 60: 185–89. [4]

Ehrenfeld, D. 1981. *The Arrogance of Humanism.* New York: Oxford University Press. [1]

Ehrlich, P. R. 1968. *The Population Bomb.* New York: Ballantine. [1]

Ehrlich, P. R. and Ehrlich, A. 1981. *Extinctions.* New York: Ballantine. [1]

Eisenberg, J. F. 1981. *The Mammalian Radiations: An Analysis of Trends in Evolution, Adaptation, and Behavior.* Chicago: University of Chicago Press. [1,8,9]

Eisenberg, J. F. and Seidensticker, J. 1976. Ungulates in southern Asia: A consideration of biomass estimates for selected habitats. *Biol. Cons.* 10: 293–308. [5]

Elias, E., Degen, A. A., and Kam, M. 1991. Effect of conception date on length of gestation in the dromedary camel *(Camelus dromedarius)* in the Negev Desert. *Anim. Repro. Sci.* 25: 173–77. [6]

Emlen, S. T. and Oring, L. W. 1977. Ecology, sexual selection, and the evolution of mating systems. *Science* 197: 215–23. [1]

Endler, J. A. 1986. *Natural Selection in the Wild.* Princeton: Princeton University Press. [9,10]

Environmental Assessment/Bison Management Plan. 1986. Jackson, Wyo.: National Elk Refuge. [2]

Espmark, Y. and Langvtan, R. 1979. Lying down as a means of reducing fly harassment in reindeer *(Rangifer tarandus* L.). *Beh. Ecol. Sociobiol.* 5: 541–54. [4]

Estes, R. D. 1972. The role of the vomeronasal organ in mammalian reproduction. *Mammalia* 36: 315–41. [7]

———. 1976. The significance of breeding synchrony in the wildebeest. *E. Afr. Wildl. J.* 14: 135–52. [6]

Estes, R. D. and Estes, R. K. 1979. The birth and survival of wildebeest calves. *Z. Tierpsychol.* 50: 45–95. [6]

Fagen, R. M. 1981. *Animal Play Behavior.* New York: Oxford University Press. [8]

Falconer, D. S. 1981. *Introduction to Quantitative Genetics.* New York: Longman. [1,9].

———. 1984. Weight and age at puberty in female and male mice of strains selected for large and small body size. *Gen. Res.* 44: 47–72. [10]

Feh, C. 1990. Long-term paternity data in relation to different aspects of rank for Camargue stallions, *Equus caballus. Anim. Beh.* 40: 995–96. [8,9]

Festa-Bianchet, M. 1988a. Seasonal range selection in bighorn sheep: Conflicts between forage quality, forage quantity, and predator avoidance. *Oecologia* 75: 58–86. [1,3]

———. 1988b. Birthdate and lamb survival in bighorn lambs *(Ovis canadensis). J. Zool., Lond.* 214: 653–61. [4,6,9]

————. 1988c. Nursing behaviour of bighorn sheep: Correlates of ewe age, parasitism, lamb age, birthdate, and sex. *Anim. Beh.* 36: 1445–54. [6]

————. 1989. Individual differences, parasites, and the costs of reproduction for bighorn ewes (*Ovis canadensis*). *J. Anim. Ecol.* 58: 785–95. [7]

————. 1991. The social system of bighorn sheep: Grouping patterns, kinship, and female dominance rank. *Anim. Beh.* 42: 71–82. [7]

Fienberg, S. E. 1980. *The Analysis of Cross-classified Categorical Data.* Cambridge: MIT Press. [3]

Fisher, R. A. 1958. *The Genetic Theory of Natural Selection.* 2d ed. New York: Dover. [8,9,10]

Fleischman, C. L. 1986. Genetic variation in musk ox (*Ovibos moshchatus*). Thesis, University of Alaska, Fairbanks. [10]

Flesness, N. 1989. Mammalian extinction rates: Background to the black-footed ferret dilemma. In U. S. Seal, E. T. Thorne, M. A. Bogan, and S. H. Anderson, eds., *Conservation Biology and the Black-footed Ferret,* pp. 3–9. New Haven: Yale University Press. [1]

Foley, R. A. and Atkinson, S. 1984. A dental abnormality among a population of Defassa waterbuck (*Kobus defassa* Ruppell 1835). *Afr. J. Ecol.* 22: 289–94. [10]

Foltz, D. W., Hoogland, J. L., and Koscielny, G. M. 1988. Effects of sex, litter size, and heterozygosity on juvenile weight in black-tailed prairie dogs. *J. Mamm.* 69: 611–14. [10]

Foose, T. J. and Foose, E. 1983. Demographic and genetic status and management. In B. B. Beck and C. M. Wemmer, eds., *Biology and Management of an Extinct Species, Pere David's Deer,* pp. 133–86. Park Ridge, N.J.: Noyse. [2,9,10,11]

Frame, L. H., Malcolm, J. R., Frame, G. W., and van Lawick, H. 1979. Social organization of African wild dogs (*Lycaon pictus*) on the Serengeti Plains, Tanzania 1967–1978. *Z. Tierpsychol.* 50: 225–49. [9]

Frankel, O. H. and Soule, M. E. 1981. *Conservation and Evolution.* Cambridge: Cambridge University Press. [2,9,10]

Frankham, R., Hemmer, H., Ryder, O. A., Cothran, E. G., Soule, M. E., Murray, N. D., and Snyder, M. 1986. Selection in captive populations. *Zoo Biol.* 5: 127–38. [9]

Franklin, I. R. 1980. Evolutionary change in small populations. In M. E. Soule and B. A. Wilcox, eds., *Conservation Biology: An Eco-evolutionary Approach,* pp. 135–49. Sunderland, Mass.: Sinauer. [10]

Franzmann, A. W., LeResche, R. E., Rausch, R. A., Oldemeyer, J. L. 1978. Alaskan moose measurements and weights and measurement-weight relationships. *Can. J. Zool.* 56: 298–306. [6]

Frison, G. C. 1978. *Prehistoric Hunters of the High Plains.* New York: Academic Press. [2,10]

Fryxell, J. M. 1987. Food limitation and demography of a migratory antelope, the white-eared kob. *Oecologia* 72: 83–91. [1]

Fryxell, J. M., Greever, J. and Sinclair, A. R. E . 1988. Why are migratory ungulates so abundant? *Amer. Nat.* 131: 781–98. [1]

Fuller, W. A. 1959. The horns and teeth as indicators of age in bison. *J. Wildl. Manage.* 23: 342–44. [3,5,6]

————. 1960. Behaviour and social organization of the wild bison of Wood Buffalo National Park, Canada. *Arctic* 13: 3–19. [4,6]

————. 1966. The biology and management of the bison of Wood Buffalo National Park. *Wildl. Manage. Bull. Ser.* 16: 1–52. [2,3,4,6]

Gabow, S. A. 1975. Behavioral stabilization of a baboon hybrid zone. *Amer. Nat.* 109: 701–12. [9]

Gadgil, M. and Bossert, W. H. 1970. Life historical consequences of natural selection. *Amer. Nat.* 104: 1–24. [8]

Gainer, R. S. and Saunders, J. R. 1989. Aspects of the epidemiology of anthrax in Wood Buffalo National Park and environs. *Can. Vet. J.* 30: 953–86. [2]

Galdikas, B. M. F. 1985. Adult male sociality and reproductive tactics among orangutans at Tanjung Puting. *Folia Primatol.* 45: 9–24. [8]

Galton, F. 1871. Gregariousness in cattle and men. *MacMillan's Mag., Lond.* 23: 353. [4]

Garretson, M. S. 1934. *A Short History of the American Bison.* New York: American Bison Society. [2,6]

Gasaway, W. C., Harkness, D. B., and Rausch, R. A. 1978. Accuracy of moose age determination from incisor cementum layers. *J. Wildl. Manage.* 42: 558–63. [3]

Geist, V. 1966. The evolution of horn-like organs. *Behaviour.* 27: 175–214. [7]

————. 1971a. *Mountain Sheep: A Study of Behavior and Evolution.* Chicago: University of Chicago Press. [1,4,7,8]

————. 1971b. The relation of social evolution and dispersal in ungulates during the Pleistocene, with emphasis on the old world deer and the genus *Bison. Quat. Res.* 1: 283–315. [2]

————. 1974. On the relationship of social evolution and ecology in ungulates. *Amer. Zool.* 14: 205–220. [7]

————. 1978. *Life Strategies, Human Evolution, and Environmental Design: Toward a Biological Theory of Health.* New York: Springer-Verlag. [4]

————. 1983. On the evolution of Ice Age mammals and its significance to an understanding of speciations. *ASB Bull.* 30: 109–33. [2]

————. 1990. Agriculture versus bison in Canada's Wood Buffalo National Park. *Cons. Biol.* 4: 345–46. [2,5]

Geist, V. and Bayer, M. 1988. Sexual dimorphism in the Cervidae and its relation to habitat. *J. Zool., Lond.* 214: 45–53. [1,4]

Geist, V. and Bromley, P. T. 1978. Why deer shed antlers. *Z. Saeugetier.* 43: 223–31. [1]

Geist, V. and Karsten, P. 1977. The wood bison (*Bison bison athabascae*) in relation to hypotheses on the origin of the American bison (*Bison bison* Linnaeus). *Z. Saeugetier.* 42: 119–27. [2,4]

Geist, V. and Petocz, R. G. 1977. Bighorn sheep in winter: Do rams maximize reproductive fitness by spatial and habitat segregation from ewes? *Can. J. Zool.* 55: 1802–10. [2]

Geyer, C. J. and Thompson, E. A. 1986. Gene survival in the Asian wild horse (*Equus przewalskii*). *Zoo Biol.* 7: 313–27. [9]

Gibson, R. M. and Bradbury, J. W. 1985. Sexual selection in lekking sage grouse:

Phenotypic correlates of male mating success. *Beh. Ecol. Sociobiol.* 18: 117–23. [7]

Gibson, R. M. and Guinness, F. E. 1980a. Differential reproductive success in red deer stags. *J. Anim. Ecol.* 49: 199–208. [7,8]

———. 1980b. Behavioural factors affecting male reproductive success in red deer *(Cervus elaphus)*. *Anim. Beh.* 28: 1163–74. [8]

Gilpin, M. E. and Soule, M. E. 1986. Minimum viable populations: Processes of species extinction. In M. E. Soule, ed., *Conservation Biology: The Science of Scarcity and Diversity*, pp. 19–34. Sunderland, Mass.: Sinauer. [9]

Ginsberg, J. R. and Huck, U. W. 1989. Sperm competition in mammals. *Trends Ecol. Evol.* 4: 74–79. [8]

Gittleman, J. L. 1986. Carnivore life history patterns: Allometric, phylogenetic, and ecological associations. *Amer. Nat.* 127: 744–71. [9]

Glenn, S. M. and Nudds, T. D. 1989. Insular biogeography of mammals in Canadian national parks. *J. Biogeog.* 16: 261–68. [1]

Gogan. P. J. and Jessup, D. A. 1985. Cleft palate in a tule elk calf. *J. Wildl. Dis.* 21: 463–66. [10]

Goldizen, A. W. 1987. Tamarins and marmosets: Communal care of offspring. In B. B. Smuts, D. L. Cheney, R. M. Seyfarth, R. W. Wrangham, and T. T. Struhsaker, eds., *Primate Societies*, pp. 34–43. Chicago: University of Chicago Press. [1]

Gosling, L. M. 1986. The evolution of mating strategies in male antelopes. In D. I. Rubenstein and R. W. Wrangham, eds., *Ecological Aspects of Social Evolution*, pp. 242–81. Princeton: Princeton University Press. [1,10]

Grafen, A. 1988. On the uses of data on lifetime reproductive success. In T. H. Clutton-Brock, ed., *Reproductive Success: Studies of Individual Variation in Contrasting Breeding Systems*, pp. 454–71. Chicago: University of Chicago Press. [9]

Grant, B. R. and Grant, P. R. 1990. *Evolutionary Dynamics of a Population*. Chicago: University of Chicago Press. [1]

Green, W. C. H. 1986. Age-related differences in nursing behavior among American bison cows *(Bison bison)*. J. Mamm. 67: 739–41. [7]

———. 1987. Mother-daughter interactions in American bison *(Bison bison):* Factors associated with individual variation. Ph.D. diss. City University of New York. [4,6,7]

———. 1990. Reproductive effort and associated costs in bison: Do older mothers try harder? *Beh. Ecol.* 1: 148–60. [6,7,8,9]

Green, W. C. H. and Berger, J. 1990. Maternal investment in sons and daughters: Problems of methodology. *Beh. Ecol. Sociobiol.* 27: 99–102. [3,6,8]

Green, W. C. H., Griswold, J. G., and Rothstein, A. 1989. Postweaning associations among bison mothers and daughters. *Anim. Beh.* 38: 847–58. [2,6]

Green, W. C. H. and Rothstein, A. 1991a. Trade-offs between growth and reproduction in female bison. *Oecologia* 86: 521–27. [6,7,10]

———. 1991b. Sex bias or equal opportunity? Patterns of maternal investment in bison. *Beh. Ecol. Sociobiol.* 29: 373–84. [5,6,8]

————. 1993a. Asynchronous parturition in bison. *J. Mamm.* 74:920–925. [6]

————. 1993b. Persistent influences of birth date on dominance, growth, and reproductive success in bison. *J. Zool., Lond.* 230: 177–86. [7]

Greene, H. W. and Losos, J. B. 1988. Systematics, natural history, and conservation. *Bioscience* 38: 458–62. [1]

Greig, J. C. 1979. Principles of genetic conservation in relation to wildlife management in southern Africa. *S. Afr. J. Wildl. Res.* 9: 57–78. [9]

Grinnell, G. B. 1892. The last of the buffalo. *Scribner's Mag.* 12: 267–86. [2,11]

Guinness, F. E., Gibson, R. M., and Clutton-Brock, T. H. 1978. Calving times in red deer (*Cervus elaphus*) on Rhum. *J. Zool., Lond.* 185: 105–14. [6]

Guinness, F. E., Lincoln, G. A., and Short, R. V. 1971. The reproductive cycle of the female red deer (*Cervus elaphus* L.). *J. Repro. Fertil.* 27: 427–38. [6,8]

Gunderson, H. L. and Mahan, B. R. 1980. Analysis of sonagrams of American bison (*Bison bison*). *J. Mamm.* 61: 379–81. [3,8]

Gunn, R. G. and Doney, J. M. 1975. Interaction of nutrition and body condition at mating on ovulation rate and early embryo survival in Scottish blackface ewes. *J. Agr. Sci.* 85: 465–70. [8]

Guthrie, R. D. 1990. *Frozen Fauna of the Mammoth Steppe.* Chicago: University of Chicago Press. [2,4]

Hackman, E., Emanuel, I., van Belle, G., and Daling. J. 1983. Maternal birth weight and subsequent pregnancy outcome. *J. Amer. Med. Assoc.* 250: 2016–20. [7]

Hall, S. J. G. 1990. Genetic conservation of domestic livestock. *Oxford Rev. Repro. Biol.* 12: 289–318. [10]

Hall, S. J. G. and Hall, J. G. 1988. Inbreeding and population dynamics of the Chillingham cattle (*Bos taurus*). *J. Zool., Lond.*. 216: 479–93. [6]

Hall, S. J. G., Vince, M. A., Walser, E. S., and Garson, P. J. 1988. Vocalisations of the Chillingham cattle. *Behaviour* 104: 78–104. [8]

Halloran, A. F. 1961. American bison weights and measurements from the Wichita Mountains Wildlife Refuge. *Proc. Oklahoma Acad. Sci.* 41: 212–18. [6]

————. 1968. Bison (Bovidae) productivity on the Wichita Mountains Wildlife Refuge, Oklahoma. *Southwest. Nat.* 13: 23–26. [6]

Hamilton, W. D. 1971. Geometry for the selfish herd. *J. Theor. Biol.* 31: 295–311. [4]

Hamilton, W. J., III, Buskirk, R., and Buskirk, W. H. 1977. Intersexual dominance and differential mortality of gemsbok, *Oryx gazella,* at Namib Desert waterholes. *Madoqua* 10: 5–19. [7]

Hanks, J. 1981. Characterization of population condition. In C. W. Fowler and T. D. Smith, eds., *Dynamics of Large Mammal Populations,* pp. 47–74. New York: Wiley. [5,11]

Harcourt, A. H. and Fossey, D. 1981. The Virunga gorillas: Decline of an "island" population. *Afr. J. Ecol.* 19: 83–97. [11]

Harper, F. 1925. Letter to the editor. *Can. Field Nat.* 39: 45. [2]

Harris, L. 1984. *The Fragmented Forest.* Chicago: University Chicago Press.[1]

Harris, R. B. and Allendorf, F. W. 1989. Genetically effective population size of large mammals: An assessment of estimates. *Cons. Biol.* 3: 181–91. [1,9]

Harris, R. B., Clark, T. W., and Shaffer, M. W. 1989. Extinction probabilities for isolated black-footed ferret populations. In U. S. Seal, E. T. Thorne, M. A. Bogan, and S. H. Anderson, eds., *Conservation Biology and the Black-footed Ferret*, pp. 69–82. New Haven: Yale University Press. [11]

Harris, R. B., Maguire, L. A., and Shaffer, M. L. 1987. Sample sizes for minimum viable population estimation. *Cons. Biol.* 1: 72–76. [1]

Hart, B. L., Hart, L. A., and Maina, J. N. 1989. Chemosensory investigation, flehman behaviour, and vomeronasal organ function in antelope. *Symp. Zool. Soc. Lond.* 61: 197–215. [7]

Harvey, W. 1651. Anatomical exercises on the generation of animals. Reprint. *Great Books of the Western World.* Chicago: Encylopædia Britannica, 1952. [8]

Haufe, W. O. 1986. Productivity of the cow-calf unit in range cattle protected from horn flies, *Haematobia irritans*, by pesticidal ear tags. *Can. J. Anim. Sci.* 66: 575–89. [4]

Haugen, A. O. 1974. Reproduction in the plain's bison. *Iowa State J. Res.* 49: 1–8. [6]

Hawley, A. W. 1989. Bison farming in North America. In R. J. Hudson, K. R. Drew, and L. M. Baskin, eds., *Wildlife Production Systems: Economic Utilisation of Wild Ungulates*, pp. 346–61. Cambridge: Cambridge University Press. [2,5]

Haynes, G. 1982. Utilization and skeletal disturbances of North American prey carcasses. *Arctic* 35: 266–81. [5]

——. 1984. Tooth wear rate in northern bison. *J. Mamm.* 65: 487–91. [3]

——. 1988. Mass deaths and serial predation: Comparative taphonomic studies of modern large mammal death sites. *J. Archaeol. Sci.* 15: 219–35. [4]

Hintz, R. L. and Foose, T. J. 1982. Inbreeding, mortality, and sex ratio in gaur (*Bos gaurus*) under captivity. *J. Heredity* 73: 297–98. [10]

Hoeck, H. N. 1982. Population dynamics, dispersal, and genetic isolation in two sympatric species of hyrax (*Heterohyrax brucei* and *Procavia johnstoni*) on habitat islands in the Serengeti. *Z. Tierspychol.* 59: 177–210. [9]

Hogg, J. T. 1984. Mating in bighorn sheep: Multiple creative male strategies. *Science* 225: 526–29. [7]

——. 1987. Intrasexual competition and mate choice in Rocky Mountain bighorn sheep. *Ethology* 75: 119–44. [7,8]

——. 1988. Copulatory tactics in relation to sperm competition in Rocky Mountain bighorn sheep. *Beh. Ecol. Sociobiol.* 22: 49–59. [7,8]

Hoogland, J. L. 1981. The evolution of coloniality in white-tailed and black-tailed prairie dogs (Sciuridae: *Cynomys leucurus* and *C. ludovicianus*). *Ecology* 62: 252–72. [11]

——. 1982. Prairie dogs avoid extreme inbreeding. *Science* 215: 1639–41. [8,11]

——. 1992. Levels of inbreeding among prairie dogs. *Amer. Nat.* 139: 591–602. [8,10]

Hornaday, W. T. 1889. The extermination of the American bison, with a sketch of its discovery and life history. *Ann. Rep. (1889) Smithsonian Inst.*, pp. 367–548. [2,3,4,10,11]

Horwich, R. H. 1990. How to develop a community sanctuary: An experimental approach to the conservation of private lands. *Oryx* 24: 95–102. [11]

Houston, D. B. 1982. *The Northern Yellowstone Elk: Ecology and Management.* New York: Macmillan. [5,7,11]

Howard, R. D. 1988. Reproductive success in two species of anurans. In T. H. Clutton-Brock, ed., *Reproductive Success: Studies of Individual Variation in Contrasting Breeding Systems,* pp. 99–118. Chicago: University of Chicago Press. [8]

Howell, A. B. 1925. Letter to the editor. *Can. Field Nat.* 39: 118. [2]

Hrdy, S. B. and Whitten, P. L. 1987. Patterns of sexual activity. In B. B. Smuts, D. L. Cheney, R. W. Wrangham, and T. T. Struhsaker, eds., *Primate Societies,* pp. 370–84. Chicago: University of Chicago Press. [1]

Hudson, R. J. and Frank, S. 1986. Foraging ecology of bison in aspen boreal forests. *J. Range Manage.* 40: 71–75. [4]

Hudson, R. J. and Watkins, W. G. 1986. Foraging rates of wapiti on green and cured pastures. *Can. J. Zool.* 64: 1705–8. [4]

Hudson, R. J. and White, R. G. 1985. *Bioenergetics of Wild Herbivores.* Boca Raton, Fla.: CRC Press. [10]

Hudson, W. E. 1991. *Landscape Linkages and Biodiversity.* Washington, D.C.: Island Press. [11]

Hughes, R. D., Duncan, P., and Dawson, J. 1981. Interactions between Camargue horses and horseflies (Diptera: Tabanidae). *Bull. Ent. Res.* 71: 227–42. [4]

Iason, G. R. 1989. Mortality of mountain hares in relation to body size and age. J. Zool., Lond. 219: 676–80. [6,10]

Iason, G. R. and Guinness, F. E. 1985. Synchrony of oestrus and conception in red deer (*Cervus elaphus* L.). *Anim. Beh.* 33: 1169–74. [6]

Ims, R. A. 1990. The ecology and evolution of reproductive synchrony. *Trends Ecol. Evol.* 5: 135–40. [1,6]

Ion, P. G. and Kershaw, G. P. 1989. The selection of snowpatches as relief habitat by woodland caribou (*Rangifer tarandus caribou*), MacMillan Pass, Selwyn/Mackenzie Mountains, NWT, Canada. *Arctic Alp. Res.* 203–11. [4]

Irving, W. 1859. *A Tour on the Prairies.* Reprint. Norman: University of Oklahoma Press, 1956. [11]

Irwin-Williams, C., Irwin, H. Agogino, G., and Haynes, C. V. 1973. Hell Gap: Paleo-Indian occupation on the high plains. *Plains Anthrop.* 18: 40–53. [2]

Jaarsveld van, A. S., Henschel, J. R., and Skinner, J. D. 1988. Improved age estimation in spotted hyaenas (*Crocuta crocuta*). *J. Zool., Lond.* 213: 758–62. [3]

Jacobsen, J. 1986. A digital photogrammetric scaling device. Humboldt State University, Arcata, Calif. Typescript. [3,6]

Janzen, D. H. 1983. No park is an island: Increase in interference from outside as park size increases. *Oikos* 41: 402–10. [1]

———. 1986a. *Guanacaste National Park.* San Jose: Editorial Universidad Estatal a Distancia. [11]

———. 1986b. The eternal external threat. In M. E. Soule, ed., *Conservation*

Biology: The Science of Scarcity and Diversity, pp. 286–303. Sunderland, Mass.: Sinauer. [11]

Jarman, P. J. 1974. The social organization of antelope in relation to their ecology. *Behaviour* 48: 215–67. [4]

Jennings, D. C. and J. Hebbring. 1983. *Buffalo Management and Marketing*. Custer, S.D.: National Buffalo Association. [2]

Jewell, P. A., Holt, S., and Hart, D., eds. 1981. *Problems in Management of Locally Abundant Wild Mammals*. New York: Academic Press. [5]

Johansson, I. 1961. Studies on the genetics of ranch bred mink. I. The results of an inbreeding experiment. *Z. Tierzuecht. Zuechtungs-Biol.* 72: 293–97. [10]

Johnson, J. R. and Nichols, J. T. 1982. Plants of South Dakota grasslands. *Bull. Agr. Exp. Sta.* 566: 1–166. [3]

Jolly, A. 1986. Lemur survival. In K. Benirshke, ed., *Primates: The Road to Self-sustaining Populations*, pp. 71–98. New York: Springer-Verlag. [11]

Jones, G. P. 1981. Spawning-site choice by female *Pseudolabrus celidotus* (Pisces: Labridae) and its influence on the mating system. *Beh. Ecol. Sociobiol.* 8: 129–42. [8]

Jones, J. K., Jr., Armstrong, D. M., Hoffman, R. S., and Jones, C. 1983. *Mammals of the Northern Great Plains*. Lincoln: University of Nebraska Press. [3,4,5]

Keeler, R. F., James, L. F., Shupe, L., and van Kampen, K. R. 1977. Lupine-induced crooked calf disease and a management method to reduce incidence. *J. Range Manage.* 30: 97–102. [10]

Kelsall, J. P., Telfer, E. S., and Kingsley, M. 1978. Relationships of bison weight to chest girth. *J. Wildl. Mgmt.* 42: 659–66. [6]

Kerley, L. 1988. Microhabitat choice and biting flies in American bison: A test of multiple hypotheses. Thesis, University of Nevada, Reno. [4]

Kiley, M. 1972. The vocalizations of ungulates: Their causation and function. *Z. Tierpsychol.* 31: 171–222. [8]

Kiltie, R. A. 1982. Intraspecific variation in the mammalian gestation period. *J. Mamm.* 63: 646–52. [6]

———. 1985. Evolution and function of horns and hornlike organs in female ungulates. *Biol. J. Linn. Soc.* 24: 299–320. [7]

King, W. J., Festa-Bianchet, M., and Hatfield, S. E. 1991. Determinants of reproductive success in female Columbian ground squirrels. *Oecologia* 86: 528–34. [7]

Kistchinski, A. A. 1971. On the formation of distinctions in an isolated insular population of wild reindeer. *Biommetehb M. O-BA. HC-II.* 76: 69–78. [10]

Kleiman, D. G. 1977. Monogamy in mammals. *Quart. Rev. Biol.* 52: 39–69. [1,8,9]

———. 1989. Reintroduction of captive mammals for conservation. *Bioscience* 39: 152–61. [11]

Kleiman, D. G., Beck, B. B., Dietz, J. M., and Dietz, L. A. 1991. Costs of a reintroduction and criteria for success: Accounting and accountability in the golden lion tamarin conservation program. *Symp. Zool. Soc. Lond.* 62: 125–42. [11]

Kleiman, D. G., Beck, B. B., Dietz, J. M., Dietz, L. A., Ballou, J. D., and Coimbra-Filho, A. F. 1986. Conservation program for the golden lion tamarin:

Captive research and management, ecological studies, educational strategies, and reintroduction. In K. Benirshke, ed., *Primates: The Road to Self-sustaining Populations*, pp. 959–79. New York: Springer-Verlag. [11]

Klevezal, G. A. and Pucek, Z. 1987. Growth layers in tooth cementum and dentine of European bison and its hybrids with domestic cattle. *Acta Theriol.* 32: 115–28. [3]

Knapp, B. Jr., Emmel, M. W., and Ward, W. F. 1937. The inheritance of screw tail in cattle. *J. Hered.* 27: 269–71. [10]

Knowles, M. 1919. A report on the Badlands of South Dakota. Files of National Park Service, Interior, South Dakota. Typescript. [3]

Knutsen, K. L. and Allendorf, F. W. 1987. Genetic variation in bison allozymes. In *North American Bison Workshop*, pp. 48–49. Missoula, Mont.: U.S. Fish and Wildlife Service, Spec. Pub. [2,10]

Kobrynczuk, F. 1985. The influence of inbreeding on the shape and size of the skeleton of the European bison. *Acta Theriol.* 30: 379–422. [10]

Kock, M. D. and Berger, J. 1987. Chemical immobilization of free-ranging North American bison *(Bison bison)* in Badlands National Park, South Dakota. *J. Wildl. Dis.* 23: 625–33. [3]

Koenig, W. D. 1988. On determination of viable population size in birds and mammals. *Wildl. Soc. Bull.* 16: 230–34. [9]

Koenig, W. D. and Albano, S. S. 1986. On the measurement of sexual selection. *Amer. Nat.* 127: 403–9. [9]

Koenig, W. D. and Mumme, R. L. 1987. *Population Ecology of the Cooperatively Breeding Acorn Woodpecker*. Princeton: Princeton University Press. [9]

Koford, C. B. 1958. Prairie dogs, whitefaces, and blue grama. *Wildl. Monog.* 3: 1–78. [11]

Komers, P. E., Messier, F., and Gates, C. C. 1992. Search or relax: The case of bachelor wood bison. *Beh. Ecol. Sociobiol.* 31: 195–203. [3,8]

Komers, P. E., Roth, K., and Zimmerli, R. 1993. Interpreting social behaviour of wood bison using tail postures. *Z. Saeugetier.* 57: 343–50. [3,8]

Krasinski, Z. A. 1967. Free-living European bisons. *Acta Theriol.* 28: 391–405. [2]

———. 1978. Dynamics and structure of the European bison population in the Bialowieza Primeval Forest. *Acta Theriol.* 23: 3–48. [2]

Krueger, K. 1986. Feeding relationships among bison, pronghorn, and prairie dogs: An experimental analysis. *Ecology* 67: 760–70. [4,11]

Kyrsiak, K. 1967. The history of the European bison in the Bialowieza Forest and the results of its protection. *Acta Theriol.* 19: 323–31. [2]

Lacy, R. C. and Clark, T. W. 1989. Genetic variability in black-footed ferret populations: Past, present, and future. In U. S. Seal, E. T. Thorne, M. A. Bogan, and S. H. Anderson, eds., *Conservation Biology and the Black-footed Ferret*, pp. 83–103. New Haven: Yale University Press. [9,10]

Lacy, R. C., Petric, A., and Warneke, M. 1993. Inbreeding and outbreeding in captive populations of wild animal species. In N. W. Thornhill, ed., *The Natural History of Inbreeding and Outbreeding*, pp. 352–74. Chicago: University of Chicago Press. [1,9,10]

Lamberson, W. R. and Thomas, D. L. 1984. Effects of inbreeding in sheep: A review. *Anim. Breeding Abstr.* 52: 287–97. [10]

Lande, R. and Barrowclough, G. F. 1987. Effective population size, genetic variation, and their use in population management. In M. E. Soule, ed., *Viable Populations for Conservation,* pp. 87–123. Cambridge: Cambridge University Press. [1,9,10]

Larson, F. and Whitman, W. 1942. A comparison of used and unused grassland mesas in the badlands of South Dakota. *Ecology* 23: 438–45. [3]

Larter, N. C. and Gates, C. C. 1990. Home ranges of wood bison in an expanding population. *J. Mamm.* 71: 604–7. [4]

Lasley, J. F. 1978. *The Genetics of Livestock Improvement.* Engelwood Cliffs, N.J.: Prentice-Hall. [1,9,10]

Laws, R. M. and Parker, I. S. C. 1968. Recent studies on elephant populations in East Africa. *Symp. Zool. Soc. Lond.* 21: 319–59. [5]

Leader-Williams, N. 1988. *Reindeer of South Georgia.* Cambridge: Cambridge University Press. [5]

Le Boeuf, B. J. and Reiter, J. 1988. Lifetime reproductive success in northern elephant seals. In T. H. Clutton-Brock, ed., *Reproductive Success: Studies of Individual Variation in Contrasting Breeding Systems,* pp. 344–62. Chicago: University of Chicago Press. [6,7,8,9]

Lee, A. K. and Cockburn, A. 1985. *Evolutionary Ecology of Marsupials.* Cambridge: Cambridge University Press. [6]

Lent, P. C. 1966. Calving and related behavior in the barren-ground caribou. *Z. Tierspychol.* 23: 702–56. [6]

Leuthold, W. 1977. *African Ungulates.* New York: Springer-Verlag. [6]

Lewis, T. 1965. The effects of an artificial windbreak on the aerial distribution of flying insects. *Ann. Appl. Biol.* 55: 503–12. [4]

Lipetz, V. and Bekoff, M. 1982. Group size and vigilance in pronghorns. *Z. Tierpsychol.* 58: 203–16. [4]

Locati, M. and Lovari, S. 1991. Clues for dominance in female chamois: Age, weight, or horn size? *Aggressive Behavior* 17: 11–15. [7]

Lott, D. 1974. Sexual and aggressive behaviour of bison. In V. Geist and F. Walther, eds., *The Behaviour of Ungulates and Its Relation to Management.* IUCN 24: 382–94. [3,7]

———. 1979. Dominance relations and breeding rate in mature male American bison. *Z. Tierpsychol.* 49: 418–32. [2,6,8,9]

———. 1981. Sexual behavior and intersexual strategies in American bison. *Z. Tierpsychol.* 56: 97–114. [2,7,8]

Lott, D. F. and Galland, J. C. 1985a. Parturition in American bison: Precocity and systematic variation in cow isolation. *Z. Tierpsychol.* 69: 66–71. [4,6]

———. 1985b. Individual variation in fecundity in an American bison population. *Mammalia* 49: 300–302. [7]

———. 1987. Body mass as a factor influencing dominance status in American bison cows. *J. Mamm.* 68: 683–85. [7]

MacArthur, R. H. and Wilson, E. O. 1967. *The Theory of Island Biogeography.* Princeton: Princeton University Press. [1]

McCarley, H. 1970. Differential reproduction in *Spermophilus tridecemlineatus. Southwest. Nat.* 14: 293–96. [9]

McClenaghan, L., Berger, J., and Truesdale, J. 1990. Genic variability and founder size in plain's bison from Badlands National Park, South Dakota. *Cons. Biol.* 4: 285–89. [2,3,10]

McClintok, M. K. 1978. Estrous synchrony and its mediation by airborne chemical communication (*Rattus norvegicus*). *Horm. Beh.* 10: 264–76. [6]

———. 1983. Pheromonal regulation of the ovarian cycle: Enhancement, suppression, and synchrony. In J. G. Vandenbergh, ed., *Pheromones and Reproduction in Mammals*, pp. 113–49. New York: Academic Press. [6]

McComb, K. 1987. Roaring by red deer stags advances the date of oestrus in hinds. *Nature* 330: 648–49. [8]

McCullough, D. R. 1979. *The George Reserve Deer Herd.* Ann Arbor: University of Michigan Press. [4,5]

McCullough, D. R., Hirth, D. H., and Newhouse, S. J. 1989. Resource partitioning between the sexes in white-tailed deer. *J. Wildl. Manage.* 53: 277–83. [1]

McDonald, J. N. 1981. *North American Bison: Their Classification and Evolution.* Berkeley: University of California Press. [2]

McDougall, J. 1898. *Pathfinding on Plain and Prairie.* Toronto: William Briggs. [2]

McHugh, T. 1972. *The Time of the Buffalo.* New York: Knopf. [2,6.10]

Mackenzie Wood Bison Management Plan. 1987. Yellowknife, Can.: Government of the Northwest Territories. [2]

MacKinnon, K. 1986. The conservation status of nonhuman primates in Indonesia. In K. Benirshke, ed., *Primates: The Road to Self-sustaining Populations*, pp. 99–126. New York: Springer-Verlag. [11]

MacNeil, M. D., Dearborn, D. D., Cundiff, L. V., Dinkel, C. D., and Gregory, K. E. 1989. Effects of inbreeding and heterosis in Hereford females on fertility, calf survival, and preweaning growth. *J. Anim. Sci.* 67: 895–901. [10]

McVey, M. E. 1988. The opportunity for selection in a territorial dragonfly, *Erythemis simplicocllis.* In T. H. Clutton-Brock, ed., *Reproductive Success: Studies of Individual Variation in Contrasting Breeding Systems*, pp. 44–58. Chicago: University of Chicago Press. [1]

Maher, C. R. and Byers, J. A. 1987. Age-related changes in reproductive effort of male bison. *Beh. Ecol. Sociobiol.* 21: 91–96. [8]

Malcolm, J. 1983. Buffalo origins charted. *Buffalo* 11: 22–23. [2,10]

Martin, P. S. 1984. Prehistoric overkill: The global model. In P. S. Martin and R. G. Klein, eds., *Quaternary Extinctions*, pp. 354–403. Tucson: University of Arizona Press. [2]

Mathews, A. 1992. *Where the Buffalo Roam.* New York: Grove-Weidenfield. [2,11]

Mattison, R. H. and Grom, R. A. 1970. History of Badlands National Monument. *Bull. Badlands Nat. Hist. Assoc.* 1: 1–56. [3]

Maury, G. 1990. *Le bison d'Europe en Margeride.* Langeac, France: Société d'Études Bison d'Europe et Margeride. [2]

Meagher, M. M. 1973. The bison of Yellowstone National Park. *Nat. Park Serv. Sci. Monog.* 1: 1–161. [2,3,6]

———. 1974. Yellowstone's bison: A unique heritage. *Nat. Park's Cons. Mag.* May: 9–14. [2]

———. 1976. Winter weather as a population regulating influence on free-ranging bison in Yellowstone National Park. In *Research in the Parks*, pp. 29–38. Washington, D.C.: Amer. Assoc. Advancement of Sciences, Ser. 1. [5,6]

———. 1989a. Evaluation of boundary control for bison of Yellowstone National Park. *Wildl. Soc. Bull.* 17: 15–19. [2,5]

———. 1989b. Range expansion by bison of Yellowstone National Park. *J. Mamm.* 70: 670–75. [2,5]

Meek, F. B. 1853. Journal of a trip to Nebraska Territory in 1853. Files of Badlands National Park. Manuscript. [3]

Melnick, D. J. and Pearl, M. C. 1987. Cercopithecines in multimale groups: Genetic diversity and population structure. In B. B. Smuts, D. L. Cheney, R. M. Seyfarth, R. W. Wrangham, and T. T. Struhsaker, eds., *Primate Societies*, pp. 121–45. Chicago: University of Chicago Press. [11]

Melnick, D. J., Pearl, M. C., and Richard, A. F. 1984. Male migration and inbreeding avoidance in wild rhesus monkeys. *Am. J. Primatol.* 7: 229–43. [9]

Melton, D. A., Larter, N. C., Gates, C. C., and Virgil, J. A. 1989. The influence of rut and environmental factors on the behaviour of wood bison. *Acta Theriol.* 34: 179–93. [4]

Michener, G. R. 1980. Differential reproduction among female Richardson's ground squirrels and its relation to sex ratio. *Beh. Ecol. Sociobiol.* 7: 173–78. [1,9]

Miller, B., Biggins, D., Wemmer, C., Powell, R., Calvo, L., Hanebury, L., and Wharton, T. 1990. Development of survival skills in captive-raised Siberian polecats. II: Predator avoidance. *J. Ethol.* 8: 95–104. [11]

Miller, B., Wemmer, C., Biggins, D., and Reading, R. 1990. A proposal to conserve black-footed ferrets and the prairie dog ecosystem. *Environ. Manage.* 14: 763–69. [11]

Miller, J. R., Jr. 1986. *Rapid City Climate.* Rapid City: South Dakota School of Mines and Technology Foundation. [3]

Miquelle, D. G. 1985. Food habits and range conditions of bison and sympatric ungulates on the Upper Chitna River, Wrangell–St. Elias National Park and Preserve. *Res. Manage. Rep. Ar.* 8: 1–112. [2]

———. 1989. Behavioral ecology of moose in Denali National Park and Preserve, Alaska. Ph.D. diss. University of Idaho, Moscow. [1,4,8]

Mishra, H. R. 1984. A delicate balance: Tigers, rhinoceroses, tourists, and park management vs the needs of the local people in Royal Chitwan National Park, Nepal. In J. A. McNeely and K. R. Miller, eds., *National Parks, Conservation, and Development*, pp. 197–205. Washington, D.C.: Smithsonian Institution Press. [11]

Mishra, H. R., Wemmer, C., and Smith, J. L. 1987. Tigers in Nepal: Conflicts with human interests. In R. L. Tilson and U. S. Seal, eds., *Tigers of the World*, pp. 449–63. Park Ridge, N.J.: Noyes. [5]

Mitani, J. C. 1988. Male gibbon (*Hylobates agilis*) singing behavior: Natural history, song variations, and function. *Ethology* 79: 177–94. [8]

Mitchell, B. and Lincoln, G. A. 1973. Conception dates in relation to age and condition in two populations of red deer in Scotland. *J. Zool., Lond.* 171: 141–52. [6,8]

Mitchell, B. D., McCowan, B. D., and Nicholson, I. A. 1976. Annual cycles of body weight and condition in Scottish red deer. *J. Zool., Lond.* 180: 107–27. [6,8]

Mitton, J. B. and Grant, M. C. 1984. Associations among heterozygosity, growth rate, and developmental homeostasis. *Ann. Rev. Ecol. Sociobiol.* 15: 479–99. [1]

Miura, S., Ohtaishi, N., Kaji, K., Wu, J., and Zheng, S. 1989. The threatened white-lipped deer *Cervus albirostris*, Gyaring Lake, Qinghai Province, China, and its conservation. *Biol. Cons.* 47: 237–44. [1]

Miyamoto, M. M., Tanhauser, S. M., and Laipis, P. 1989. Systematic relationships in the Artiodactyl tribe Bovini (family Bovidae), as determined from mitochondrial DNA sequences. *Syst. Zool.* 38: 342–49. [2]

Moore, J. and Ali, R. 1984. Are dispersal and inbreeding avoidance related? *Anim. Beh.* 32: 94–112. [1]

Morris, D. W. 1987. Sexual differences in habitat use by small mammals: Evolutionary strategy or reproductive constraint? *Oecologia* 65: 51–57. [4]

Mortenson, I. L. 1988. *Badlands National Park Statement for Management.* Denver: National Park Service. [3]

Munsell Soil Color Chart. 1954. Baltimore: Munsell Color Company. [10]

Murie, J. O. and Boag, D. A. 1984. The relationship of body weight to overwinter survival in Columbian ground squirrels. *J. Mamm.* 65: 688–90. [6,10]

Murie, J. O. and Dobson, F. S. 1987. The costs of reproduction in female Columbian ground squirrels. *Oecologia* 73: 1–6. [7]

Myers, N. 1985. A look at the present extinction spasm and what it means for the future evolution of species. In R. J. Hoage, ed., *Animal Extinctions*, pp. 47–57. Washington, D.C.: Smithsonian Institution Press. [1]

National Park Service. Unpublished bison document, Interior, South Dakota..

Nei, M., Maruyama, T., and Chakraborty, R. 1975. The bottleneck effect and genetic variability in populations. *Evolution* 29: 1–10. [10]

Nei, M., and Tajima, F. 1981. Genetic drift and estimation of effective population size. *Genetics* 98: 625–40. [10]

Nelson, K. L. 1965. Status and habits of the American buffalo (*Bison bison*) in the Henry Mountains area of Utah. Salt Lake City: Utah State Dept. Fish and Game Publ. 65: 2. [2]

Newmark, W. D. 1986. Species-area relationship and its determinants for mammals in western North American national parks. *Biol. J. Linn. Soc.* 28: 83–98. [1]

———. 1987. A land-bridge island perspective on mammalian extinctions in western North American parks. *Nature* 325: 430–32. [1]

Nicholson, A. J. 1957. The self-adjustment of populations to change. *Cold Springs Harbor Symp. Quant. Biol.* 22: 153–73. [7]

Nishida, T. 1989. Is lifetime data always necessary for evaluating the "intensity" of selection? *Evolution* 43: 1826–27. [9]

Norland, J. E. 1984. Habitat use and distribution of bison in Theodore Roosevelt National Park. Thesis, Montana State University, Bozeman. [4]

Oates, J. F. 1986. African primate conservation: General needs and specific priorities. In K. Benirshke, ed., *Primates: The Road to Self-sustaining Populations*, pp. 21–30. New York: Springer-Verlag. [11]

O'Brien, P. H. 1982. Flehman: Its occurrence and possible functions in feral goats. *Anim. Beh.* 30: 1015–19. [6]

O'Brien, S. J., Roelke, M. E., Marker, L., Newman, A., Winkler, C. A., Meltzer, D., Colly, L., Evermann, J. F., Bush, M., Wildt, D. E. 1985. Genetic basis for species vulnerability in the cheetah. *Science* 227: 1428–34. [10]

Oftedal, O. T. 1985. Pregnancy and lactation. In R. J. Hudson and R. G. White, eds., *The Bioenergetics of Herbivores*, pp. 215–38, Boca Raton, Fla.: CRC Press. [4]

Ogilvie, W. 1890. Furs. *Sessional Papers of Victoria* 53: 91–92. [2]

O'Hara, C. C. 1920. The White River badlands. *So. Dakota School Mines Bull.* 13: 1–81. [3].

Olech, W. 1987. Analysis of inbreeding in European bison. *Acta Theriol.* 32: 373–87. [2,10]

Oosenbrug, S. M. and Carbyn, L. N. 1985. Wolf predation on bison in Wood Buffalo National Park. Canadian Wildlife Service, Edmonton. Manuscript. [2,4]

Orford, H. J. L., Perrin, M. R., and Berry, H. H. 1988. Contraception, reproduction, and demography of free-ranging Etosha lions (*Panthera leo*). *J. Zool., Lond.* 216: 717–33. [5]

Owens, M. and Owens, D. 1984. *Cry the Kalahari*. New York: Houghton Mifflin. [11]

Owen-Smith, N. 1977. On territoriality in ungulates and an evolutionary model. *Q. Rev. Biol.* 52: 1–38. [9]

———. 1979. Assessing the foraging efficiency of a large herbivore, kudu. *S. Afr. J. Wildl. Res.* 9: 102–10. [4]

———. 1988. *Megaherbivores*. Cambridge: Cambridge University Press. [1,5]

Packer, C. 1979. Male dominance and reproductive activity in *Papio anubis*. *Anim. Beh.* 27: 37–45. [8,11]

———. 1986. Sexual dimorphism: The horns of African antelopes. *Science* 221: 1191–93. [7]

Packer, C., Herbst, L., Pusey, A. E., Bygott, J. D., Hanby, J. P., Cairns, S. J., and Borgerhoff Mulder, M. 1988. Reproductive success in lions. In T. H. Clutton-Brock, ed., *Reproductive Success: Studies of Individual Variation in Contrasting Breeding Systems*, pp. 363–83. Chicago: University of Chicago Press. [7,8]

Packer, C. and Pusey, A. E. 1982. Cooperation and competition within coalitions of male lions: Kin selection or game theory? *Nature* 296: 740–42. [1]

———. 1983a. Adaptations of female lions to infanticide by incoming males. *Amer. Nat.* 121: 91–113. [1,6]

———. 1983b. Male takeovers and female reproductive parameters: A simulation of oestrus synchrony in lions (*Panthera leo*). *Anim. Beh.* 31: 334–40. [6]

Packer, C., Pusey, A. F., Rowley, H., Gilbert, D. A., Martenson, J., and O'Brien, S. J. 1991. Case study of a population bottleneck: Lions of the Ngorongoro Crater. *Cons. Biol.* 5: 219–30. [1,10]

Parker, G. A. 1974. Assessment strategy and the evolution of fighting behavior. *J. Theor. Biol.* 47: 223–43. [8]

Partridge, L., Hoffmann, A., and Jones, J. S. 1987. Male size and mating success in *Drosophila melanogatser* and *D. pseudoobscura* under field conditions. *Anim. Beh.* 35: 468–76. [9]

Peek, J. M., Miquelle, D. G., and Wright, R. G. 1987. Are bison exotic in the Wrangell–St. Elias National Park and Preserve? *Environ. Manage.* 11: 149–53. [2]

Pemberton, J. M., Albon, S. D., Guinness, F. E., Clutton-Brock. T. H. and Berry, R. J. 1988. Genetic variation and juvenile survival in red deer. *Evolution* 42: 921–34. [10]

Pemberton, J. M., Albon, S. D., Guinness, F. E., Clutton-Brock, T. H., and Dover, G. A. 1992. Behavioral estimates of male mating success tested by DNA fingerprinting in a polygynous mammal. *Beh. Ecol.* 3: 66–75. [8]

Pemberton, J. M., King, P. W., Lovari, S., and Bauchau, V. 1989. Genetic variation in the alpine chamois, with special reference to the subspecies *Rupicapra rupicapra cartusiana* Couturier, 1938. *Z. Saeugetier.* 54: 243–50. [10]

Pemberton, J. M. and Smith, R. H. 1985. Lack of biochemical polymorphism in British fallow deer. *Heredity* 55: 199–207. [10]

Pennycuick, L. 1975. Movements of the migratory wildebeest population in the Serengeti area between 1960 and 1973. *E. Afr. Wildl. J.* 13: 65–87. [1]

Peterson, M. J., Grant, W. E., and Davis, D. S. 1991. Bison-brucellosis management: Simulation of alternative strategies. *J. Wild. Manage.* 55: 205–13. [2]

Peterson, R. O. 1988. The pit or the pendulum: Issues in large carnivore management in natural ecosystems. In J. K. Agee and D. R. Johnson, eds., *Ecosystem Management for Parks and Wilderness*, pp. 105–17. Seattle: University of Washington Press. [11]

Petrie, M. 1983. Female moorhens compete for small fat males. *Science* 220: 413–15. [7]

Pfeifer, S. 1985. Flehman and dominance among captive adult female scimitar-horned oryx (*Oryx dammah*). *J. Mamm.* 66: 160–63. [6]

Pianka, E. R. and Parker, W. S. 1975. Age-specific reproductive tactics. *Amer. Nat.* 109: 453–64. [8]

Picton, H. D. 1979. The application of insular biogeographic theory to the conservation of large mammals in the northern Rocky Mountains. *Biol. Cons.* 15: 73–79. [1]

Pilgrim, G. E. 1947. The evolution of the buffaloes, oxen, sheep, and goats. *J. Linn. Soc. Zool.* 41: 272–86. [2]

Pimm, S. L., Gittleman, J. L., McCracken, G. F., and Gilpin, M. E. 1989. Plausible alternatives to bottlenecks to explain reduced genetic diversity. *Trends Ecol. Evol.* 4: 176–78. [10]

Pope, T. R. 1992. The influence of dispersal patterns and mating systems on genetic differentiation within and between populations of the red howler monkey (*Alouatta seniculus*). *Evolution* 46: 1112–28. [9,11]

Popenoe, H. 1983. *Little-known Asian Animals with a Promising Economic Future.* Washington, D.C.: National Academy Press. [2]

Popper, D. E. and Popper, F. J. 1987. The Great Plains: From dust to dust. *Planning* (December): 12–18. [2,11]

Prins, H. H. T. and Iason, G. R. 1989. Dangerous lions and nonchalant buffalo. *Behaviour* 108: 262–96. [4]

Pruett-Jones, S. G. and Pruett-Jones, M. A. 1990. Sexual selection through female choice in Lawes parotia, lek-mating bird of paradise. *Evolution* 44: 486–501. [8]

Pucek, Z. 1992. IUCN, Bison Specialist Group files, Gland, Switzerland. Memo.[2]

Rachlow, J. and Bowyer, T. 1991. Inter-year variability in birth synchrony in Dall sheep. *J. Mamm.* 72: 487–92. [6]

Ralls, K. 1976. Mammals in which females are larger than males. *Quart. Rev. Biol.* 51: 245–76. [1,7]

Ralls, K. and Ballou, J. 1983. Extinction: Lessons from zoos. In C. M. Schoenwald-Cox, S. M. Chambers, B. MacBryde, and L. Thomas, eds., *Conservation and Genetics*, pp. 164–84. Menlo Park, Calif.: Benjamin Cummings. [1,10]

————. 1986a: Captive breeding programs for populations with a small number of founders. *Trends Ecol. Evol.* 1: 19–22. [1]

————. 1986b. Preface to the proceedings of the workshop on genetic management of captive populations. *Zoo Biol.* 5: 81–86. [1]

Ralls, K., Brownell, R. L., Jr., and Ballou, J. 1980. Differential mortality by sex and age in mammals with specific reference to the sperm whale. *Rep. Int. Whal. Comm., Spec. Is.* 2: 223–43. [1]

Ralls, K., Brugger, K. and Ballou, J. 1979. Inbreeding and juvenile mortality in small populations of ungulates. *Science* 206: 1101–3. [1,10]

Ralls, K. Brugger, K. and Glick, A. 1980. Deleterious effects of inbreeding in a herd of captive Dorcas gazelle. *Int. Zoo Yrbk.* 20: 137–46. [10]

Ralls, K., Harvey, P. H., and Lyles, A. M. 1986. Inbreeding in natural populations of birds and mammals. In M. E. Soule, ed., *Conservation Biology: The Science of Scarcity and Diversity*, pp. 35–56. Sunderland, Mass.: Sinauer. [1,11]

Rao, P. S. S. and Inbaraj, S. G. 1980. Inbreeding effects on fetal growth and development. *J. Med. Gen.* 17: 27–33. [10]

Redford, K. H. 1985. Emas National Park and the plight of the Brazilian cerrados. *Oryx* 19: 210–14. [11]

————. 1987. The pampas deer (*Ozotoceros bezoarcticus*) in central Brazil. In C. Wemmer, ed., *Biology and Management of the Cervidae*, pp. 410–14. Washington, D.C.: Smithsonian Institution Press. [11]

Redhead, B. 1987. The management of brucellosis and tuberculosis in bison in Wood Buffalo National Park. In *North American Bison Workshop*, pp. 62–64. Missoula, Mont.: U.S. Fish and Wildlife Service, Spec. Pub. [2]

Reed, J. M., Doerr, P. D., and Walters, J. R. 1986. Determining minimum population sizes for birds and mammals. *Wildl. Soc. Bull.* 14: 255–61. [9]

Reeves, B. O. K. 1978. Heads-Smashed-In: 5500 years of bison jumping on the Alberta plains. *Plains Anthrop.* 23: 151–74. [2]

Reher, C. A. 1974. Population study of the Casper site bison. In G. C. Frison, ed., *The Casper Site,* pp. 113–24. New York: Academic Press. [4]

————. 1978. Buffalo population and other deterministic factors in a model of adaptive process on the shortgrasss plains. *Plains Anthrop.* 23: 23–39. [2]

Reichman, O. J. 1987. *Konza Prairie: A Tallgrass Natural History.* Lawrence: University of Kansas Press. [11]

Reiter, J. and Le Boeuf, B. 1991. Life history consequences of variation in age at primiparity in northern elephant seals. *Beh. Ecol. Sociobiol.* 28: 153–60. [6,7,10]

Reiter, J. R., Panken, K. J., and Le Boeuf, B. J. 1981. Female competition and reproductive success in northern elephant seals. *Anim. Beh.* 29: 670–87. [8]

Reynolds, H. 1982. An endangered species program brings wood bison to Nahanni. *Zoonoos* (July): 4–8. [5,6]

Reynolds, H. W., Glaholt, R. D., and Hawley, A. W. L. 1982. Bison. In J. A. Chapman and G. A. Feldhamer, eds., *Wild Mammals of North America,* pp. 972–1000. Baltimore: Johns Hopkins University Press. [2,6]

Reynolds, H. W. and Hawley, A. W. L. 1987. Bison ecology in relation to agricultural development in the Slave River lowlands, N.W.T. *Occ. Pap. Can. Wildl. Serv.* 63: 1–73. [5,6]

Ribble, D. O. 1992. Lifetime reproductive success and its correlates in the monogamous rodent, *Peromyscus californicus. J. Anim. Ecol.* 61: 457–68. [9]

Ribble, D. O. and Millar, J. S. 1992. Inbreeding effects among inbred and outbred laboratory colonies of *Peromyscus maniculatus. Can. J. Zool.* 70: 820–24. [10]

Rideout, C. B. and Worthen, G. L. 1975. Use of girth measurement for estimating weight of mountain goats. *J. Wildl. Mgmt.* 39: 705–8. [6]

Risenhoover, K. L. and Bailey, J. A. 1985. Relationships between group size, feeding time, and agonistic behavior of mountain goats. *Can. J. Zool.* 63: 2501–6. [4]

Riska, B. 1991. Introduction. In *Maternal Effects in Evolutionary Biology: Symposium. Proc. Fourth Int. Congress Syst. Evol. Biol.,* Portland: Disoscordides Press. [10]

Robbins, C. T. 1983. *Wildlife Feeding and Nutrition.* New York: Academic Press. [4]

Robinette, W. L. and Olsen, O. A. 1944. Studies of the productivity of mule deer in central Utah. *Trans. No. Amer. Nat. Res. Conf.* 9: 156–61. [8]

Roe, F. G. 1970. *The North American Buffalo.* 2d ed. Toronto: University of Toronto Press. [2,4,10]

Rogers, L. L. 1987. Effects of food supply and kinship on social behavior, movements, and population growth of black bears in northeastern Minnesota. *Wildl. Monog.* 97: 1–72. [9]

Rood, J. 1980. Mating relationships and breeding suppression in the dwarf mongoose. *Anim. Beh.* 28: 143–50. [8]

Roosevelt, T. 1899. *Hunting Trips of a Ranchman.* New York: Putnam's Sons. [3]

Rossdale, P. D. 1976. A clinician's view of prematurity and dysmaturity in thoroughbred foals. *Proc. Royal Soc. Med.* 69: 27–28. [6]

Rothstein, A. 1988. Social organization in juvenile bison bulls *(Bison bison):* Nonlinear dominance and dyadic associations. Ph.D. dissertation, City University of New York. [3]

Rothstein, A. and Griswold, J. G. 1991. Age and sex preferences for social partners by juvenile bison bulls, *Bison bison. Anim. Beh.* 41: 227–37. [8]

Rowell, T. E. 1974. The concept of social dominance. *Beh. Biol.* 11: 131–54. [7]

Rutberg, A. T. 1983. Factors influencing dominance status in American bison cows *(Bison bison). Z. Tierpsychol.* 63: 202–12. [7]

———. 1984. Birth synchrony in American bison *(Bison bison):* Response to predation or season? *J. Mamm.* 65: 418–23. [2,4,6]

———. 1986a. Lactation and fetal sex ratios in American bison. *Amer. Nat.* 127: 90–94. [2,4,5,6]

———. 1986b. Dominance and its fitness consequences in American bison cows. *Behaviour* 96: 62–91. [4,6,7]

———. 1987. Adaptive hypotheses of birth synchrony in ruminants: An interspecific test. *Amer. Nat.* 130: 692–710. [6]

Ryan, M. J. 1985. *The Tungara Frog.* Chicago: University of Chicago Press. [8]

Sadlier, R. M. F. S. 1969. *The Ecology of Reproduction in Wild and Domestic Mammals.* London: Methuen. [6]

Sage, R. D. and Wolff, J. O. 1986. Pleistocene glaciations, fluctuating ranges, and low genetic variability in a large mammal *(Ovis dalli). Evolution* 40: 1092–95. [10]

Saharia, V. B. 1984. Human dimensions in wildlife management: The Indian experience. In J. A. McNelley and K. R. Miller, eds., *National Parks, Conservation, and Development* pp. 190–96. Washington, D.C.: Smithsonian Institution Press. [11]

Samuels, A. and Altmann, J. 1986. Immigration of a *Papio anubis* male into a group of *Papio cynocephalus* baboons and evidence for an *anubis-cynocephalus* hybrid zone in Amboseli, Kenya. *Int. J. Primatol.* 7: 131–38. [9]

———. 1991. Baboons of the Amboseli Basin: Demographic stability and change. *Int. J. Primatol.* 12: 1–19. [9]

Sargeant, A. B., Allen, S. H., and Hastings, J. O. 1987. Spatial relationships between sympatric coyotes and red foxes in North Dakota. *J. Wildl. Manage.* 51: 285–93. [11]

Sargent, R. C., Gross, M. R., and Van Den Berghe, E. P. 1986. Male mate choice in fishes. *Anim. Beh.* 34: 543–50. [8]

Schaller, G. B. 1967. *The Deer and the Tiger.* Chicago: University of Chicago Press. [11]

———. 1972. *The Serengeti Lion.* Chicago: University of Chicago Press. [4,6]

———. 1976. Aggressive behaviour of the domestic yak. *J. Bombay Nat. Hist. Soc.* 73: 385–89. [2]

———. 1977. *Mountain Monarchs: Wild Sheep and Goats of the Himalaya.* Chicago: University of Chicago Press. [2,11]

Schaller, G. B., Jinchu, H., Wenshi, P., and Jing, Z. 1985. *The Giant Pandas of Wolong*. Chicago: University of Chicago Press. [1,11]

Schaller, G. B. and Junrang, R. 1988. Effects of a storm on Tibetan antelope. *J. Mamm.* 69: 631–34. [7]

Schonewald-Cox, C. M. 1983. Conclusions: Guidelines to management: A beginning attempt. In C. M. Schonewald-Cox, S. M. Chambers, B. MacBryde, and L. Thomas, eds., *Genetics and Conservation*, pp. 414–45. Menlo Park, Calif.: Benjamin-Cummings. [1,11]

Schwagmeyer, P. L. 1988. Scramble-competition polygyny in an asocial mammal: Male mobility and mating success. *Amer. Nat.* 131: 885–92. [8]

Schwagmeyer, P. L. and Parker, G. L. 1990. Male mate choice as predicted by sperm competition in thirteen-lined ground squirrels. *Nature* 348: 62–64. [8]

Schwartz, C. C. and Ellis, J. E. 1981. Feeding ecology and niche separation in some native and domestic ungulates on the shortgrass prairie. *J. Appl. Ecol.* 18: 343–53. [4]

Seidensticker, J. 1987a. Bearing witness: Observations on the extinction of *Panthera tigris balica* and *Panthera tigris sondaica*. In R. L. Tilson and U. S. Seal, eds., *Tigers of the World*, pp. 1–9. Park Ridge, N.J.: Noyes. [1,11]

——. 1987b. Managing tigers in the Sunderbans: Experience and opportunity. In R. L. Tilson and U. S. Seal, eds., *Tigers of the World*. pp. 416–26. Park Ridge, N.J.: Noyes. [11]

Seip, D. R. and Bunnell, F. L. 1984. Body weights and measurements of Stone sheep. *J. Mamm.* 65: 513–14. [6]

Sekulnic, R. 1982. Daily and seasonal patterns of roaring and spacing in four red howler *Alouatta seniculus* troops. *Folia Primatol.* 39: 22–48. [8]

Selander, R. K. 1966. Sexual dimorphism and differential niche utilization in birds. *Condor* 68: 113–51. [4]

——. 1976. Genic variation in natural populations. In F. J. Ayala, ed., *Molecular Evolution*, pp. 21–27. Sunderland, Mass.: Sinauer. [3]

Selander, R. K., Smith, M. H., Yang, S. Y., Johnson, W. E., and Gentry, J. B. 1971. Biochemical polymorphism and systematics in the genus *Peromyscus*. I. Variation in the oldfield mouse (*Peromyscus polionotus*). *University of Texas Publ.* 7103: 49–90. [3]

Senft, R. L., Rittenhouse, L. R., and Woodmansee, R. G. 1985. Factors influencing selection of resting sites by cattle on shortgrass steppe. *J. Range Manage.* 38: 295–99. [4]

Shank, C. C. 1982. Age-sex differences in the diets of wintering Rocky Mountain bighorn sheep. *Ecology* 63: 627–33. [1,4]

Sharps, J. 1988. Politics, prairie dogs, and the sportsman. In D. W. Uresk and G. Schenbeck, eds., *Eighth Great Plains Wildlife Damage Control Workshop Proc.*, pp. 117–18. Rapid City, S.D.: U.S. Department of Agriculture. [11]

Shaw, J. H. and Carter, T. S. 1989. Calving patterns among American bison. *J. Wildl. Manage.* 53: 896–98. [5]

Sheire, J. W. 1969. The badlands: Historic basic data study. U.S. Department of Interior, Office of Archaeology and Historic Preservation, Washington, D.C. Manuscript. [3]

Shelley, K. J. and Anderson, S. H. 1989. A summary on genetics and sterilization in a free-ranging herd of bison near Jackson, Wyoming. Wyoming Game and Fish Department, Cheyenne. Manuscript. [5]

Sherman, P. W. 1989. Mate guarding as paternity assurance in Idaho ground squirrels. *Nature* 338: 418–20. [8]

Shields, W. M. 1982. *Philopatry, Inbreeding, and the Evolution of Sex*. Albany: State University of New York Press. [10]

———. 1987. Dispersal and mating systems: Investigating their causal connections. In D. B. Chepko-Sade and Z. T. Halpin, eds., *Mammalian Dispersal Patterns: The Effects of Social Structure on Population Genetics*, pp. 3–24. Chicago: University of Chicago Press. [1]

———. 1993. The natural and unnatural history of inbreeding and outbreeding. In N. W. Thornhill, ed., *The Natural History of Inbreeding and Outbreeding*, pp. 143–69. Chicago: University of Chicago Press. [10]

Shirley, E. P. 1867. *Some Account of English Deer Parks with Notes on the Management of Deer*. London: Murray. [9]

Shoemaker, H. W. 1919. *The Gray Wolf of South Dakota*. Altoona, Penn.: Altoona Tribune. [3]

Short, J. 1986. The effect of pasture availability on food intake, species selection, and grazing behaviour. *J. Appl. Ecol.* 23: 559–71. [4]

Shueler, J. 1989. *A Revelation Called the Badlands*. Interior, S.D.: Badlands Natural History Assoc. [3]

Shull, A. M. and Tipton, A. R. 1987. Effective population size of bison on the Wichita Mountains Wildlife Refuge. *Cons. Biol.* 1: 35–41. [2,9,10,11]

Siegel, S. 1956. *Non-parametric Statistics for the Behavioral Sciences*. New York: McGraw-Hill. [3]

Siegel, S. and Castellan, N. J. 1988. *Non-parametric Statistics for the Behavioral Sciences*. 2d ed. New York: McGraw-Hill. [3,10]

Silk, J. B. 1983. Local resource competition and facultative adjustment of sex ratios in relation to competitive abilities. *Amer. Nat.* 121: 56–66. [10]

Sinclair, A. R. E. 1977. *The African Buffalo: A Study of Resource Limitations of Populations*. Chicago: University of Chicago Press. [2,4,5,6,7]

———. 1989. Population regulation in animals. In J. M. Cherrett, ed., *Ecological Concepts*, pp. 197–241. Oxford: Blackwell. [5]

Sinclair, A. R. E. and Wells, M. P. 1989. Population growth and the poverty cycle in Africa: Colliding ecological and economic processes? In D. Pimental and C. Hall, eds., *Food and Natural Resources*, pp. 439–84. New York: Academic Press. [11].

Skinner, J. D. and van Jaarsveld, A. S. 1987. Adaptive significance of restricted breeding in southern African ruminants. *S. Afr. J. Science* 83: 657–63. [6]

Skinner, M. F. and Kaisen, O. C. 1947. The fossil bison of Alaska and preliminary revision of the genus. *Bull. Amer. Mus. Nat. Hist.* 89: 123–256. [2]

Skogland, T. 1988. Tooth wear by food limitation and its life history consequences in wild reindeer. *Oikos* 51: 238–42. [3]

Skorupa, J. P. 1986. Responses of rain forest primates to selective logging in Kibale

Forest, Uganda: A summary report. In K. Benirshke, ed., *Primates: The Road to Self-sustaining Populations,* pp. 57–70. New York: Springer-Verlag. [11]

Slatis, M. A. 1960. An analysis of inbreeding in the European bison. *Genetics* 45: 275–87. [2,10]

Smith, A. T. and Peacock, M. 1990. Conspecific attraction and the determination of metapopulation colonization rates. *Cons. Biol.* 4: 320–23. [11]

Smith, D. G. 1986. Incidence and consequences of inbreeding in three captive groups of rhesus macaques (*Macaca mulatta*). In K. Benirshke, ed., *Primates: The Road to Self-sustaining Populations,* pp. 859–74. New York: Springer-Verlag. [10]

Smith, D. G., Lorey, F. W., Suzuki, J., and Abe, M. 1987. Effects of outbreeding on weight and growth rate of captive infant rhesus macaques. *Zoo Biol.* 6: 201–12. [10]

Smith, D. G. and Smith, S. 1988. Parental rank and reproductive success of natal rhesus males. *Anim. Beh.* 36: 554–62. [8]

Smith, J. L. D. and McDougal, C. 1991. The contribution of variance in lifetime reproduction to effective population size in tigers. *Cons. Biol.* 5: 484–90. [10]

Smith, M. H., Scribner, K. T., Carpenter, L. H., and Garrott, R. A. 1990. Genetic characteristics of Colorado mule deer (*Odocoileus hemionus*) and comparisons with other cervids. *Southwest. Nat.* 35: 1–8. [10]

Smith, R. H. 1979. On selection for inbreeding in polygynous animals. *Heredity* 43: 205–11. [9]

Smuts, B. B. 1986. Sexual competition and mate choice. In B. B. Smuts, D. L. Cheney, R. L. Seyfarth, R. W. Wrangham, and T. T. Struhsaker, eds., *Primate Societies,* pp. 385–99. Chicago: University of Chicago Press. [8]

Snead, J. S. and Alcock, J. 1985. Aggregation formation and assortative mating in two meloid beetles. *Evolution* 39: 1123–31. [8]

Sokal, R. R. and Rohlf, F. J. 1981. *Biometry.* San Francisco: W. H. Freeman. [3,6,7]

Soper, D. 1941. History, range, and home of the northern bison. *Ecol. Monog.* 2: 347–412. [2,4,6]

Soule, M. E. 1980 . Thresholds for survival: Maintaining fitness and evolutionary potential. In M. E. Soule and B. A. Wilcox, eds., *Conservation Biology: An Eco-evolutionary Approach,* pp. 151–69. Sunderland, Mass.: Sinauer. [1]

Soule, M. E., Wilcox, B. A., and Holtby, C. 1979. Benign neglect: A model of faunal collapse in the game reserves of East Africa. *Biol. Cons.* 5: 259–72. [1]

Speth, J. D. 1983. *Bison Kills and Bone Counts.* Chicago: University of Chicago Press. [2,4,10]

Spinage, C. A. and Brown, W. A. 1988. Age determination of the West African buffalo *Syncerus caffer brachyceros* and the constancy of tooth wear. *Afr. J. Ecol.* 26: 221–27. [3]

Stacey, P. B. and Taper, M. 1992. Environmental variation and the persistence of small populations. *Ecol. Appl.* 2: 18–29. [9].

Stanley, S. M. 1985. Extinction as part of the natural evolutionary process: A paleobiological perspective. In R. J. Hoage, ed., *Animal Extinctions*, pp. 31–46. Washington, D.C.: Smithsonian Institution Press. [1]

Stanley-Price, M. R. 1989. *Animal Re-introductions: The Arabian Oryx in Oman.* Cambridge: Cambridge University Press. [1,9,10,11]

Stormont, C. J. 1982. Blood groups in animals. *J. Amer. Vet. Med. Assoc.* 181: 1120–24. [10]

Struhsaker, T. T. 1975. *The Red Colobus Monkey.* Chicago: University of Chicago Press. [1]

Stuwe, M. and Nievergelt, B. 1991. Recovery of alpine ibexes from near extinction: The results of effective protection, captive breeding, and reintroduction. *Appl. Anim. Beh. Sci.* 29: 379–87. [10,11]

Stuwe, M. and Scribner, K. T. 1989. Low genetic variability in reintroduced alpine ibex (*Capra ibex ibex*) populations. *J. Mamm.* 70: 370–73. [1]

Sukumar, R. 1986. The elephant populations of India: Strategies for conservation. *Proc. India Acad. Sci.* (November): 59–71. [5,11]

Sunquist, F. and Sunquist, M. E. 1988. *Tiger Moon.* Chicago: University of Chicago Press. [5,11]

Sunquist, M. E. 1981. The social organization of tigers in Royal Chitwan National Park. *Smith. Contrib. Zool.* 336: 1–98. [11]

Tashiro, H. and Schwardt, H. H. 1953. Biological studies of horseflies in New York. *J. Econ. Ent.* 46: 813–22. [4]

Taylor, R. D. 1988. Age determination of the African buffalo, *Syncerus caffer* (Sparrman) in Zimbabwe. *Afr. J. Ecol.* 26: 207–20. [3]

Templeton, A. R. 1987. Inferences on natural population structure from genetic studies on captive mammalian populations. In D. B. Chepko-Sade and Z. T. Halpin, eds., *Mammalian Dispersal Patterns: The Effects of Social Structure on Population Genetics*, pp. 257–72. Chicago: University of Chicago Press. [9,10]

Templeton, A. R. and Read, B. 1983. The elimination of inbreeding depression in a captive herd of Speke's gazelle. In C. M. Schonewald-Cox, S. M. Chambers, B. MacBryde, and L. Thomas, eds., *Genetics and Conservation*, pp. 241–62. Menlo Park, Calif.: Benjamin-Cummings. [1,10]

Terborgh, J. 1974. Preservation of natural diversity: The problem of extinction-prone species. *Bioscience* 24: 715–22. [1]

Teska, W. R., Smith, M. H., and Novak, J. M. 1990. Food quality, heterozygosity, and fitness correlates in *Peromyscus polionotus*. *Evolution* 44: 1318–25. [10]

Tessaro, S. V. 1989. Review of diseases, parasites, and miscellaneous pathological conditions of North American bison. *Can. Vet. J.* 30: 416–22. [2]

Thompson, E. A. 1986. Ancestry of alleles and extinction of genes in populations with defined pedigrees. *Zoo Biol.* 5: 161–70. [9]

Thompson, K. V. 1991. Flehman and social dominance in captive female sable antelope, *Hippotragus niger*. *Appl. Anim. Beh. Sci.* 29: 121–33. [6]

Thorne, E. T., Meagher, M. and Hillman, R. 1991. Brucellosis in free-ranging bison: Three perspectives. In R. Keiter and M. Boyce, eds., *The Greater Yellowstone Ecosystem*, pp. 275–88. New Haven: Yale University Press. [2]

Thoules, C. R. 1990. Feeding competition between grazing red deer hinds. *Anim. Beh.* 40: 105–11. [7]

Tilson, R. L. and Norton, P. M. 1981. Alarm duetting and pursuit deterrence in an African antelope. *Amer. Nat.* 118: 455–62. [8]

Treus, V. D. and Labanov, N. V. 1971. Acclimitisation and domestication of the eland *Taurotragus oryx* at Askanya Nova Zoo. *Int. Zoo Yrbk.* 11: 147–56. [10]

Trites, A. W. 1991. Fetal growth of northern fur seals: Life history strategy and sources of variation. *Can. J. Zool.* 69: 2608–17. [10]

Trivers, R. L. 1972. Parental investment and sexual selection. In B. Campbell, ed., *Sexual Selection and the Descent of Man*, pp. 136–79. Chicago: Aldine. [1]

Trombulak, S. C. 1991. Maternal influence on juvenile growth rates in Belding's ground squirrel (*Spermophilus beldingi*). *Can. J. Zool.* 69: 2140–45. [10]

Trudell, J. and White, R. G. 1981. The effect of forage structure and availability on food intake, biting rate, bite size, and daily eating time of reindeer. *J. Appl. Ecol.* 18: 63–81. [4]

Turner, R. W. 1974. Mammals of the Black Hills of South Dakota and Wyoming. *Univ. Kansas, Mus. Nat. Hist. Misc. Publ.* 60: 1–178. [3]

Underwood, R. 1982. Vigilance behaviour in grazing African ungulates. *Behaviour* 79: 82–107. [4]

Uresk, D. W. 1985. Effects of controlling black-tailed prairie dogs on plant production. *J. Range Manage.* 38: 466–68. [11]

Uresk, D. W. and Bjugstad, A. J. 1983. Prairie dogs as ecosystem regulators on the northern high plains. In *Seventh Proceedings North American Prairie Conference*, pp. 91–94. Springfield, Mo.: U.S. Department of Agriculture. [11]

Uresk, D. W. and Paulson, D. B. 1989. Estimated carrying capacity for cattle competing with prairie dogs and forage utilization in western South Dakota. In R. C. Szaro, K. E. Severson, and D. R. Patton, eds., *Symposium on Management of Amphibians, Reptiles, and Small Mammals in North America*, pp. 387–90. U.S. Department of Agriculture, Gen. Tech. Rep. 166. [11]

Urick, J. J., Brinks, J. S., Pahnish, O. F., Knapp, B. W., and Riley, T. M. 1968. Heterosis in postweaning traits among lines of Hereford cattle. *J. Anim. Sci.* 27: 323–30. [10]

USFWS. n.d. Files of U.S. Fish and Wildlife Service, Valentine, Nebraska. Manuscript. [10]

Van Camp, J. 1987. Predation on bison. *Occ. Pap. Canadian Wildl. Serv.* 63: 25–33. [4]

———. 1989. A surviving herd of endangered wood bison at Hook Lake, NWT? *Arctic* 42: 314–22. [1,5]

Van Camp, J. and Calef, G. W. 1987. Population dynamics of bison. *Occ. Pap. Canadian Wildl. Serv.* 63: 21–24. [4]

Van Schaik, C. P. and Van Noordwijk, M. A. 1988. Scramble and contest in feeding competition among female long-tailed macaques (*Macaca fascicularis*). *Behaviour* 105: 77–98. [7]

Van Vuren, D. 1980. Ecology and behavior of bison in the Henry Mountains, Utah. Thesis, Oregon State University, Corvallis. [2,4]

————. 1983. Group dynamics and summer home range of bison in southern Utah. *J. Mamm.* 329–32. [4]

————. 1984. Abnormal dentition in the American bison *Bison bison*. *Can. Field Nat.* 98: 366–67. [10]

————. 1987. Bison west of the Rockies: An alternative explanation. *Northwest Sci.* 61: 65–69. [2]

Van Vuren, D. and Bray, M. P. 1983. Diets of bison and cattle on a seeded range in southern Utah. *J. Range Manage.* 36: 499–500. [2]

————. 1985. The recent geographic distribution of *Bison bison* in Oregon. *Murrelet* 66: 56–58. [2]

————. 1986. Population dynamics of bison in the Henry Mountains. *J. Mamm.* 67: 503–11. [2,5]

Van Vuren, D. and Coblentz, B. E. 1988. Dental anomalies of feral goats (*Capra hircus*) on Aldabra Atoll. *J. Zool., Lond.* 216: 503–6. [10]

van Zyll de Jong, C. G. 1986. A systematic study of recent bison, with particular consideration of the wood bison (*Bison bison athabascae* Rhoads 1898). National Museum Canada, *Publ. Nat. Sci.* 9: 1–69. [2]

————. 1990. Action plan for North American bison conservation. Species Survival Commission, IUCN, Gland, Switz. Typescript. [2]

Verrell, P. A. 1985. Male mate choice for large fecund females in the red-spotted newt, *Notophthalmus viridesens:* How is size assessed? *Herpetologica* 41: 382–86. [8]

Verts, B. J. and Carraway, L. N. 1980. Natural hybridization of *Sylvilagus bachmani* and introduced *S. floridanus* in Oregon. *Murrelet* 61: 95–98. [10]

Vetter, C. 1991. The buffalo wars. *Outside* (May): 54–59. [2]

Vincent, J. 1970. The history of Umfolozi Game Reserve, Zululand, as it relates to management. *Lammergeyer* 11: 7–48. [11]

Wade, M. J. 1987. Measuring sexual selection. In J. W. Bradbury and M. B. Andersson, eds., *Sexual Selection: Testing the Alternatives.* pp. 197–207. Chichester: Wiley. [9]

Walker, B. H., Emslie, R. H., Owen-Smith, R. N. and Scholes, R. J. 1987. To cull or not to cull: Lessons from a southern African drought. *J. Appl. Ecol.* 24: 381–401. [11]

Walker, R. E. 1987. Buffalo herd management in Custer State Park. In *North American Bison Workshop*, pp. 22–23. Missoula, Mont.: U.S. Fish and Wildlife Service, Spec. Pub. [2]

Wallace, A. R. 1876. *The Geographical Distribution of Animals.* Vol. 1. London: Macmillan. [1]

Wasser, C. H. 1977. Bison-induced stresses on canyon bottom ecosystems in Colorado National Monument. Files of Colorado National Monument, Fruita, Colo. Typescript. [10]

Weedon, R. R. 1990. The badlands. In S. G. Froiland, ed., *Natural History of the Black Hills and Badlands,* pp. 177–95. Sioux Falls, S.D.: Center for Western Studies Press. [3]

Welsh, D. A. 1975. Population, behavioural, and grazing ecology of the horses of

Sable Island, Nova Scotia. Ph.D. diss., Dalhousie University, Dalhousie, New Brunswick. [7]

Western, D. 1979. Size, life history, and ecology in mammals. *Afr. J. Ecol.* 17: 185–204. [9]

———. 1989. Population, resources, and environment in the twenty-first century. In D. Western and M. Pearl, eds., *Conservation for the Twenty-first Century,* pp. 11–25. New York: Oxford University Press. [1]

Western, D. and Pearl, M., eds. 1989. *Conservation for the Twenty-first Century.* Oxford University Press, New York. [1]

Western, D. and Ssemakula, J. 1981. The future of the savannah ecosystem: Ecological islands or faunal enclaves? *Afr. J. Ecol.* 19: 7–19. [1]

Whicker, A. D. and Detling, J. 1988. Ecological consequences of prairie dog disturbances. *Bioscience* 38: 778–84. [4,11]

White, G. C. and Garrott, R. A. 1990. *Analysis of Wildlife Radio-tracking Data.* San Diego: Academic Press. [appendix 4]

Wildt, D. E., Bush, M., Goodrowe, K. L., Packer, C. Pusey, A. E., Brown, J. L., Joslin, P., and O'Brien, S. J. 1987. Reproductive and genetic consequences of founding isolated lion populations. *Nature* 329: 328–31. [10,11]

Williams, G. C. 1966. *Adaptation and Natural Selection.* Princeton: Princeton University Press. [1,8]

Willson, M. F. 1984. *Vertebrate Natural History.* Philadelphia: Saunders. [1]

Wilson, E. O. 1988. The current state of biological diversity. In E. O. Wilson, ed., *Biodiversity,* pp. 3–18. Washington, D.C.: National Academy Press. [1]

Wilson, E. O. and Bossert, W. H. 1971. *A Primer of Population Biology.* Sunderland, Mass.: Sinauer. [5]

Wilson, M. 1978. Archaeological kill site populations and the Holocene evolution of the genus. *Bison. Plains Anthrop.* 23: 9–22. [2]

Wirtz, P. 1981. Territorial defense and territory takeover by satellite males in the waterbuck *Kobus ellipsiprymnus* (Bovidae). *Beh. Ecol. Sociobiol.* 8: 161–62. [1]

———. 1982. Territory holders, satellite males, and bachelor males in a high density population of waterbuck (*Kobus ellipsiprymnus*) and their associations with conspecifics. *Z. Tierpsychol.* 58: 277–300. [1]

Wirtz, P. and Kaiser, P. 1988. Sex differences and seasonal variation in habitat choice in a high density population of waterbuck, *Kobus ellipsiprymnus* (Bovidae). *Z. Saeugetier.* 53: 162–69. [4]

Wolff, J. O. 1988. Maternal investment and sex ratio adjustment in American bison calves. *Beh. Ecol. Sociobiol.* 23: 127–33. [6,8]

Wright, S. 1931. Evolution in Mendelian populations. *Genetics* 16: 97–159. [9,10]

———. 1978. *Evolution and the Genetics of Populations.* Vol. 4, *Variability Within and Among Natural Populations.* Chicago: University of Chicago Press. [1,10]

Yamazaki, T. and Maruyama, T. 1974. Evidence that enzyme polymorphisms are selectively neutral, but blood group polymorphisms are not. *Science* 183: 1091–92. [10]

Yellowstone Bison: Background and Issues. 1990 (Mammoth, Wyo.). State of Montana, U.S. Department of Interior and U.S. Department of Agriculture. [2,5]

Zabinski, J. 1976. European bison pedigree book 1973. *Polish Sci. Publ.* 179–229. [2]

Zar, J. H. 1984. *Biostatistical Analyses*. Engelwood Cliffs, N. J.: Prentice-Hall. [3]

Zirkel, C. 1941. Natural selection before the "Origin of Species." *Proc. Amer. Phil. Soc.* 84: 71–123. [1]

Zullinger, E. M., Rickleffs, R. E., Redford, K. H., and Mace, G. M. 1984. Fitting sigmoidal equations to mammalian growth. *J. Mamm.* 607–36. [10]

Index